LORENZO
the Magnificent

Also by
DAVID LOTH

THE BROWNINGS
A Victorian Idyll

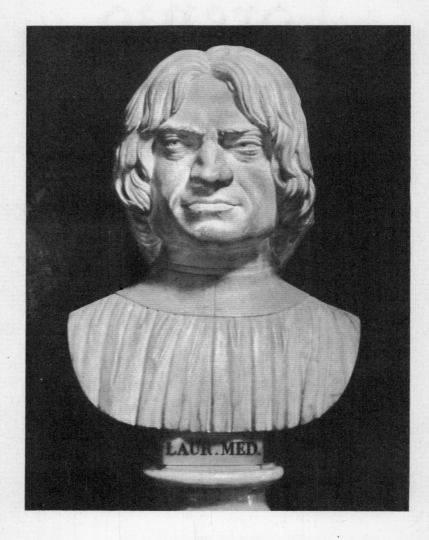

Lorenzo the Magnificent

"Equally formed for every pursuit"

Lorenzo the Magnificent

By David Loth

New York

Brentano's ✢ Publishers

To L. M. S.

ILLUSTRATIONS

Illustrations

LORENZO
the Magnificent

I

Lorenzo di Piero di Cosimo de' Medici was engaged to be married and all business was suspended in Florence. For when the Medici celebrated a family event, their patriarchal generosity was broad enough to include most of Tuscany in the treat. They always organized a festivity well worth leaving work to see, but when the gay, improvident, resourceful Lorenzo turned his talents to producing a show, the populace could be sure that even family tradition would be excelled.

This particular show had been impatiently anticipated. Long ago the young Magnificence had promised the mistress of his heart that he would stage for her the most brilliant tournament ever seen in Italy. For weeks Florence had watched him directing his workmen and artists as they prepared to redeem that promise. Now almost the entire population was hurrying towards the Piazza Santa Croce to see their host of the day shiver a lance for his lady.

In the square and on the housetops they were so closely packed that they could hardly breathe. But in the cold of early February they welcomed the crowding. It kept them warm as they surged helplessly around the tilting ground waiting for the show to begin, the whole mass swaying backwards and forwards to the shock of new arrivals pushing for place.

At last they had something to see, for the beautiful Lucrezia Donati, surrounded by the fairest of Florentine maidens, was being enthroned above the lists as the Queen of Love. For one moment she held the centre of the stage alone, smiling proudly on her subjects of a day as she stood there high above them, tall, majestic, her bright dark eyes carefully treated to appear even more brightly dark under the intricately coiffed pile of her fair hair. Then her ladies clustered around her and the brasses blew a loud appreciation of the tableau.

Every man in the crowd had his favorite in that feminine court and shouted his admiration to his fellows. Every woman admired and envied the gleaming, heavily embroidered silks of the gowns and the furs and velvets of the cloaks. But they all turned from the Court of Love to cheer Lorenzo as he rode into the square for the formal parade that preceded the equally formal battle.

Truly he vindicated his claim to the title of "Magnificent," which in a world of flattery he shared with every man of whom someone had a favor to ask. So much splendor concentrated in one young person had never been seen in Florence until that day. The crowd scarcely realized that before them rode the ugliest young man in town. Normally his face was arresting by its homeliness, but today the beauty of his gaudy trappings drew the eye from the plainness of his features. The Medici treasure vaults had been looted to provide the heir of the House with a costume that would dazzle all observers. The other gallants needed but one look to know that they were beaten before they placed a lance in rest.

A hum of gratified approval greeted Lorenzo's five pages as, surrounded by fifers and drummers sounding away right merrily, they rode into the Piazza. Behind them came their knight, blazing in red, white and a glitter of gems, proud in the knowl/ edge that the heights of personal adornment had at last been reached.

Above his head waved a banner which he had designed himself for the occasion. It depicted the beautiful Lucrezia, in the gold and silver robes she wore as Queen of Love, standing in the sunshine weaving a wreath of laurel. No one doubted for whom the wreath was intended. In a scroll at the lady's feet, among the fallen leaves, was worked in pearls, although misspelled, her champion's motto for the day, "Le Tems Revient."

The banner was almost as much admired as the cavalier's dress. This was founded on a scheme of red and white silk, slashed and puffed in the French manner and spangled with jewels. Across the young man's shoulders was flung a scarf embroidered with fresh and withered roses. His cap was black velvet surmounted by a golden feather which dripped pearls and diamonds. Pearls were lavished even on the red and white velvet with which his horse was capari/

soned. The steed himself was the finest to be found in the Kingdom of Naples, whose ruler had selected him from the best stud in Europe as an appropriate gift for Lorenzo de' Medici. The animal pranced and reared admirably, enabling the rider to display his only martial accomplishment, horsemanship.

But the kingly gift was no war horse. Lorenzo, encircled by ten mounted cavaliers almost as splendid as himself, dismounted and changed into his fighting clothes. In place of the silk coat he put on a doublet of velvet fringed with gold and embroidered with the Lilies of France, a privilege newly bestowed upon his family. The velvet cap was laid aside in favor of a helmet sporting three long blue plumes. Taking up his shield, also embossed with the fleurdelys and with Il Libro, the great Medici diamond, set in the centre, Lorenzo mounted his charger, this one the gift of Borso d'Este, Duke of Ferrara, and the trumpet sounded the signal for the fight to begin.

The jousting of Italy had little in common with the crude, rough combats in which the transalpine barbarians delighted. Everything was so ordered that no man need be afraid to risk his best clothes in the fray. Italians made of bloodshed a serious business, not a game. They did their killing without ostentation or parade, and did it very well. But they did not want their pageants marred by torn, dusty costumes and the groans of injured men.

Of course unforeseen contingencies might arise. These were, however, amply provided for in an old ruling of the Florentine Signoria entitled "A Provision Against Cases of Accident." No man, it was stipulated, could be punished if he killed another in the course of a regularly organized tournament. A more practical safeguard was furnished by the tilting ground itself. The contestants galloped down parallel alleys, fenced off from each other so that the horses could not collide. Blows were exchanged over the fence in passing. Furthermore, professional soldiers, who might be presumed to know too much of the art of battle and to forget their company manners in the heat of the strife, took no part in these amateur proceedings.

Song and gladness were held to be much more desirable than blows in any Italian tournament. So from their post on the roof of the Church of Santa Croce, the musicians broke forth into sprightly tunes as Lorenzo put the spurs to his steed and rode out against Carlo Borromeo to start the real business of the day. Two lances splintered, two horses faltered in their strides, two riders rocked a little in their saddles, the trumpet blared triumphantly, the crowd cheered happily and the judges leaned their heads closer together. Lorenzo trotted back to the head of the lists to take on his kinsman, Braccio de' Medici. Braccio was almost unhorsed but not quite, the nearest to an upset that the day of fighting witnessed. Against his third antagonist, Carlo

[7]

da Forme, Lorenzo showed even more remarkable prowess. With a lucky stroke he cleanly split Carlo's helmet, a rarely difficult achievement which sent the crowd into ecstasies. Then, after exchanging a blow with Benedetto Salutati, the host felt that the demands of honor had been satisfied. He retired to the stands with his retinue to watch the other seventeen competitors win their laurels.

They did well, but not too well, for at the end of the afternoon's sport not a single man had been parted from his saddle and the judges were able without shame to announce that Lorenzo de' Medici was the victor. He had paid well for his triumph. The day's festivities cost him ten thousand ducats, but he did not begrudge the expense for, besides keeping his promise to Lucrezia, he could write:

"Although I was not highly versed in the use of weapons and the delivery of blows, the first prize was given to me, a helmet fashioned of silver with Mars as the crest."

It was this helmet instead of the laurel wreath which the Queen of Love placed upon his head as he knelt before her in the sight of all Florence. They made such a pretty picture of aristocratic happiness as they faced each other on the dais that it would have been unkind amid so much splendor to recall that it was not many weeks since they had scorned all that, since Lorenzo had addressed and Lucrezia had received with delight the sonnet

Seek he who will in grandeur to be blest,
  Place in proud halls, and splendid courts, his joy,
  For pleasure or for gold his arts employ,
  Whilst all his hours unnumbered cares molest.
A little field in native flowerets dressed,
  A rivulet in soft murmurs gliding by,
  A bird whose love-sick note salutes the sky,
  With sweeter magic lull my cares to rest.
And shadowy woods, and rocks, and towering hills,
  And caves obscure, and nature's free-born train,
  And some lone nymph that timorous speeds along,
Each in my mind some gentle thought instils
  Of those bright eyes that absence shrouds in vain;
  Ah gentle thoughts! soon lost the city cares among.

But although this poem was forgotten, the day had been such a splendid tribute to the Goddess of Love, so stirring, so romantic, that Luigi Pulci could not restrain his Muse. Even as the home-going throngs milled about the Piazza, reminding each other of the day's glories, he was murmuring to himself the exalted stanzas which he hoped would make both the tournament and himself immortal. But the men and women who jostled him did not need Pulci to tell them that the day had been a grand success. They all agreed that Lorenzo had kept his promise and upheld gloriously the family tradition.

He was very busy receiving congratulations on his entertainment, but not too busy to think of his betrothed, who after all might be interested to know

[9]

what he had done for her. He found time to send off a few lines to Rome to assure Clarice Orsini that he, her future husband, had given a tournament in honor of their engagement and that he had acquitted himself well. Clarice was properly appreciative, at least so Lorenzo's diplomatic uncle, Francesco Tornabuoni, wrote him. Francesco's letters had been picturing a beautiful, accomplished girl bowed under a load of anguish greater than she could bear, suffering from a severe headache caused by incessant worry over possible injury to her young man. The news of his success worked a miraculous cure, and once again the dear girl went singing happily about the house "and was quite merry." But when she answered Lorenzo's letter, she was able to control the exuberant gayety which so much impressed Francesco. Nor were there traces of past pain. She was just as calm as Lorenzo.

"I have had a letter from you which pleases me greatly," she wrote after only a short delay, "since it told me about the tournament in which you gained so much honor. I am very glad you have been satisfied by a thing which gives you so much pleasure, and if my prayers have been heard it is an especial joy to me, for I am so anxious to please you. I commend myself to you. No more."

Lucrezia Donati figured not at all in this tender correspondence.

II

It was the "age of baſtards and adventurers," but Lorenzo de' Medici was neither. Born into a world of Papal nephews, condottieri chiefs and illegitimate nobles, he boaſted a descent of remarkable respect-ability from the jovial founder of the family fortunes who gave the Medici their name and was remembered in legend as one man to whom that amorous Nea-politan, Queen Giovanna la Superba, refuſed her favors.

Having received her short and simple answer to his advances, he returned to Florence, where his talents were more generously appreciated. He was a medico, whence the family name, and gained great repute for the marvellous curative powers of his pills. The sign outside his shop was adorned with six of the capsules, and the later, greater representatives of the family took their coat of arms from the sign. It also furnished the war-cry of "Palle! Palle!" with which the Medici adherents entered upon civil dis-putes.

Nearer than the physician to the roots of the family tree, the envious maintained, was the Queen of the Witches, whose minions were ſtill active when the greateſt of her descendants ruled in Florence. The poet Poliziano himself had seen them walking about the streets, plucking out their eyes in a casual manner and putting them back again, working all sorts of mischief and generally carrying on the traditions of the legendary past. Poliziano saw so much of them that he lectured on the subject at the University, where he was professor of philosophy, but he did not mention his patron's ancestress. Nevertheless, others said that it was this malignant female's legacy which established the family power, wealth and luck, for she left a key to that enchanted garden where would be found the spells of a successful sorcerer.

"Thus," she explained to her heirs, "you can do all the evil and enjoy all the crime that a great ruler can desire; spare not man in your vengeance, nor woman in your passion, for he lives best who wishes for most and gets what he wants."

Insofar as they followed the precepts of this out⁄spoken and practical dame, her descendants fulfilled the spirit of the lines

> *Take all that's evil and unto it add*
> *All that is glorious, and the result*
> *Will be, in one brief word, the Medici.*

They early found, however, that banking was a much better key than either medicine or sorcery to the enchanted garden of power and wealth. Ever since the doctor's day they had been catering to the financial needs of their fellows. As Florence grew into a middle⁄class paradise where merchant and banker could speak on terms of equality with Pope and King, the Medici grew with it. In the wars of the Guelphs and Ghibillines, the old nobility was driven from power and deprived of all property and civil rights. The middle class ruled alone, and very often not too wisely. The dominant faction was usually a little too domineering, while many of the leaders of commerce neglected business for the even more hazardous risks of politics.

In the constant turmoil of a hundred years, the Medici kept their heads. They devoted themselves exclusively to their private affairs, except on the rare occasions when an emergency compelled every man to take a side. The Medici were then always with the masses, but never so zealously as to lose all favor with the minority.

The offices of the Republic—except the judge-ships, which were held by foreigners who would be more impartial than natives—were filled by lot from the middle-class business men and prosperous arti-sans who alone possessed the boon of citizenship. The Medici had to take their turn, but the terms were short and they never performed the duties of office with offensive heartiness. They spent all their energies on finance. Branches of the Medici Bank spread all over the continent of Europe, even to England and the Levant. They did so well that when Giovanni de' Medici died in 1428 he left to his sons, Cosimo and Lorenzo, the second largest fortune in the second richest city of Europe.

That was not enough for Cosimo. He had always

listened with respect while his father preached about tranquillity, minding one's own business, letting politics as severely alone as the peculiar constitution of Florence would permit, making no enemies and serving all men well—at an equitable price. For forty years the son had heard these words of wisdom, but hardly were old Giovanni's affairs settled than Cosimo began to put into effect a more ambitious policy of his own. Giovanni had made no will—the Medici seldom bothered about such trifles, knowing how easily the most strictly drawn testament could be upset—and Cosimo's first care was to see that his brother's estate remained united to his own. Even the second largest fortune in Florence was not going to be big enough for him.

Once assured of Lorenzo's co-operation and the bank's continued prosperity, Cosimo plunged into politics. Tall, lean, handsome, generous and persuasive, he was seen and heard at all important public meetings and private conferences. He recruited followers, intrigued against his rivals, played the munificent patron to the populace and the arts. He worked so hard and so formidably that five years after his father's death he was in a small cell-like room high up in the tower of the Palazzo Publico, a prisoner of state, afraid to eat lest the food be poisoned and expecting at any moment to be thrown from the narrow window to the pavement, a favorite Florentine mode of execution.

He had aroused the serious attention of the Albizzi,

the family who had for years maintained themselves by a well calculated mixture of force and fraud at the head of the government. Rinaldo degli Albizzi was not minded to allow a mere Medici to dispute his power. But he made one bad mistake. He shrank from the summary execution of so popular a figure as Cosimo, who was the most surprised man in Florence when, after six weeks of imprisonment, he was still alive. His jailer was friendly and shared the banker's food to prove that it was not poisoned. Meanwhile friends outside were acting, and for a bribe of only a thousand ducats secured from the Gonfalonier of Justice, the ostensible head of the state, the secret release of his prisoner, who was smuggled hurriedly out of town.

There remained only one dignified course for the Albizzi. They exiled Cosimo to Venetian territory along with Lorenzo and a few chiefs of the defeated party. Cosimo bore the blow philosophically. After all, the lot of the vanquished was usually more severe. He still had his health, his money and—what the Albizzi did not realize—his popularity in Florence. Venice was a pleasant place. The aristocrats of the islands were pleased to honor him, for they were shrewd and knew that the exiled Florentine of today might be the ruler of tomorrow. Cosimo knew it too and kept up a voluminous correspondence with friends at home.

He was more successful at long range than he had been on the ground. The Albizzi's pride and brag

were getting a little on Florentine nerves. Within a
year the men of the family were flying to escape
Cosimo's vengeance, and the head of the House of
Medici came riding into Florence in triumph. Welcomed as the saviour of his country from tyranny, he
spent the next thirty years in proving to her that she
could take tyranny and like it. He had his own
brand, so judicious that only a few recognized it, and
these few could be ignored in public as envious,
malicious malcontents who did not know what was
good for them.

The necessary show of legality was easy. The
Albizzi had shown how it was done. Not long after
Cosimo returned from Venice, the bells of the
Palazzo Publico summoned the people to the great
Square where important affairs were settled. An
army of mercenaries was drawn up around the big
open space, and most of those citizens known to be
hostile to the Medici found it impossible to get
through the ranks. The rest of the burghers were
asked if they would care to entrust the government's
reorganization to a committee of Cosimo's friends—
yes or no? The ayes had it, and Cosimo had earned
the right to manipulate republican forms of administration at his own sweet will.

And now he remembered the lectures of old
Giovanni. There was something in them, Cosimo
decided. He would make his tyranny as unostentatious as possible. In the sight of the populace he remained only a banker, a generous patron of arts, big

Cosimo de' Medici Welcomed Home from Exile

hearted in dispensing charity and possessed of a
passion for building. But foreign kings and princes
knew that when they were dealing with Florence, it
would save time to go direct to Cosimo de' Medici.

The family was doing very well. Lorenzo never
tried to cross his elder brother and could be trusted
with the most delicate foreign missions. Two sons,
Piero and Giovanni, were growing up to carry on
the family ambition. Florence was prosperous and
the Medici fortune had become the largest in a city
of wealthy men. Cosimo settled down to enjoy the
fruits of his success and extend his financial opera-
tions still further.

First of all he needed a new house, and on a large
plot on the Via Larga he prepared to erect a palace
whose exterior would maintain the unostentatious
appearance of his policy but which would give scope
within for his lavish tastes. His favorite architect,
Brunelleschi, then engaged on the enormous project
of the Cathedral of Santa Maria del Fiore, offered
a plan that was altogether too magnificent. Michelozzi, the second architect of the day, came nearer
fulfilling the banker's ideas. He produced a rather
hybrid creation, a blockhouse below, Doric on the
second story and Corinthian on the third, but it
conveyed the impression of solid respectability and
plainness which Cosimo desired.

The whole family took up their residence here,
and Contessina, Cosimo's very capable wife, had
now all she could manage to keep in that order which

was the pride of her life the big new house and the two country villas at Careggi and Cafaggiuolo. The poor woman had a hard time after the comparative simplicity of the Bardi Palace, which had been part of her dowry, but she was one of those dutiful women who derive a perverse pleasure from domestic success. She talked of cheeses and wines and servants and clothes with enormous animation and volubility. She was always fussing around Cosimo when he was at home, taking much better care of him than that busy man desired. On her two sons, delicate young men, she spent her energies happily.

She rather resented her husband's increasing consequence in the State. It took him often away from her, and he never wrote letters, a failing of which she complained bitterly. Furthermore the cares of his position sat heavily upon him and made him rather uninteresting company for a wife who longed for an appreciative listener to her tales of household adventures, of what she had said to the butcher and what the wine merchant said to her and how the children were always wearing out their clothes. Cosimo was patient. The nearest he came to temper in reply to her scoldings about his silence was in his old age when he remarked plaintively:

"When we are going to our country house you are busy for a fortnight preparing for the move, but since I have to go from this life to another does it not seem to you that I ought to have something to think about?"

Both his sons brought their wives home to Contessina's admirably run house. Here also, among the several dozen domestics, was the Circassian slave girl, Maddalena, for whom Cosimo had paid sixty ducats when she was young and handsome. Their son, Carlo, was being trained for the Church and to be the family representative at Rome.

The marriages of the legitimate children strengthened friendships between the Medici and leading families of Florence. Piero's wife was Lucrezia Tornabuoni, a great acquisition, for she was a beautiful, intelligent girl with a large number of able brothers who could be used to good advantage. Ten years later Giovanni married Ginevra degli Alessandri, and her family too was influential.

Contessina might have expected to have a proper audience now. But these modern girls were not like the home-loving young women of Contessina's day. They were interested in the strangest things, books— they actually read books—pictures, statues, music, even the philosophic discourses so dear to their husbands. Contessina could not be angry, for the younger women did their share of the work well enough, but she was puzzled. Even when Lucrezia and Ginevra were blessed with children they did not adopt their mother-in-law's views. The old woman devoted herself more entirely than ever to the house and left the others to their own kind of talk.

There was plenty of it, whether they were in the city palace or the country villas. Cosimo was always

willing, when business permitted, to discuss philosophy or the arts. Men of learning and of wit too
thronged his hospitable houses. It was fashionable
just then to encourage scholars, and Cosimo took
the lead in everything. He did not boast much learning himself, but he was a discerning patron. The
best writers, artists and talkers of the day were glad
to accept subsidies from the great man who demanded in return only the privilege of listening to
their debates. He heard so much of their arguments
that at last he was able to take a respectable part in
the conversation.

It was about this time that Italy discovered Plato.
So much dialogue appealed irresistibly to men who
were just beginning to realize what leisure is for.
Plato became a literary style as well as a philosophic
necessity, and everywhere his disciples began to study
Greek. That was too much for Cosimo; he was too
old. But there were other ways in which he could
show his superlative recognition of the prevailing
fetish. He established a Platonic Academy and
selected a bright lad named Marsilio Ficino to be
the future head of it. Marsilio was twenty, old enough
to have displayed capacity for the task and young
enough to be taught by the best masters in Italy.
Within a few years the meetings of the Academy were
the talk of Florence. Nowhere else was such ripe
wisdom, such acute logic, such vast information,
such caustic wit. Nowhere else was so much that
would have astounded Plato read into the philoso

pher's teachings. Any day the most perplexing problems of humanity were settled forever on the basis of Platonic principles. But the next day they would be settled all over again, and quite differently. There was no end save sheer exhaustion to the talk or the principles.

Cosimo enjoyed it hugely. He was a most philosophic person these days. There was no one in Florence to dispute his authority. Every few years he had an army and the people summoned to the Piazza della Signoria—the army first and then the people—to confirm the system on which his authority rested. There were few dissenting voices. The men of the Albizzi, the Strozzi and many lesser families were scattered over Italy bemoaning the hardships of exile.

Such irreconcilables as remained in Florence were treated to a new kind of persecution. Cosimo knew better than most that the greatest political weapon is money, so he used his hold on the government to make his enemies poor and keep them that way. A wayward citizen's first offense of opposition to the established order was a substantial increase in his tax assessment. If he failed to take the hint, a series of crushing levies quickly ruined him, and Cosimo had nothing to fear from any bankrupt. His people entertained too great a respect for wealth and expected too expensive favors from their rulers to be led astray by any penniless demagogue.

The scholarship to which Cosimo bowed in his

hours of leisure was no protection for the political foe. Death after the torture might be reserved for cruder spirits, but learning never conferred entire immunity from punishment. Gianozzo Manetti, the great Humanist whose eloquence had so charmed King Alfonso that the Neapolitan monarch sat immovable through a long oration without noticing a fly that crawled about his nose, was ruined by taxation. Francesco Filelfo, a turbulent though scholarly professor, had been one of the few who in 1433 had urged Rinaldo degli Albizzi to kill Cosimo while he could. Since then Filelfo had been using his unexcelled powers of invective against the Medici. One day as he was walking to the University an assassin employed by the family set upon him with a dagger. The professor defended himself ably, but soon decided to accept the offer of a chair outside Tuscany.

While his foes grew poorer, Cosimo became richer. The bulk of the Medici wealth was concentrated in his hands. His brother died in 1440, leaving only a minor son, Pier Francesco, and an immense estate "which Cosimo," his grandson recorded, "kept for the use and benefit of the said Pier Francesco and for Piero and Giovanni, his own sons, until they were of proper age." The division of this property was not made until 1451 when, the young Lorenzo reports approvingly, "a liberal half" was assigned to Pier Francesco.

This fortune, now unequalled in Europe, enabled Cosimo not only to increase his popularity at home but made him the arbiter of international quarrels. Kings could not make war without Cosimo's consent, for where else could they get ready money to pay their troops? Popes looked to him for loans to maintain the dignity of the Church. Edward IV of England was to owe his throne to timely Medici credit, a debt he never paid.

But it was in Italy that Cosimo's money power was most felt. A war in which Naples and Venice were allied against Florence and which must have crushed the smaller state, was averted when Cosimo called his notes and left the enemies of his country without money for their condottieri. Later, reconciled to Venice, he provided the financial resources which enabled the maritime republic to fight France and Milan at the same time. Florence was very proud of him.

Under him the city became the unquestioned centre of cultivated society, much resorted to by the aspiring nobility of surrounding states, great and small. To Cosimo's court—as it was called everywhere but in Florence—came the young Sigismondo Pandolpho Malatesta, who at seventeen had made himself Lord of Rimini by virtue of his own fierce military talents and the completeness with which he interpreted in his life and person the spirit of the age.

At home the handsome, cheerful youth had already learned those secrets of the torture chamber and poison vial which he used for the gratification of his passions, his ambitions and his hates. In Florence he acquired a devotion to art and scholarship which all his life rivalled his cruelty and lust. He went back to Rimini to adorn that city with beautiful buildings, works of art and the writings of the best scholars, all bought with the proceeds of the most savage raids upon his neighbors. He wrote really very pretty sonnets to his mistresses before he killed them. He heaped favors upon the learned. He was willing to fight for culture as quickly as for loot, and he honestly regarded the ashes of a Greek philosopher as a splendid prize of victory. He never ceased to admire Florence and the Medici.

Sigismondo came to the city at the height of its glory under Cosimo. Pope Eugenius IV was meet⁄ ing the Greeks there in an effort to bring about reunion of the Eastern and Western Churches. The Council, which drew the best theological debaters from all Christendom, was begun at Ferrara, but the plague necessitated hasty removal to a healthier city. Cosimo's brother, as the last diplomatic act of his life, secured the meeting for Florence, carrying out nobly the instructions of the Signoria, which opened:

"Present thyself at the feet of H. H. Pope Eugenius, commending to him our city and its Signoria and our whole people as faithful and devout sons of Holy Church and of His Holiness, offering our city and our people to His Holiness.

"To descend now to substantial matters. . . ."

In the negotiation of these substantial matters Lorenzo proved his capacity. The sum Florence should pay for the privilege of housing the Council, the accommodations to be offered, the protection to be given were details which he worked out so well that in spite of the competition of many other cities the streets of Florence were soon filled with Cardinals, Bishops, Patriarchs, Metropolitans and their suites. The Council halls resounded with debates on the nature of the Trinity and the position of the Bishop of Rome. The Emperor of the East, John Paleologus, was present to hear the disputes, and the earnings of the Medici Banks all over the world were poured out for his entertainment. Pageantry became a daily custom, but the Florentines never tired of the show. They were sorry when the Council broke up in an agreement which those prelates of the Greek Church who had remained at home refused to accept.

There was no practical result from all the talk, but Florence was not left altogether desolate to mourn past splendors. Excuses were easily found after the great ecclesiastics had gone for giving the people plenty of shows. Visiting celebrities, feast days, the arrival of foreign embassies, the marriages of prominent citizens, all became public spectacles. While looking back at the last good time and forward to the next one, the artisans and clerks were content to work hard for their masters, and the masters never failed to furnish the good time. It was all one big happy family.

III

Piero's elder boy was developing into the favorite
of this family. But he was a husky youngster and
bore up well under the strain. Indeed, he thrived
on it. He was one of those pushing children who
want to do everything and know everything as soon
as they can talk. His parents and his tutors took
advantage of his willing spirit. They burdened his
infant schoolroom with a curriculum from which he
would have shrunk in horror if he had not been too
young to know. As it was, he only lapped it up and
sought further information about all sorts of things,
religion and politics and art, how things are made,
how games are played.

By the time he was eight years old he was trying
to be a teacher himself. He undertook the education
of his four-year-old brother, Giuliano, a docile child
and enduring. In a corner of the gardens at Careggi
or a room in the Via Larga palace, Giuliano patiently tried to satisfy Lorenzo with a repetition of
what the older child had learned that day. But
fortunately for the younger, Lorenzo was kept too
busy to devote much time to pedagogy.

For when he was eight the teaching staff was en-
larged. His first tutor, the learned Gentile Becchi,
could no longer cope with the pupil single-handed.

Cristoforo Landino for polite letters and rhetoric, Argyropylus for Greek and the philosophy of Aristotle, Marsilio Ficino for Platonism, a music master, a mathematics instructor, a riding master, a fencer and a religious mentor were all turned loose upon the young prodigy at once, and he satisfied all of them. He did it so quickly that he had spare moments to play in the fields with the farm boys or around the stable with the grooms or with little Lucrezia Donati in the villa whose gardens adjoined his own at Careggi.

He also learned from his mother the arts of dancing and practical piety. Every morning when the family was in Florence, Lucrezia took her four children— there were two girls, Bianca and Nannina, besides the boys—to pray at the chapel of the Confraternity of St. Paul. They were always attended by swarms of the beggars that infested Florence, for Lucrezia had taught her children never to refuse alms.

The dancing served a purpose when distinguished guests were entertained in the Via Larga. By the time Lorenzo was ten, Cosimo was boasting that his grandchildren had appeared before crowned heads. No less a personage than the Duke of Milan had applauded diplomatically the evolutions performed for his edification.

The family was not often in Florence, though. Lucrezia was never very well—she had borne seven children, three of whom died in infancy—and was

constantly seeking health in the country. Careggi
and the half villa, half fortress which Michelozzi had
built for Cosimo at Cafaggiuolo were her favorite
resorts when her own weakness or a recurrence of
the plague, an epidemic which hovered over Italy
almost constantly, drove her from the city. Most of
the horde of teachers went with her, and in 1461,
when Lorenzo was twelve, Becchi was able to write
to Piero:

"We are well on with Ovid, and have read four
books of Justin, both history and fable."

It was time for the boy to enter on the serious
business of life. He was rather young, perhaps, but
the family needed him. He could take some of the
burden of splendid appearances from his weary elders.
For Cosimo had entered upon his seventy-fifth year
and was finding himself possessed of a love of repose.
He delegated more and more of his affairs to his
sons, and spent his own time thinking about life and
talking about philosophy. But the sons both worked
under disadvantages. The elder was already known
as Piero the Gouty. His malady when it did not
completely incapacitate him for business, prevented
his travelling.

Giovanni was in equally bad health. All his life
he had eaten and drunk too much, and had never
obeyed his mother's repeated injunctions about keeping his feet dry and staying out of the poisonous night
air. Lorenzo was the only other man in the family.
Somebody had to recognize the presence of Duke

John of Anjou, for part of the Medicean foreign policy was a friendship, political and financial, with the French royal house.

So Lorenzo went on his first diplomatic mission. It was lots of fun. He had a new suit, that of a French boy, much more ornate and colorful in its slashed doublet, puffed sleeves, tight hose and plumed cap than the simple jacket of Florentine youth. He liked to dress up and he was not a bad looking little boy. His bobbed black hair was worn in bangs on his forehead and rather long behind. His cheeks were round and smooth and pink. His eyes, nearsighted and peering, were rather small, but his chin had not yet attained its final massive proportions and his lips were a little fuller than they would be later. All in all he was such a good figure that Becchi, who was part of the retinue, wrote home proudly:

"The boy made so charming an appearance that we were immediately surrounded by an immense concourse which followed us to the King's son."

Lorenzo made his little speech with so much assurance and conducted himself in so manly, dignified a way when complimented that the tutor exclaimed—the French having even then a reputation for lightness:

"His gravity belied his costume."

He came home to receive the approval of his elders and take his place in the family councils, a listener rather than a talker, but on the job. He was grown up, and he never regretted his lost childhood. Being a man was a great deal more amusing than listening to ghost stories in the nursery and being told at every turn a list of the things he must not do.

Italy in 1461 was no place for children anyway, but a man could enjoy life as long as the plague and the daggers of his enemies left him in health. Even a very young man of twelve, if he had plenty of money, an inquiring mind, a taste for reading and the position of heir to a State, could have a good time. Not the least of such a young man's pleasures was the getting acquainted with the great men among whom he would have to fight his way. A ruthless lot all of them, rulers, ecclesiastics, merchants, painters, writers, sculptors, soldiers. They knew what they wanted, and they were not fussy about how they got it. A man learning to be governor of Florence must know how to walk carefully in their midst.

First of all he must learn to keep an eye on Venice, mightiest and most incomprehensible of the powers of Italy, for the aristocrats in their palaces on the canals might decide at any moment to turn their incomparable resources from fighting with the Turk for the trade of the Levant to oppressing their Italian neighbors.

Next door, Milan was rather a place for spending money. The Sforza ruled there, inheriting cruelty from the Viconti whom they had dispossessed and greed from their peasant ancestor who had raised himself to the front rank of condottieri. The peasant's son, Francesco, had seized the Duchy of Milan for himself after amassing an ample fortune by the sale of his sword, but he could still be bought, and to a Florentine ruler was usually worth the price.

In Rome Aeneas Silvius Piccolomini, Pope Pius II, was quarrelling with his rival princes over the extent of the Holy See's temporal power and trying to get them to support the great crusade which was the ambition of his life. The ugly, bald, weak-eyed little man, crippled by a long pilgrimage barefoot through the snows of Scotland, was a poet and scholar of renown. Italy in general and the Medici in particular had hailed with joy his election as the successor to Alonso Borgia, Calixtus III, the "barbarous Spaniard," who had so little reverence for the ornaments of civilization that he scattered or destroyed the literary and artistic treasures painfully collected by his predecessors. Calixtus left behind him only empty coffers in the Vatican and a rich, handsome young nephew named Rodrigo in the Sacred College.

Pius, it was believed, would be a peaceful Pope, probably devout, certainly a good ruler and patron of arts. But once elevated to the throne, the feeble, prematurely old man developed an unexpected strain of bellicosity. He made war on the smaller principalities which he thought should acknowledge themselves as Papal vassals. To organize his crusade he used money which his early admirers hoped would be spent in promoting research and building. To attain his warlike objects he wielded temporal and spiritual weapons ambidextrously.

His bitterest quarrel was with Sigismondo Mala-testa, whose greed and ferocity were a good match in the game of trouble making for the Pope's preten-sions. When he was not cultivating the aesthetic tastes acquired in Florence, Sigismondo was selling his army and his own military genius to the highest bidder, usually Venice, or trying to enlarge the boundaries of Rimini. He had just defeated the Papal army, but Pius always had another resource than vulgar strength. He excommunicated Mala-testa for the crimes of heresy, sacrilege, rebellion against the Holy See, rape, adultery, violation, incest, parricide, felony and murder. The Lord of Rimini was actually guilty of most of these offences, and a few others which the Pope in his hasty rage forgot to mention, but he declined the Pontiff's invitation to come to Rome and be burned for his sins. Pius had to be content with consigning his effigy to the flames.

His Holiness was equally unfortunate in his cru-sade. That form of adventure was just a little old fashioned. There was a discouraging lack of response even to the Bull in which the Pope expressed a determination to lead the sacred army in person.

"We will not fight with the sword because our feeble hand can scarcely raise itself to bless the people," he explained. "We will fight not with the sword but with prayer; we will stand high on the poop of the ship or on a high hill near the battle to bless our friends and to curse our enemies."

Naples watched such a Pope jealously. The Holy See had certain claims on the Kingdom which were generally satisfied with formal gestures of submission and the tribute of one white horse a year. But the head of the Church might at any moment demand more. Frequently he did. Every time that happened the French and Spanish pretenders to the Neapolitan throne were reminded of their rights, and all Italy was disturbed. King Ferrante was inspired by the fright of one such occasion to start his unique collec/ tion of the corpses of men he distrusted. Neatly embalmed and dressed in their best clothes, they occupied a special room in the palace and served to hearten their owner with the memory of plots that had failed.

Ferrante's rights to his throne were none too legitimate. He said he was the bastard of Alfonso the Good and a Spanish woman, but it was more commonly believed that she had deceived her royal lover with a half/caste Moor from Valencia. A dark, handsome but over/fed Spaniard of cultivated tastes —he had been brought up by Alfonso as a son— Ferrante was strong enough to seize Naples, but he had a good deal of trouble holding it against foreign and domestic enemies.

In between the five important powers, a host of smaller states, independent or semi/independent, struggled for existence and aggrandizement. Ferrara,

[*33*]

Siena, Lucca, Genoa and even tinier counties, baronies, duchies and free cities went their own way or acknowledged the nominal lordship of whoever pleased them most or promised most.

In Florence Lorenzo was learning that his grand-father ruled the State largely because he knew just what was going on in all these places and what it meant. There were plenty of other men in the city able and willing to play the Magnificent. Some of them were nearly as rich as Cosimo and shared his popularity. But none of them had so many friends in high places abroad. As soon as manhood over-took him, Lorenzo began to appreciate the advan-tages of friends in high places. He observed with interest the little acts of reciprocal kindness which kept these friendships cemented. A loan, a quiet tip about an enemy's movements, a word of praise at a timely moment, trifling but well chosen gifts, gal-lantry to the right woman—these are the ties that bind.

In his new life Lorenzo might have been freed from the army of tutors if he had desired. But they had done their work so well that he kept them as friends and still devoted himself to study and con-versation. Becchi, Landino, Ficino and the rest were supposed to be the tutors of Giuliano, but they spent almost as much time on Lorenzo's education.

The young man was much oftener in Florence now, for he had to take his chance with the other men on the plague while the women and children went to the country. He could no longer spend his summers at the villa, but he was permitted to travel elsewhere to learn statecraft with the Florentine embassies.

His financial education was neglected. The Medici were getting a little proud. Though they clung to the Bank, which gave them the money to enjoy and keep their position, they were beginning to believe that the future head of the house should be something more than just a banker. Piero's boyhood had been afflicted with many weary months in the Medici branches abroad, studying finance. He still spent more time in the counting house than in the Palazzo Publico. But his son, whose visits to the office were hardly more than courtesy calls, was given only a rudimentary understanding of the firm's vast affairs. While Piero attended to business and Cosimo spent his days in remembering past triumphs, Lorenzo represented them officially on those public occasions when a splendid and amiable presence was the sole requisite. His uncle was too ill now for any business and in 1463, shortly after the death of his infant son, Giovanni died too. Cosimo had hoped for great things from the young gourmand, and wandered disconsolately about his palace muttering:

"This is a large house for so small a family."

For the first time he began to entertain doubts about the destiny of the Medici. He himself was so old, seventy-six, and Piero so crippled by gout that strength seemed to have departed from the family.

Of course Lorenzo was a promising boy, but what could any boy do in the face of such competition as would surely arise after the old man's death? Cosimo knew his Florence too well to suppose that loyalty alone would hold the proud chiefs of the Medici party in allegiance to an invalid and a child. Desperately he tried to fortify the family position by matrimonial alliances. Bianca, Lorenzo's elder sister, was betrothed to a son of the ambitious and wealthy Pazzi. Negotiations were begun for the marriage of the younger girl to Bernardo of the Rucellai, an equally wealthy family who boasted sixty armed retainers and had hitherto held aloof from the Medici if they did not oppose them. There was even talk of engaging Lorenzo himself to the daughter of Luca Pitti, a vain, extravagant man, popular in the city and one of Cosimo's ablest lieutenants.

But all this marrying and giving in marriage was a poor substitute, the old man knew, for some one as strong as himself to carry on the government of Florence. His only comfort when he contemplated the probable fate of his prosperity was Lucrezia, who had already shown a shrewdness which Florentines were not too stubborn to recognize and use in a woman.

"She is the best man among us," Cosimo would say, and blessed the inspiration that had led him to select her as a wife for his elder son.

IV

Cosimo did not have long to worry. In the summer of 1464 he was very sick. So was Piero, and together they retired to Careggi. The son improved, but the father grew rapidly worse until soon there was little hope that the doctor could do anything more for him. They kept trying, but Piero reported:

"The physician is hourly expected to arrive from Milan, but for my part I place my confidence in God."

Cosimo himself had no doubts. He knew he was dying, and it was an old family tradition that men in his condition should give their sons some last good words of advice. No one making such speeches could ask for a better listener than Piero. Strict attention to business, for power depends on wealth, a well ordered and harmonious home, modesty in the administration of government, for jealousy comes without being courted—these were the theses on which the dying man elaborated. Piero was so much impressed that he did not wait for Cosimo to die before passing the lecture on to his own sons. A few days later, in the heat of midsummer, Cosimo de' Medici passed quietly out of life, congratulating himself to the last that all his affairs—personal, financial, governmental—were in the best possible order.

Piero was still too weak to travel and remained with his mother at Careggi. On Lorenzo fell the burden of arranging the funeral with the simplicity which Cosimo had desired, receiving unending visits of condolence and keeping a watchful eye on the tranquillity of the State. He was fifteen and had learned dignity. The prettiness of boyhood had departed. His cheeks had sunk, his lips thinned, his flat nose, which completely lacked a sense of smell, had lengthened and his chin grown. He was very knobby as to joints, long in the limb and rather clumsy in his movements.

But he presided with great composure in the Via Larga, thanking friends of the family in tones as stilted as their own, tactfully, and a little reluctantly, rejecting proposals for making the burial a gorgeously mournful pageant, and apportioning mourning clothes for the household. There were yards and yards of black cloth, veils and kerchiefs for the women, the amount varying from huge mounds of material for the dowager Contessina to skimpy gowns for the maids and slaves. On Lorenzo fell the task of arranging for innumerable masses in all the churches and chapels Cosimo had helped build or support.

Once the ceremonies were over, he went back to having a good time. For that there was no better city in the world than Florence. In exchange for a worthless political freedom that they never knew what to do with, her people had gained complete liberty to enjoy themselves in their own way. It was a little dangerous, perhaps, but they were too restless to be satisfied with the pleasures of ease and security. They sacrificed both gladly for excitement.

Of nights the young Lorenzo descended into the streets seeking adventure, and was never disappointed. Often enough it was quite mild, the simple adventure of defining life and human nature and truth with other talkative spirits on the marble platform between the Cathedral and the Baptistery, where on the hottest nights a breeze blew across the cool stone. Next evening he might join some band of clerks and weavers who felt their youth and wanted to sing. The old and sometimes bawdy songs were not enough for them. They wanted novelty and were not ashamed to improvise. Lorenzo de' Medici was always a welcome addition to such parties, for he improvised charmingly. Even at fifteen he could be sentimental or salacious, sad or gay, martial or pastoral, just as the occasion demanded. True, he had a voice like a frog with a head cold, but once he had provided the words his companions could always drown him out.

Other times Lorenzo found his way to many little houses in Florence where the wine was perhaps a little rougher than in the homes of the wealthy but flowed just as freely. And the daughters were as charming and bold as Lorenzo's own sisters. The respectability of their parents made the girls of Florence neither dull nor demure. They were as

ready as any rich damsel for a jest, a kiss or an as-
signation. They all liked Lorenzo as much—well,
almost as much—as if he had been handsome. For
he was amusing and generous.

Their brothers found him a good comrade for an
evening's gayety, and if it came to a bit of a brawl, as
it often did, he could swing a cudgel handily and use
his feet well. He was Cosimo's grandson, but he was
also one of the boys. The formal "Your Magnificence" of his appearances on the stage of public
affairs was never heard in the dark, narrow streets at
night when Lorenzo went out to play.

These were not the only pleasures the young man
was learning. He discovered the joy of putting down
on paper his thoughts—or what he took to be his
thoughts—his hopes, his feelings, his vaguely formed
notions of the world. Poetry was the ideal medium
for such unsubstantial writing, and Lorenzo did not
see why it should not be done in his native Tuscan.
Latin seemed unduly dignified to express a fanciful
mood that was anything but dignified. He could
write Latin verses, of course, and did so in order to
prove it, but Tuscan could be beautiful too. Look at
Dante and Boccaccio and Petrarch. The world had
not followed their example, but Lorenzo read some
of the products of his own pen aloud and was pleased
to listen to the approving words his verses provoked.

From his study, he turned with fresh enthusiasm
to the organizing of receptions, celebrations and processions. He never got over a childish love of dressing

Lorenzo de' Medici at 12
"His gravity belied his costume"

up, of seeing others dress up, of taking part in
pageantry. Piero, warned by gout and the growing
worries of a position which taxed too much his
ftolid imagination, approved this trait in his son,
but could not underftand it. He moaned bitterly
whenever he had to do some entertaining without
Lorenzo's aid. Once, when relieved unexpectedly
by a friend of the burden of some visiting princelings,
Piero wrote to his son:

"I am aftounded that Giovanni de' Pazzi, having
done it once, undertakes it again."

Lorenzo was not aftonished. He himself welcomed the inauguration of the new Signoria every
two months because it was an excuse for a party. He
would scrutinize with as much care as Piero the
names of the petty tradesmen, merchants, professional
men and even artisans who were to be the oftensible
rulers of Florence for the next sixty days. But while
Piero withdrew to Careggi for the office taking,
Lorenzo assumed a leading place among the dancers
at the bi-monthly celebration and arranged the
musical programmes. Only his youth kept him from
being among the speakers who extolled the virtues
of republican inftitutions, the greatness of the Florentine people and the wisdom of their rulers. Lorenzo
felt he would be very good at that sort of thing, but he
admitted that it hardly became one of his years to
make such orations. From time to time he was permitted to gratify his taftes for public speaking in a
subordinate address of welcome to a foreign embassy.

Less formal, but just as much fun as affairs of state, were the horse races, tournaments, football games and hunts organized for feast days, family celebrations or no reason at all. Racing was Lorenzo's favorite sport, and he was always a guest at the Alessandri Palace on race day. This fortunate family lived right at the finish of the course down the Borgo degl' Albizzi. The Alessandri were famous horse owners themselves, and the house was decorated lavishly with the gorgeously embroidered banners, the only prize offered for victory, which their stable had won for them.

Lorenzo, who was just beginning his career as owner, envied them their trophies, but was glad to watch from the Alessandri windows as the collection was increased.

Three strokes of the bell from the Palazzo Publico would start the horses, sometimes ridden by jockeys but more often urged on only by the shouts of the crowd and a set of spurs ingeniously devised so that the faster the horse galloped the deeper the rowels bit. They ran between lanes of yelling enthusiasts who carpeted the course with flowers thrown into the street with a little prayer for the entry that carried the thrower's money while boys on the housetops signalled to the watchers further along how the race was going. Lorenzo lost considerable sums on these races, for at sixteen he had not yet conquered the Borgo degl' Albizzi.

In other respects his tastes were so literary and

democratic that Piero was a little worried. He had come within the year to rely on Lorenzo for every‑ thing but finance. He consulted the boy about the final negotiations for Nannina's marriage, about the new list of citizens eligible for public office, about what to write to Louis XI in reply to his professions of undying regard. Louis in memory of certain timely loans from Cosimo benevolently addressed the patri‑ arch's son as "Cousin" and conferred upon the family the honorable distinction of adding the fleur‑ de‑lys to their shield. Both King and banker con‑ sidered that the loans had been well repaid. Men so honored, Piero felt, should make a more imposing show abroad than Lorenzo's nightly diversions made at home.

The young man was away on many embassies this year, to Bologna, Ferrara, Venice, Milan and to the new Pope, Paul II, the Venetian merchant who had deserted his counting house for the Church when his uncle was elected to the Holy See as Eugenius IV.

Piero repeatedly urged his son not to stint himself in impressing his hosts with the importance and wealth of the Medici. He realized only when the bills came in that such advice was needless. Lorenzo dis‑ covered ways of spending money that Piero did not know existed. His visits were ostensibly a tour of inspection of the Medici Banks, but Lorenzo saw only so much of the working of these institutions as was possible in the time necessary to draw funds for the more serious business of diplomacy.

[43]

It was a leisurely business. He spent most of his days on horseback, riding over Italy with an escort of writers and orators to exchange high-flown speeches with the rulers of the peninsula. Everything was done with a minimum of haste. Ambassador and Prince gave each other copies of newly discovered antique manuscripts, debated the respective merits of Plato and Aristotle, joined in praising a new painter—and once in a while dropped a few words about their political intentions. This, in the midst of processions, banquets, dancing and games, was a prelude to the long, formal speeches in which the orators endeavoured to out-do each other in flattery. Only then could there be serious talk of alliances, mutual assistance, tariffs, trade regulations, military contingents and subsidies. After elaborate farewells, the Ambassador would take horse for the many days' ride to the next capital, resting on the way from one set of festivities in preparation for the next.

Lorenzo's missions to Rome and Milan were especially important. It was essential that the Medici —and Florence—should be on good terms with the new Pope and the new Duke. Pius had died with his dreams of a modern Crusade shattered, and Paul was much more concerned with temporal affairs than with converting the heathen. He was far from being a scholarly priest. He had all the arrogant Venetian merchant's dislike of learning and wanted no students in the domains of the Church. Lorenzo had a large contempt for the Papal attitude, but there was too much at stake for him to show it. He dissembled so well that Paul became quite fond of him, and the Medici remained in favor at Rome.

He paid a high price in discomfort for his success. The Eternal City was not the sort of place to commend itself to a fastidious taste. It was here that Lorenzo first began to refer jocularly to the divine mercy which had permitted him to come into the world without a sense of smell. The young connoisseur was horrified by the indifference to all that he loved. Monuments of the beautiful, revered paganism were allowed to crumble into neglected ruins or were actually torn down to provide building material for the wretched hovels in which the Romans lived. Narrow streets paved with mud and filth were filled with quarrelsome crowds of unhealthy idlers. In the country round about an unfortunate peasantry who might have been happy in their immunity from taxation, since the Popes were still content to live on their spiritual revenues, were kept miserably poor and subjected to endless suffering by the incessant feuds of the Colonna and the Orsini, families too powerful to be controlled by the Vatican and too weak to establish the despotism at which they aimed. Lorenzo was very glad to escape from the domains of the Church to happier, cleaner, more cultured cities.

The importance of his embassy to Milan lay in the fact that Francesco Sforza had recently died, and there was some doubt that his son, Galeazzo Maria, would be able to hold the Duchy, for he was following out only the last of the three precepts which his father had considered sufficient to secure success in this world:

"Leave other men's wives alone.

"Strike none of your followers, or if you do send the injured man far away.

"Never ride a hard-mouthed horse or one who drops his shoe."

In spite of the young Duke's follies and short-comings, the Medici needed the Sforza alliance, and Lorenzo was able to give the Milanese the impression that the family millions were behind the new dynasty.

Of all his missions, however, Lorenzo most enjoyed a trip to Pisa to meet Federigo, son of Ferrante of Naples. The youth was escorting southward Ippolita Sforza, the bride of his elder brother, Duke Alfonso of Calabria. The cruelty, greed and belligerence of his family had missed Federigo, who preferred study and poetry to the martial sports which were more common in Naples than in any other part of Italy.

He was a couple of years younger than Lorenzo, and so obviously impressed by the Florentine's talents that immediate friendship was assured. Ippolita was clever, too, and with what was already being called the arrogance of youth the three agreed passionately that Dante and Boccaccio deserved to be ranked with Homer and Virgil, even if they had chosen to write in the vulgar tongue. Lorenzo wrote in the vulgar tongue himself. He justified the ex-

cessive modernism by making for Federigo a collection of his favorite Tuscan poems, to which he
appended four sonnets of his own. He included also
a prose argument for Italian which was just as
worthy as any classical language, he insisted, to express beautiful and noble thoughts. For years after-
wards men who dared to write Italian quoted
Lorenzo in answering the classicists who sneered at
men so ignorant of Latin that they must use the
jargon of the peasantry.

In spite of his radicalism, Lorenzo shared with
the most applauded poets of his day a belief that a
man's writing and a man's life were very far apart.
A pedantic style came naturally to him; he did not
need to learn it from the Humanists who surrounded
him, and he could with complete intellectual sincerity deliver himself oracularly of advice which he
scorned to follow.

Better than being a poet oneself, he thought, was
to acquire the glory that comes from being a patron
of poetry. To hear others sing in praise of his magnificence pleased him more than to make verses himself.
It was a point of view he impressed upon Federigo,
saying it was thus that men proved their claim to real
aristocracy.

His colleagues in the Muse's service were not long
in discovering this preference. They approved of it
heartily. It removed a formidable competitor and
added greatly to the rewards obtainable by those who
were left. Any writing man in whom Lorenzo be-

lieved—and he had a great capacity for faith—could be sure of at least a trifle to help him on his way to fame, if he asked for it nicely. Before long the army of suspected genius which Cosimo had bequeathed to Piero was transferring its allegiance to Lorenzo and gaining new recruits along the way. In but a little time they had found that the young man meant just what he said to Federigo. Soon they were almost all as confident of Lorenzo's benevolence as was Luigi Pulci when he wrote:

"If you do not wish people to believe or know that I am your friend and have some influence with you, placard it on the walls—at your own expense of course—as for some time past, having had no money to pay away, I have been paying with your name instead. Wherever I show myself people whisper, 'That is Lorenzo's great friend.'"

V

The prestige that was so great as to cause awed whispers in the streets was the result of that rivalry which Cosimo had known would develop after he was dead. Scarcely had the city finished its mourning for the man she honored posthumously with the title "Pater Patriae" than the chiefs who had feared and obeyed him began to wonder why they should serve with the same zeal an invalid whom they all regarded as too stupid to serve himself.

Luca Pitti, Diotisalvi Neroni, Agnolo Acciajuoli and Niccolo Soderini talked it over frequently. They agreed that Luca would be a much more attractive head of the State than the gouty, retiring Piero, who permitted his wife or his son to guide him in affairs of real importance. The four started carefully, basing their campaign on the fact that Cosimo had often spoken highly of Diotisalvi's sagacity. The object of his praise now proved that it was well deserved.

A great part of Cosimo's popularity with his fellow business men was the reward of his willingness to lend money on easy terms for long periods— to those whose politics were "right." Neroni, with that lofty expression assumed by men about to deliver themselves of disinterested advice, suggested to Piero

[49]

that the Bank had too much money tied up in the
enterprises of others. It was an argument appreciated
by a man trained for business rather than for politics.
Piero still thought that money had only commercial
uses. He innocently called the debts.

The result was a near panic, so widely had Cosimo
scattered his resources, and for some time Piero was
cordially detested. Debtors went around the markets
and counting houses telling each other that the
Medici were getting rather above themselves. The
arrogant Piero, near bankrupts maintained, was ruin-
ing the prosperity of Florence in his selfish desire to
augment a fortune that was already too large for one
man.

Luca Pitti and his friends were most sympathetic.
But they were too cautious to do anything about it
just yet, and before they could work the discontent
up to useful proportions Piero, who was neither as
stupid as he looked nor as his enemies believed, saw
his error. He protested that he was only trying to put
his father's affairs in order, that he merely wanted to
see where the Bank stood, that he had no intention
of pressing his very good friends and loyal supporters
for inconvenient payments. Most of the debtors were
satisfied with the explanation and a renewal of their
notes. The rest were squeezed, and as ruined men
ceased to count for much in the opposition.

Still Piero had no suspicion of treachery. His most
eminent followers, enraged by the failure of their
guile, now decided to resort to cruder but more often

successful methods. If Piero would not ruin himself, he could be removed entirely. The conspirators were in no hurry and spent months in maturing their next scheme, which was to be the murder of Piero and the simultaneous arrival of a mercenary force strong enough to oversee a new election. From the turmoil that would be sure to follow, Luca Pitti would rise as the saviour of his country, and the Medici would be put back where they belonged.

It was a nice scheme but over-complicated. It took so long to prepare that Lucrezia heard something of it. She had always tried to be on good terms with everybody; she was in correspondence with many Florentine exiles, for they all knew that the best way to win favor with Piero was through her intercession, and her sister, Dianora, was married to Soderini's brother, Tomasso.

Her information was vague enough, but it quite thoroughly alarmed her husband. Any revolutionary attempt, he knew, would seek to enlist the support of those exiles who were always trying to find a way to come home. Many of them were in Naples, and some of them were influential there. Piero wondered anxiously what the Kingdom's attitude would be at a show-down. He sent Lorenzo to find out.

The boy soon learned that Ferrante was rather on the fence. Obviously he would be on the side of the party which seemed the stronger when the struggle began. Lorenzo, ably introduced by Federigo, Ippolita and an army of scholars, convinced

His Majesty that this party could only be the Medici.

The King, who knew as well as Piero the value of the exiles to any Florentine opposition party, was impressed by the friendship Lorenzo was able to inspire in men who had no cause to love his family. It was easy for the young man to forgive offences committed long ago against his grandfather, and he discovered that some of the exiles were quite nice people. He particularly liked Filippo and Lorenzo Strozzi, who had been driven from Tuscany as children for the crime of being male members of an undesirable family. They had acquired wealth in Naples and wanted to spend it in Florence. The efforts of their mother, Alessandra, who had spent thirty years in intrigues designed to annul the sentence of banishment, had accomplished nothing. But Lorenzo promised to see what he could do. The Strozzi thought that was likely to be much, and the young man left Naples with assurances that the conspiracy would receive no support there.

He came home to report the success of his mission and to find that everything seemed quiet, except for the confusion attendant upon Nannina's marriage. Terms had at last been fixed with the Rucellai, and all Florence was asked to celebrate. The bridegroom's family fêted the town for three days, spending several times the amount of the girl's dowry to do it. The most precious ornaments of every Florentine family were borrowed to increase the splendor of the festivities. For the three days nobody did any work. Dancing and eating and drinking took up all their time, and when it was over Piero retired to Careggi for a good long rest.

The quartet of his enemies had by this time completed their plans. Even the formal accession of the Rucellai and their sixty armed followers could not frighten the conspirators. They had hired Ercole d'Este, brother of the Marquis of Ferrara, to march into Florence with fifteen hundred men as soon as Piero was dead. To hasten that death a band of bravos was recruited in the city. And it was all done so neatly that as yet the party in power had heard nothing of it.

Quite unostentatiously Este moved close to the frontier, the assassins were being entertained by their employers just inside the city gates and Piero was on his way down from Careggi in a litter. It had been many years since he could sit a horse, and his enemies complained that their ruler was so decrepit he travelled like an old woman. Even young women rode mules or horses, for the roads were not made for carriages.

Piero moved too slowly to suit his impatient son and Lorenzo was almost in Florence by the time the litter was half way down Careggi hill. An unusual number of men, all armed, were loitering about the gate, but Lorenzo pretended not to notice. He stopped to pass the time of day, and some of them seemed embarrassed. Again Lorenzo pretended not to notice. Someone asked politely after his father's health. Lorenzo replied that Piero was much better, thanks, was in fact following close behind and would not be long delayed. He waved a cheerful goodbye and left the men lounging with an even greater ap- pearance of nonchalance against the towering walls. But once out of sight, Lorenzo sent a messenger galloping back to warn Piero that trouble was wait- ing for him. The ruler of Florence prudently changed his route and entered the city by another gate.

He immediately summoned a great council at the Medici house. The four leaders of the conspiracy did not attend. They were busy holding a council of their own. It was too late for them to pretend that nothing had happened. Este's approach to the border was now well known, and he thought it no longer necessary or desirable to conceal the names of his employers. The conspirators were obliged to choose between flight, compromise and civil war. At first they inclined towards war, but only the sagacious Neroni seemed to realize that it was their last chance. When it came to the point, the others decided to see what words would accomplish. As Florentines they always preferred talk to fighting.

Meanwhile Florence divided for the conflict. Pitti's adherents adopted the name of "the Party of the Hill" because their chief was building on an eminence across the Arno the most pretentious palace a private citizen ever attempted. Florence was very proud of his initiative. Hundreds of his admirers had contributed treasures for the new house. It was one of the reasons the conspirators believed his popularity invincible. But the Medici knew a little more about that sort of thing. They called themselves "the Party of the Plain." They boasted that Piero was content with his modest little palace on the Via Larga and spent his honorable gains on public works and charity rather than the glorification of his vanity. It was an effective argument.

The spokesmen of the factions met on the neutral ground of the Palazzo Publico. The excitement and worry had done Piero's gout no good, so he was unable to attend the verbal controversies. This duty fell upon Lorenzo. Fortified with the sound advice of a cautious father, which he tempered with the audacity of self confidence, the youth of seventeen out-talked and out-guessed politicians trained in his grandfather's school.

He persuaded the vacillating Luca to see Piero alone and secretly. A few effective words recalling the memory of Cosimo, the duty of a Florentine citizen to place the State above his personal interests, a speech about old friendship, a hint that Lorenzo's hand might be bestowed upon Luca's daughter, and the two old friends were clasped in each other's arms, dropping tears on each other's shoulders. Every Florentine was trained to weep at will. The reconciliation was complete and lasted until Luca got back to his companions. With them too he enjoyed a reconciliation, and the game of words began all over again.

There were more conferences in the Palazzo Publico, but nothing came of them except lessons in politeness. Meanwhile Lorenzo and Neroni continued to prepare for civil war. Lorenzo organized into troops all the young men he could recruit on his side of the river. The streets resounded with yells for the "Party of the Plain" and with the war-cry of the Medici, "Palle! Palle! Palle!" His nights of rioting with the common people were proving useful.

Neroni across the Arno could not persuade his comrades to agree to force. Este was still at the frontier, but his aid was now more than counter-balanced by the arrival nearby of an army twice as strong, lent to the Medici by Galeazzo Sforza of Milan. The conspiracy was breaking up in talk. Soderini could not induce his brother, Tomasso, even to remain neutral. Pitti could no longer be trusted by either side, and the great liberal movement disintegrated into pitiful pleas for forgiveness by the lesser offenders and the stoical acceptance of their luck by the leaders.

A new set of edicts of banishment was issued by an obliging Signoria. To compensate for the loss of so many prominent citizens, the sentences against Cosimo's old enemies were revoked. Soderini, Acciajuoli and Neroni, with a few of their chief supporters, went hurriedly out of Florence, but Luca Pitti received the reward of his treachery. He did not like it. Officially his status was not changed. But of course his daughter could no longer be thought of as

Lorenzo's bride and might consider herself lucky to be given to Giovanni Tornabuoni instead. The Pitti Bank lost much of its trade, and no failure was ever popular in Florence. The very workmen refused to resume their labors on his house, and the huge shell stood empty and forlorn for years until the Medici decided to finish it for themselves.

The number of exiles was fewer than usual after such civil commotions, and their tragedy was easily forgotten in the rejoicing with those who were coming back after many years.

"Return to your mother who awaits you with such great longing," Alessandra Strozzi wrote to Filippo.

With others of the pardoned, the son wound up his affairs in Naples joyously and set out for home with the glad cry:

"Try to arrange that we sup upon something else besides sausages."

The whole affair was a great triumph for the young Lorenzo. He took most of the credit for saving his family, and his fame spread so widely that Ferrante of Naples wrote paternally:

"Already we loved you on account of your excellent qualities and the services done by your grandfather and father. But as we have lately heard with what prudence and manly courage you behaved in the late revolution, and how courageously you placed yourself in the foremost ranks, our affection to you has grown remarkably. We wish then the illustrious Piero all happiness with so worthy a son, and congratulate the Florentine people on so eminent a protector of their freedom, and ourselves on a friend whose excellent gifts increase visibly every day. Perhaps it would be our wish to incite you to praiseworthy action, but your noble and active nature does not need encouragement, not to mention that you have the example of your grandfather and your father constantly before your eyes."

Almost as much as the conspiracy itself, the mildness of the punishments was discussed in Florence. Not a single life was taken. It was a new family policy, and one which Lorenzo had a hand in shaping.

"He only knows how to conquer who knows how to forgive," he said pompously.

Almost as much as Lucrezia he was deluged with prayers to intercede on behalf of members of the defeated party. The Medici always disliked refusing requests—it was not part of the character they wished to assume in the public eye. But some had to be refused, and Lorenzo and Piero together worked out quite a satisfactory formula for answering those whom it would be impolitic to refuse.

"For offences against ourselves," they explained kindly, "we bear no ill will. For such, pardon is freely and gladly given."

The tone was gracious, but there was a catch in it, the petitioners found.

"Offences against the Republic," the formula continued, "are quite another matter. We are merely private citizens like yourselves. Who are we to pardon enemies of the State? It hurts us, but surely you can appreciate our position."

It was an effective silencer for those who pleaded that past services condoned future treacheries, and the new set of exiles turned to the old game of plotting their return. Meanwhile the Albizzi, the Strozzi and the rest were resuming their share in the government and becoming, if not ardent "Palleschi," at least men on whose memories of bitterness the Medici could rely more surely than on other men's forgetfulness of favor.

Florence was so quiet that Lorenzo could safely resume his diplomatic travels. His first mission took him again to the court of Paul II, and there he made the only brilliant commercial transaction of his life. He persuaded Paul to lease to the Medici the Papal alum mines at La Tolfa. The terms in themselves were advantageous, for the lease gave the Medici a monopoly of alum in Italy. But Paul went further. When the Holy See went into business, it could show the value of the spiritual approach. His Holiness pronounced a blanket excommunication upon anyone who should threaten the profits of the monopoly by importing alum from the land of the hated Turk. It was a favor Paul was glad to confer upon a faithful son of the Church, and Lorenzo left Rome filled with gratitude to his mother for raising him so piously.

He got home in time to have his first taste of war.

Most of this year's exiles had gone to Venice where they conceived the bright idea of regaining their old places at the head of a Venetian army. Venice was always ready to fight for a good cause, if the reward was tempting, and the exiles offered her Milan. They were poor enough to promise everything, and they assured the Republic that the Duchy would be an easy prey as soon as Medici support was withdrawn from the Sforza.

On that understanding war began. Lorenzo was eighteen, and a big healthy lad too. But there was no thought of his partaking of anything so vulgar as battle. The Medici were not low adventurers like the Sforza nor military princelings like the Malatesta. Plenty of soldiers could be hired; the lives of diplomats and bankers must not be risked.

So naturally Lorenzo was very far away from danger as the Florentine army under the joint command of Federigo d'Urbino and Galeazzo Maria manoeuvred carefully out of the way of Bartolomeo Coglione's Venetian troops. Federigo and Coglione were two of the most skillful commanders in Italy. No others of that day could keep the pay going so long with so little fighting. Coglione needed no excuse for confining his activities to loot, for he was in the enemy country. The reason Federigo gave for doing the same thing was that Galeazzo Maria interfered too much. The Signoria then invited the Duke to come to Florence for a discussion of affairs more worthy of his talents than war.

Lorenzo did his bit for the country by entertaining the visitor. Galeazzo had come into the city with an empty purse wide open at his belt, for he was a poor man and found it hard to maintain the style to which he thought the Dukes of Milan should be accustomed. The Signoria had prepared Santa Maria Novella for him, but Galeazzo did not think his empty purse could be filled in a Church. His experience was that the Church took, but never gave to such as he. So he asked the Medici to put him up. They should, he said with his mouth watering, treat him just like one of the family.

It was hardly worth the expense. Federigo, relieved of the Duke's presence, forced a battle on the enemy, but did it so skillfully that not a single man on either side was killed. It was a great triumph for Italian arms, but hardly for the employers. Both commanders were wildly cheered by their troops as they retired from a trampled but not gory field to the security of winter quarters.

VI

They were very busy arranging Lorenzo's marriage, but he was not much interested. He was too busy with love and the poetry of love to concern himself with such a dull financial transaction as matrimony. While Piero and his older advisers canvassed the young womanhood of Italy, Lorenzo was discovering ever new charms in the little girl with whom he had played on the Careggi hillside years ago. They had been only children then, but they were eighteen now and knew Life. They were becoming acquainted all over again, and Lorenzo was wondering if the lady preferred poetry or pageantry as the expression of his passion. He decided to try both.

While he was making up his mind, his family finished their inspection of the eligibles of Italy. Choice seemed to fall upon a daughter of the Orsini, Clarice, if that suited Lorenzo. Piero prided himself on being a modern parent; he consulted his son's wishes before mating him. Lorenzo thought the girl would do. He remembered that he had seen her once on his last visit to Rome. Fifteen, wasn't she? Yes, she seemed all right. Anything Piero wanted. He left it all to his father, for just now he was himself too much occupied. Braccio Martelli was giving a tournament to celebrate his marriage. Lorenzo was to be one of the warriors, and Lucrezia Donati would be watching. The matter of a suitably splendid costume and the problem of horses took up all his time.

He planned so well that on the day of the jousting Lucrezia crowned him with a chaplet of violets woven by her own hands. Her knight had been far from carrying off military honors in the fight, but he did not mind, for he had been the best dressed. He had worn Lucrezia's colors, and she with the wreath of violets had publicly acknowledged that she loved him. In his joy he pledged himself to give in her honor the most magnificent tournament that Florence had ever seen.

Meanwhile he took the Muses into his confidence, explaining to them in prose and verse what love was and how his girl excelled all others. He told the patient goddesses that he could not make up his mind whether he loved her more for her beauties of person or excellencies of mind.

"She was," he wrote, "of a just and proper height; her complexion extremely fair, but not pale; blooming but not ruddy. Her countenance was serious without being severe; mild and pleasant without levity or vulgarity. Her eyes were lively, without any indication of pride or conceit. Her whole shape was so finely proportioned that amongst other women she appeared with superior dignity, yet free from the least degree of formality or affectation. In walking, in dancing, or in other exercises which display the person, every motion was elegant and appropriate."

But she was even better than that. She had a brain—Lorenzo had wondered about that before he committed himself to love—and he could record proudly:

"Her sentiments were always just and striking; she always spoke at the proper time, and always to the purpose, so that nothing could be added, nothing taken away. Though her remarks were often keen and pointed, yet they were so tempered as not to give offence. Her understanding was superior to her sex, but without the appearance of arrogance or presumption; and she avoided an error too common among women, who when they think themselves sensible become for the most part insupportable. There was nothing that could be desirable in a beautiful and accomplished woman which was not in her most abundantly found. By these qualities I was so captivated that not a power or faculty of my body or mind remained any longer at liberty."

A young man in such a condition could do no less than write poetry. Most of Lorenzo's contemporaries would have burst into Latin song. Some of them would have attempted Greek. But the language of Dante and Beatrice, Lorenzo said modestly, was good enough for him, and in common, unscholarly Tuscan he informed Florence about the state of his affections, crying:

Alas for me! whene'er my footSteps trace
Those precinEts where eternal Beauty reigns,
The sanguine currents from a thousand veins
Flow round my heart, and pallid grows my face;
But when I mark that smile and heavenly grace,
Its wonted powers my drooping soul regains;
WhilSt Love, that in her eyes his state maintains,
Points to my wandering heart its reSting place,
And Stooping from his beamy mansion swears
"By all that forms my power and points my dart,
The living luStre of those radiant eyes,
I Still will guide thy way; dismiss thy fears;
True are those looks of love." My truSting heart
Believes th' insidious vow—and from me flies.

His heart was never very securely moored. While
his mother set out for Rome to see for herself whether
Clarice was worth negotiating for, Lorenzo was in
Pisa judging a beauty conteSt. Lucrezia Donati was
not one of those who competed for the prize, but her
lover could appreciate beauty wherever he found it.
His discrimination when confronted with the charms
of the three nymphs who reached the final examina-
tion was so great that Luigi Pulci reported to a friend
at home that the award was made "by a better man
than Paris."

Lorenzo came back to Florence and Lucrezia
Donati well pleased with himself. He learned without emotion that his mother had probably found him
a wife. The match, she reported, seemed certain to

give the Medici that desired alliance with wealth, the Church and the temporal lords of the Papal territory. The Orsini "are rich and likely to become richer," she said; they divided with the Colonna the important fiefs of the Romagna, and one of Clarice's uncles was a power in the Sacred College.

The girl herself was not so bad. Lucrezia took pains to make the first meeting rather casual—it would not be diplomatic to display too great eager-ness—and was introduced one day at mass. She saw a typical Roman, rather shy, but Lucrezia thought that fault would be speedily remedied in Florence. Clarice "seemed to me handsome, fair and tall, but being so covered up I could not see her to my satisfaction." So next day, hints of her mission having been sent on ahead, Lucrezia paid a courtesy call at the Orsini home. This visit too "was managed quietly, without ceremony, so should nothing come of it you will lose naught, as there has been no parleying." But something did come of it, and the young man's mother wrote to her husband:

"We talked for some time and I looked closely at the girl. She is of good height and has a nice com-plexion, her manners are gentle though not so winning as those of our girls, but she is very modest and would soon learn our customs. She has not fair hair because here there are no fair women; her hair is reddish and abundant, her face rather round but it does not displease me. Her throat is fairly elegant, but it seems to me a little meagre, or to speak better slight. Her bosom I could not see as here the women are entirely covered up, but it appeared to me of good proportions. She does not carry her head proudly like our girls, but poked it a little forward; I think she was shy, indeed I see no fault in her save shyness. Her hands are long and delicate. In short, I think the girl is much above the common."

But Lucrezia hastened to add that her own daughters were far superior, and she concluded with the pious exhortation:

"Let us leave the issue to God."

This letter filled the cautious Piero with misgivings. He detected what he thought was a coldness, a suspiciously temperate praise, a certain lack of enthusiasm in Lucrezia's description. But she assured him she had written only so as "not to raise your hopes too high; there is no handsomer girl at present unmarried in Florence."

Piero was satisfied with this and with his wife's verbal report when, after a cheerless, rainy journey, she came home. Lorenzo's only apparent interest in the affair was a sentimental proposal to Lucrezia Donati that since he was going to marry a Roman, it would be romantically appropriate if she married a Roman too. He promised to look out for a suitable husband next time he visited the Eternal City, but of this he did not speak when his own matrimonial problems were discussed in the Via Larga.

These problems were vastly complicated. The marriage of a Medici required more negotiating than any Florentine treaty and almost as much as a big loan to a foreign monarch. Both families plunged into the transaction with traditional Italian love of bargaining, for it gave zest to the solemnity of such alliances. Plenipotentiaries were appointed by both sides. Uncle Giovanni Tornabuoni and Filippo de' Medici, Archbishop of Pisa, represented Lorenzo. Giacopo Orsini, Clarice's father, and his brother-in-law, the Cardinal, acted for the girl. No one was in a hurry and the conferences dragged on and on and on. The size of the dowry, the part each family was to pay, the ultimate disposition of it under all conceivable circumstances, the form of the announcement, the date of the wedding—such details provided meaty subjects for a debate remarkable in its politeness and endurance.

Months rolled by. Clarice pursued the monotonous round of household duties and religious exercises which made every respectable Roman girl long for a husband. She could read and write but with some difficulty and never for pleasure. Her hours of leisure were spent mostly in wondering what Lorenzo was like and whether life in Florence was as gay as even she in her sheltered existence had heard. Clarice was young, but she had firm ideas about gayety. She did not approve of it at all, for she was not very bright and never knew that there could be anything better in the world than the dull primness to which she had been reared. She was one of the proudest members of a proud family, and it would never

occur to her that a different plan of life than her own
stupid one could possibly recommend itself to others
save for depravity or perversity.

Lorenzo, for his part, did not care what she
thought or would think. If his mother believed the
girl was a good match for him, he was quite content
to make her the mother of his children. More than
that she would not expect. Meanwhile he would be
enjoying himself, for there would always be Lucrezia
Donati and nymphs at Pisa and girls around the
corner back of San Lorenzo.

All the passion that went into the courtship was
displayed by the negotiators as they argued about the
dowry. They did it all secretly, for neither family was
quite ready to make public announcements. The
Florentines were at war, and the Orsini wanted to see
how that struggle turned out before they came to any
definite conclusion. Giacopo did not want an exile
for a son-in-law.

Piero was for reticence because he was afraid of
the Florentine temper. He knew his people would
think him proud for seeking a foreign wife for his
son. There were sure to be many, especially the
parents of marriageable girls, to complain that the
Medici no longer thought Florentine merchant stock
good enough for them. Piero did not want the
bargaining disturbed by such gossip. But at last it was
no longer possible to keep the secret. The Pazzi,
wealthiest and proudest of the families remaining in
Florence to rival the Medici, had heard of the nego-

tiations and were spreading the news. The Pazzi Bank hoped to create a little discord which might enable them to obtain the lucrative Papal account. So finally terms were hastily agreed upon—a dowry of six thousand florins in money, jewels and clothes, the husband, after the Florentine fashion, paying none, and the whole, after the Roman fashion, to revert to the Orsini should Clarice die childless and intestate.

Everybody in the family except Lorenzo was pleased and excited. He did not express any opinions at all. The further formalities did not take long, and on a day in December, 1468, the Archbishop wrote happily to his young relative:

"I hardly know how to express to Your Magnificence with what pleasure and contentment I have this day espoused in your name the Magnificent and noble Madonna Clarice degl' Orsini, a maiden whose looks, carriage and manners, I conceive, merit the bridegroom who was, I think, destined for her by Heaven. For this Your Magnificence ought devoutly to thank God who in this as in other matters wherein you have been so well treated by fortune, has protected you; and I, who desire your well being and honor as ardently as anyone, for many reasons have longed for this day and congratulate Your Magnificence *ex intimo cordis;* may it be productive of all good. I pray our Lord Jesus Christ to grant to both a happy and a long life together and to let you see *filios filiorum vestrorum usque in quartam et quintam generationem.*"

Lorenzo, telling his own story several years later, recorded the blessed event in much simpler, less lyrical language. All he found to say of it was:

"I, Lorenzo, took to wife Clarice, daughter of the lord Giacopo Orsini, or rather she was given to me, in December, 1468."

He spent the next months in thinking up excuses for not visiting the Orsini. Formal wedding cere monies were to be held in Florence in June, but Clarice's family kept urging Lorenzo to honor them with his presence before then. At first there was al ways the excuse that the tournament he was to give in February prevented his leaving home. It was rather annoying to have the fun of preparation inter rupted by the unending letters from Rome. June, Lorenzo thought, was quite early enough for him and Clarice to meet, but it was hard to say so tactfully.

Uncle Francesco Tornabuoni was now taking a hand in the correspondence. So many people as sured Lorenzo that Clarice was the pink of all perfection it could scarcely be surprising if he shrank from facing such a paragon. No one, except possibly Lucrezia Donati, could be all that the letter writers said Clarice was. Uncle Francesco waxed positively poetic and indulged a lyric strain that ill became his years and reputation for good sense.

"Of a truth you have the most perfect bride in Italy," he concluded after extolling the girl's beauty, charm, modesty, grace, intelligence, learning, man ners and quickness of perception. At least, the banker reproved his nephew, if Lorenzo could not come to Rome, he might write the girl once in a while. That seemed reasonable, and the young man dashed off a few lines conveying the most dignified and correct sentiments. Brighter girls than Clarice would have found it hard to evolve entertaining replies to such epistles, and the Orsini were never very entertaining. Clarice's letters gave the lie direct to Uncle Francesco's eulogies on her intelligence and learning. Lorenzo sighed, and went to call on his Lucrezia.

June was drawing nearer, and Uncle Francesco's pen was never tired. Now that the tournament was over Lorenzo really ought to visit Rome. Madonna Maddalena, Clarice's mother, was most anxious to entertain him. It would put the final seal upon her happiness "for she says she wants you to see your merchandise before you take it home; it improves every day."

And then on the first of June the merchandise was delivered. There was more of it than Lorenzo had seen casually in Rome three years before, but not too much. They sent it to Benedetto degl' Alessandri's house to be kept until the formal ceremonies, which would begin on the fourth, a Sunday. The whole city was making a long week end of it, and Florence was decorated as for a feast day. Every palace displayed its banners and trophies. Every square was adorned with flags and allegorical works. The eighty-odd silk shops in the Por' Santa Maria were draped

Clarice Orsini

"The most perfect bride in Italy"

with the most gorgeous specimens of their wares just as though it were San Giovanni's Day.

A few staunch republicans grumbled that the affair was taking on all the marks of a royal wedding, but their complaints were quite lost in the general buzz of pleasant anticipation. The Medici would put on as good a show as any royalty in Europe, and would not tax their fellow citizens to pay for it, or at least the fellow citizens would not know they were being taxed.

All Friday and Saturday people milled about the Via Larga watching the wedding gifts being brought into the Medici house. Jewels and plate and brocade and impossibly ornate works of art from the princely friends of both families were cheered impartially, but the yelling was not a circumstance to that which greeted the arrival of wagon loads of produce, the gifts of Tuscan cities and communes paying their tribute of loyalty to the ruling family. For on Saturday afternoon "with great noise and rejoicing," as one chronicler reported, all the meat, wine, vegetables and sweets which had been received were distributed among the people. That night the feasting began.

The formal banquets in honor of the young couple did not start until Sunday. To these—there were five of them in three days—all Italy and even barbarian countries contributed. Piero Parenti, a youth of nineteen who was one of Lorenzo's friends to partake of all five feasts, was so impressed that he wrote out an elaborate account of it all, "particularly as regards sweetmeats and sugar plums." There were tons of these delicacies, although sweets were scarce and considered the greatest luxury any gourmet could enjoy. The sugar plums, Parenti wrote ecstatically, were "as big as arbutus berries" and in such quantities that he could not calculate them. Hundreds of casks of wine were stacked at strategic points to keep the merriment at a pitch worthy of the occasion, and for days no one had a chance to be thirsty.

Prayers for the weather were benevolently answered, and Sunday morning was hot and clear. The costumes on which the women of Florence had been working for months appeared at their best. The men were not so gorgeously apparelled, for weddings were a purely feminine business, once the financial details had been settled. Clarice was the centre of all the festivities, and no one noticed whether Lorenzo was there or not.

The display was worthy of him, however. It was so great that Fiametta, the careful wife of Filippo Strozzi, tried to be excused from it on the plea of a recent confinement. But the Medici were determined to make a success of their show. Lucrezia was so insistent upon the attendance of the women of all the leading families that the Strozzi, after a correspondence worthy of a domestic crisis, finally decided to spend the money necessary to equip Fiametta with a new wardrobe of expensive brocade gowns. She had her reward, for she was widely admired as one of the handsomest women present.

The horse which had borne Lorenzo so well to his tournament now carried Clarice from the Alessandri Palace to the Via Larga where, enthroned among thirty of Florence's fairest maidens—Lucrezia Donati was one of the most conspicuous among them—she watched an exhibition of dancing on a platform in front of the Medici house. Then the first dinner was served, and for three days, with only brief intervals for rest, the long tables in the palace were crowded with the banqueters. There was none of that promiscuous seating arrangement which deadened the elaborate functions for future generations. The young men had their own tables, separated, but not too far, from the girls, while the "women of a certain age" were quietly segregated on the balcony. Piero and his friends discussed politics, business and the good old days over their wine in the loggia.

Relays of musicians kept feet tapping through the dinners and the symbolic ceremonies essential to any prosperous marriage. An olive tree was hoisted in at a window amid tremendous cheering to insure marital peace. There was a small tournament to show the foreign bride that the men she was to live among were warriors of prowess. And after the actual wedding ceremony in the Medici church of San Lorenzo, Clarice was escorted with much parade and blowing of trumpets back to the home of Alessandri, who was acting for her *in loco parentis*. This, a mark of true Florentine courtesy, was a delicate tribute to the old Roman custom of the bride returning, without her husband, to her father's house to spend the nuptual night in the independence of maidenhood. With such a start to married life, the Romans said, a wife never lost her rights nor passed altogether into her husband's power. Florence had no such custom, but was ready to give the newcomer every opportunity.

VII

Lorenzo did not linger long at home to ac-
custom himself to married life. Only a few days
after the wedding the call of diplomacy took him to
Milan. Duke Galeazzo Maria had a new son and
wanted Piero to be the godfather. The ruler of
Florence, worn out by his son's marriage celebration
and suffering terribly from gout, which the festivities
had aggravated, was far too ill to go. He sent Lorenzo
instead, and with a select band of retainers and
scholars to amuse him on the long ride, the bridegroom departed gayly.

He was not the kind of a husband who writes
letters. He corresponded voluminously with all sorts
of people—with relatives, statesmen, businessmen,
writers, painters, soldiers, priests—but Clarice heard
of his doings from Gentile Becchi, who chronicled
in carefully selected detail the splendid progress of
the ambassadorial party along the sunlit roads to
Milan. A brief scrawl from the head of the procession
was all that Clarice received.

"I have arrived safely and am quite well," Lorenzo
wrote at last. "This I believe will please you better
than any other news save that of my return."

But he ended with the conventionally ardent

phrase which the complete letter-writer of the day ordained for all epistles to intimates:

"I will soon come back to you, for it seems a thousand years till I can see you again. Pray to God for me, and if there is anything here you want, let me know before I leave."

He was too busy being magnificent to the Milanese to write more. Piero had long since been relieved of his fears that Lorenzo would not make a sufficiently impressive show abroad. He was now worried by his son's insistence on outdoing everybody in everything, especially if it were expensive. Piero was very explicit in his instructions, which were mostly exhortations to modesty in display, before the expedition set out, but even so he was not quite easy in his mind.

"Tell Lorenzo," he wrote after the party was on its way, "not to exceed his orders and not to make so many oranges (so much show); he is not an ambassador."

Lorenzo paid no attention to his father's cautious remarks, and made a great many oranges. Nor was he sorry, for he recorded proudly:

"I went to Milan at the request of the Illustrious Duke Galeazzo to stand proxy for Piero, our father, to his first born child. I was received with much honor, more so than the others who came for the same purpose, although they were persons more worthy than I. We paid our duty to the Duchess by presenting her with a necklace of gold with a large diamond which cost near two thousand ducats. The consequence was that the said Lord desired that I should stand godfather to all his children."

Piero thought it a doubtful honor, but Lorenzo quite ignored his expostulations. Indeed, he hardly heard them, for when he came back to Florence he fell in love. The new passion made his affairs of the heart very absorbing, as he was by no means pre-pared to give up Lucrezia Donati. Clarice gave no trouble. She was accustoming herself to a firm and steady disapproval of Florentine society as she saw it, but she had been too well trained in the maxim of good wifeliness—"do not annoy your husband"—to disturb Lorenzo unnecessarily about his women friends.

After all, the young man was very discreet. His share in the negotiations for Lucrezia's marriage to Niccolo Ardenghelli, who was not a Roman, was most unostentatious. In fact no one knew that he had anything to do with it, not even Ardenghelli. As for the new love—well, all Florence was at the feet of Simonetta Vespucci.

She was a Genoese girl, and had arrived as the bride of Marco di Vespucci during Lorenzo's visit to Milan. She was sixteen, just Marco's age, and Florence could not remember ever having seen any-thing so beautiful. She quickly displaced Marietta Strozzi as the reigning belle of town. The young bloods of the city now came in bands with their songs and gifts to the Vespucci Palace instead of the Strozzi home. Every time Simonetta walked along the streets, the impressionable artisans left their work to follow her, rolling their eyes amorously in the fine old Italian manner. Men who could never hope to speak to her fought each other furiously and often bloodily because of some fancied disparagement of her beauty.

Lorenzo always boasted that he was a true Florentine, so it was only natural that he should follow the example of his fellow citizens. But he was not content to ogle the girl during chance meetings or break a cudgel on behalf of her fair name. He went to work more directly. Almost the first thing he learned was that his brother and Marco Vespucci had been playmates for years. He realized suddenly that Giuliano and his friends were growing up. He really ought to see more of the boy and teach him to entertain fittingly. It was the brotherly thing to do.

Apologizing for the delay, Lorenzo gave a dinner at Careggi in honor of the young Vespuccis, and from then on the two families saw much of each other. Giuliano was not far behind Lorenzo in declaring his love, and soon Simonetta was favoring the Medici boys above all her other cavaliers. Quite gradually she came to see more of Giuliano than of the elder brother. The younger was one of the hand-somest youths in town, nearly as learned and ac-complished as Lorenzo, much less talkative, better at games and gave such a deceptive impression of aloofness that Poliziano once exclaimed:

For Julian many a maiden heaved the sigh,
And many a glance the tender flame confessed;
But not the radiance of the brightest eye
Could melt the icy rigor of his breast.

No girl could be expected to resist the challenge. Besides, Giuliano had much more time to himself than did Lorenzo, whose love songs may have been more polished and articulate but whose habits were not monogamous. Giuliano had no public business to keep him from amusing his mistress, and Simonetta found that a lover who was always at her command was better than a sonnet, however well turned. She still liked Lorenzo, and showed it, but he thought of so many other things besides love and even when in an amorous mood he did not always think of her.

He was almost alone now in ruling the family councils. Piero was so sick he seldom appeared, could hardly give his son verbal instructions. In his leisure Lorenzo was fully as much occupied with the state of the arts and learning or with the gay celebration of public festivals as with women. He had as much fun writing carnival songs as sonnets to a lady. It was gloriously intoxicating to listen to the gay crowds swirling through the streets roaring out his verses and his philosophy:

Lorenzo

Fair is youth and void of sorrow
And it hourly flies away—
Youths and maids enjoy today;
Naught ye know about tomorrow.

This is Bacchus and the bright
Ariadne, lovers true;
They, in flying time's despite
Each with each find pleasure new.

These the nymphs with all their crew
Keep perpetual holiday.
Youths and maids enjoy today;
Naught ye know about tomorrow.

Young and old together playing,
Boys and girls be bright as air,
Every sorry though forswear!
Keep perpetual holiday.
Youths and maids enjoy today;
Naught ye know about tomorrow.

Ladies and gay lovers young,
Long live Bacchus, live desire!
Dance and play; let songs be sung;
Let sweet love your bosoms fire,
In the future come what may!
Youths and maids enjoy today;
Naught ye know about tomorrow.

Fair is youth and void of sorrow,
But it hourly flies away.

He was taking his own advice, too. Despite the burdens that Piero's illness heaped upon him he found time to write, to read the new books that agents were sending him from all over the world, to watch artists at their work of beautifying Florentine churches, palaces and gardens, to debate the Platonic theory of life with the apostles of the new learning and to ride out for an exceedingly unplatonic adventure when the day's work was done.

In the studios he was already a familiar figure. He was considered to have a very nice discrimination in painting and sculpture, and his interest led him to seek the companionship of the masters. The Verrochio brothers were just then showing a new understanding of the human anatomy. Antonio Pollajuolo was excelling them as a painter if not as a sculptor. Benozzo Gozzoli was hard at work on a series of frescoes which were becoming the despair of every rival except the somewhat younger Domenico Ghirlandaio, who had in mind some designs even more ambitious. Andrea Verrochio had a new apprentice, and the handsome, good-natured seventeen-year-old Leonardo da Vinci was extremely popular with his fellow students, even though Lorenzo had never noticed him.

The young connoisseur was much more attracted by one of the artists in Pollajuolo's studio. Sandro Botticelli was plump, jolly, festively inclined, twenty-five years old and serious only where painting was concerned, as befitted the best pupil the genial Fra

Lippo Lippi had ever had. And as was also fitting for the good Friar's disciple, Sandro was the beneficiary of Medici patronage. Old Cosimo had been Fra Lippo's steady protector, and Lorenzo was prepared to extend the same favors to the pupil. He greatly enjoyed the painter's merry, rather coarse wit and ardent dissertations on the beautiful possibilities which no brushman had yet realized but of which they all dreamed.

When the argument turned on those broad abstractions which were the delight of the sages, Lorenzo was a match even for such a scholar as Ficino. The Greek philosophy was a game, not a chore to them, and in their lighter moments they undertook to interpret in plain Italian the creed of the great master, Ficino in prose and Lorenzo in verse. The poet, with all a city man's idealization of rural life and all a young man's cynicism concerning life in general, addressed his version of Plato's theories to a Tuscan shepherd, and without knowing very much about it wrote:

> *. . . I know no happier life,*
> *No better riches than you shepherds boast,*
> *Freed from the hated jars of civil strife,*
> *Alike to treachery and to envy lost.*
> *The weed ambition 'midst your furrowed fields*
> *Springs not, and avarice little root can find.*
>
> *Not like the world where wisest he who knows*
> *To hide the secret closest to his breast.*

Ficino thought it such a good interpretation of Plato—the scholars of the fifteenth century could find anything in Plato—that he felt his share of the bargain was done when he had rendered Lorenzo's verses into prose.

However, Lorenzo was quite content these days to leave pastoral joys, with their attendant evils such as raids by condottieri, poverty, hardship, squalid lives and servility, to the peasants. For himself the lower pleasures of collecting books and objects of art, of ruling the State in Piero's name, of celebrating the charms of his mistresses, of spending money with both hands were enough.

For actual experience of rural life he would repair to the monastery of Camaldoli, almost buried in the woods of the Casentino. Here, with Giuliano and a few literary men from Florence, he would exchange jests with the Abbot, Mariotto Arlotta, the most polished wit in Tuscany. There too came the accomplished Leo Battista Alberti, whose versatility was the wonder of his contemporaries. Never, said his friends, quite unconscious of young da Vinci's existence, had so many talents been united in a single body. Poet, antiquarian, philosopher, mathematician, mechanic, painter, architect, musician, lawyer, the venerable scholar was perhaps the most respected man of learning the middle of the century could boast. As a man of action he was equally acclaimed. He was a tireless athlete, a famous horse breaker and, long after his hair was white, was said to be the strongest man in Italy. In short, as the idiom of the time had it, he was one "with a beard upon his breast."

At Camaldoli he quite naturally took the lead, but Lorenzo was not far behind. As the party re-clined under the trees, gazing up at the green slopes of the Apennines, Alberti broke into one of those discourses in praise of solitude which the warm drowsiness of a summer sun and the vast calm of mountain scenery naturally inspire. He took the young Medici for his target as they sprawled, atten-tive but indolent, on the grass. He lectured them on their duty to their finer natures, which demanded of them complete abstention from all worldly pursuits. Study, meditation and elevating conversation with a few kindred spirits far from the call of business, politics or frivolity, he declared, is the goal of all who sincerely embrace the Platonic doctrine.

Lorenzo promptly took up the challenge. He could find in the Greek dialogues plenty of excuses for his chosen mode of life. After all, he asked the white-haired old athlete, where would the world be if all men abandoned government and commerce for the simple life of the peasant or the contemplative life of the philosopher? He grew quite warm as he argued, his long, graceful hands punctuating his re-marks with emphatic gestures while at his side Giuliano nodded approvingly. The blood of gener-ations of hard-headed bankers still predominated in the Medici.

VIII

Lorenzo needed that hard Medici heritage. Piero was dying, and the fortunes of the House, which old Cosimo had feared no youth could ever maintain, seemed to be dying with him. All through the fall of 1469 Piero suffered so terribly from gout that he could not give his children the benefit of those golden words of advice which every boy had a right to hear at his father's bedside.

The cold rains of the Tuscan autumn dripped mo-notonously outside the windows at Careggi. Couriers and anxious members of the family splashed along the muddy roads to Florence. None of them ever had good news. Those who rode their slipping horses down the hill to the city carried nothing but bad reports of Piero's health. Those who struggled up-wards to the villa brought rumors of hidden in-trigues. There were a great many people passing in and out of the Palazzo della Parte Guelpha in whose high, dark rooms many strange schemes had been wrought in the past. The Guelph Party no longer had the power it wielded when opposed by the full might of the Ghibbelines, but the old name still had weight and could be dangerous if it were raised against the newer Parte Medici.

Just what went on in the panelled council hall

off the Mercato Nuovo no one knew, but elsewhere there were gloomy conferences on the keeping of power. Only two members of the ruling family seemed indifferent to the political consequences of Piero's death. Piero himself thought of it only as a welcome relief from intolerable pain. Lorenzo showed concern only for the sufferings of a father he respected for qualities which he did not himself possess.

As to his position in society and politics, the heir apparent to Medici greatness was quite nonchalant. He believed the best way to lose that position was to display anxiety over those mysterious Guelph doings. He had supreme confidence in his own abilities, and he was not so young as to regard youth as a handicap. Of all the family, he alone preserved the composure which he considered appropriate in a crisis.

But he was not idle. At the big family gatherings, which took their tone from the gloom of the heavens, he was a silent, aloof spectator. But he had many quiet, confidential chats with the leaders of his party. He made it plain to all of them that his father's powers would descend to him; he took it for granted. The problem as he saw it, he said, was how to make the transfer as tranquil as possible. He inclined gracefully and almost deferentially to the views of his elders, looking to them to protect his and Giuliano's heritage.

Before the day when all this diplomacy was to prove its worth, it was driven completely from the young man's mind by pity for his father's dying torments. No amount of Greek philosophy could console him as he stood helplessly by watching while the prematurely aged and broken man lay on his bed, too stupefied by pain even to pray for death. The long agony was protracted until early December. At last, on the third of the month, Piero the Gouty died.

There was great excitement in the town when the news was known. Everywhere men discussed the possible results, but no one seemed to realize that the dead man had been little more, these last years, than the chairman of a committee. He had never been such a despot as old Cosimo. In the last months of his life, he had been tortured by suspicions of his fellow committeemen and had talked of getting rid of them, but they were still functioning. Popular fears that the new régime, whatever it might be, would be inaugurated amid tumult and disorder were not justified.

Lorenzo's refusal during his father's illness to worry about the future was partly responsible for the peaceful state of the city. The leaders of his party were in general well satisfied with the existing order. They did not object to having a nominal chairman to sanction their decisions. Lorenzo's attitude led them to believe that he would be just what they wanted. It hardly seemed possible that a young man so absorbed in study, women and extravagant dis-play could find the time to be a serious rival to men of years and experience. The lesson of the Pitti conspiracy they ignored as the product of necessity, not ambition, and resolved that there would never be another such emergency.

The new head of the House of Medici observed this belief with pleasure. His grief did not at all interfere with his plans now. He found it quite easy to maintain composure, for it had been his father's anguish that upset him most; death was a blow he could bear with equanimity.

He knew there were men who were urging Tomasso Soderini to assume charge of the government, although the doings at the Palazzo della Parte Guelpha were only vaguely revealed to him. But Soderini remained just as loyal to Lorenzo as he had been to Piero during the Pitti conspiracy. The older man, for all his abilities, was not personally ambitious. He had a love of repose, a dislike of responsibility that was quite foreign to most of his fellow citizens. He was a kindly man, always ready to put forth on behalf of friends efforts which he would have scorned to use for his own advancement. Lorenzo had no scruples about employing them, and the whole business, quietly managed by Tomasso with a self effacement which Cosimo could not have improved upon, proceeded according to plan.

"What is that Prince worth who is not obeyed by his own subjects, especially at the beginning?" Lorenzo once asked, and added: "The ruler of a government must make his position secure within the first four days."

So two days after Piero's death, Tomasso suggested to the heads of all the powerful families in Florence that they should meet to consider the future of their party and their caste. The gathering in the convent of San Antonio had all the characteristics of a national convention. There were speeches about loyalty and principles and the continued welfare of Florence under Medici leadership which had contributed so much to the city's prosperity. Everything was carefully directed towards one end, and the opponents of that end never had a chance to interrupt the ponderous turnings of the political machine which ground steadily towards the nomination of Lorenzo and Giuliano.

Led by the politic Tomasso, the delegates were swept into a unanimous pledge to regard Piero's two sons as their own children. The youngsters promptly repaid the compliment by promising to look upon the members of that reverend assemblage as their fathers. The party was agreed that the lads should wield jointly the authority which had belonged to their father and grandfather.

The notification ceremonies were held in the Via Larga that night. The men who had most influenced Piero called to condole with the family and repeat the pledges of support. But they all knew that a two man rule could not last for very long. Some of them may have thought that Soderini would be the real power, working through his two young kinsmen, but Lo-renzo had other ideas. Ever since he had hectored

Giuliano in the nursery, he had found his brother a
docile, devoted servant. Despite the boy's popularity,
charm and quite considerable talents, Lorenzo knew
that he would never be a rival. Indeed, so purely
formal did the elder consider Giuliano's inclusion
in the nomination that he did not even mention it
when he recorded briefly the events of the time. He
was always at his best in the first person singular; it
came naturally to him.

"Although I was very young, being twenty years
of age," his description ran, "the principal men of
the city and of the state came to us in our house to
condole with us on our loss and encourage me to
take charge of the city and of the state, as my grandfather and father had done. This I did, although on
account of my youth and the great responsibility and
perils arising therefrom, with great reluctance, solely
for the sake of our friends and our possessions. For it
is ill living in Florence for the rich unless they rule
the state."

The Lorenzo who penned this modest account
was twenty-three and had had three years in which to
develop a strong resentment against the demands
which politics made upon his time. Ruling the State,
he told himself repeatedly when his studious, artistic
and playful moods had to be repressed in the interest
of statecraft, was a mug's game. But power fascinated
him, and he could no more do without it than he
could do without books or pictures or conversation
or shows or mistresses.

[92]

He wanted everything and got it—at a price. The price he paid for power was a certain measure of self-contempt. He, Lorenzo de' Medici, was wasting time on the trivia of life instead of enjoying himself. For these moments, when he forgot that the exercise of power was also enjoyment of a kind, he invented the excuse that the rich must rule to remain rich. It was true enough up to the point that separates partici-pation in government from autocracy, but if Lorenzo had really desired the repose of which he sang so sweetly, he could very easily have delegated many of his responsibilities to others.

He had to fight hard at first to keep those responsi-bilities. He was not the only man who believed the rich should rule. Florence was full of them. They wanted, and expected, to take a good deal of the burden from Lorenzo's shoulders. They required very discreet management. He could not ignore them after that affecting scene in which they had promised to be fathers to him. He could not em-ploy them as tools, for one cannot with honor use one's father basely. He would not admit them to the share in the government to which they aspired, for that would mean abdication.

There remained but one course. He smothered rivalry in abundant honors. All the men he sus-pected of setting their ambitions too highly were called, one by one, into earnest conference. Lorenzo deferred politely to his guest's years, dignity, ex-perience and worth. In France, or Germany, or

Turkey, anywhere that was very far away, the older man's talents were needed for the safety of the State. Foreign complications were so embarrassing, the young diplomat confided, that only the person to whom he happened to be talking could serve Florence in that particular capital. Would the distinguished citizen once more sacrifice his personal preferences to his patriotism and accept the delicate mission?

The appeal, reinforced by the commands of Lorenzo's hand-picked Signoria, served a double purpose. It removed from Tuscany men with whom Lorenzo could neither work nor quarrel. And it greatly enhanced his prestige abroad. Foreign courts noted with respect the increased splendor and consequence of the Florentine embassies now that this young Medici was at the head of affairs. Foreign rulers began to believe that the expressions of esteem which they had addressed to him on his father's death were not such exaggerated flattery as that sort of missive usually turned out to be.

Lorenzo had no doubts of his ability to rule Florence without the help of experienced counsellors. He entered very happily upon his new role, although he governed with his left hand to save his right for more enjoyable things. There were many experiments he wanted to try, and many of them were only very remotely connected with anything Cosimo would have regarded as political. The young man had his own theories. Now that all the vast resources of the family were at his absolute command, he could test them.

One of these theories was that the people could be educated by a discerning master to have a better time. Ribaldry and buffoonery were all very well, but he wished a little more subtlety could be introduced into the amusements of the mass. As a theatrical manager, Lorenzo had modern ideas, and he never had to consider the box office. There was no box office. But there were plenty to tell him that he had to give the public the rough vulgarity to which they were accustomed. Otherwise, the wise men told him, his shows would not attract the crowds. Failure to amuse would start the break away from the loyalty which Florence had learned to bestow upon the Medici. Nevertheless Lorenzo clung to his idealistic faith in the ability of his people to appreciate better things.

They could have afforded them even if Lorenzo had not paid the bills. There was not another city in the world where so much money flowed so freely. The wealth of Florence was based upon her hundreds of textile factories, her wood, metal and stone workers and her banks. Wool came all the way from England and Spain to be made into cloth and sold back to the growers at a nice profit. Florentine carving was in great demand everywhere, and in all the chief industries of the city skilled, well paid workmen predominated. They knew how to protect themselves too. The guild system had reached the height of its power, so that members, comprising most of the male population of Florence from Lorenzo de'

Medici down, shared well in the prosperity which their superiority in craftsmanship had won for the city.

Lorenzo began to put his ideas into force from the very moment he felt that nothing could be done without him. The most skillful engineers, the best artists in town were put to work on floats, costumes and fireworks for the next feast day. Nothing that the world was learning in the way of beauty and mechanical progress was ignored in preparing the show. Lorenzo himself undertook to improve the musical taste of the celebrants. Instead of the old, worn-out songs, he offered verses of his own composition, set to newly composed music. The verses were much more polished, much more delicately phrased and much more witty than the songs they replaced. They were also spiced liberally with dashes of rollicking ribaldry which endeared them mightily to the public taste.

There was another theory, closely related to the improvement in popular dramatic criticism. Lorenzo believed that the great majority of Florentines were not a bit concerned about their government so long as it left them reasonably prosperous and well entertained. He was quite ready to debate the point with Plato himself, and he was called upon to do so with Plato's disciples. For the republican theory of that day was largely derived from Greek philosophy, although the practice had been plentifully corrupted. The select group of citizens, set apart from the rest of the population, were supposed to value civic honor above life itself. Bribery, tax dodging and intrigue were so much a part of every day politics that no one bothered to square them with the spotless dogma which the bribers, dodgers and intriguers espoused. The heads of Italian republics really believed that their fellow citizens watched a magistrate's every official act jealously.

Lorenzo begged to differ. He maintained that a normal citizen's jealousy could only be aroused by politics when politics went astray and damaged the citizen in his personal preoccupations. The citizen, said Lorenzo confidently, would even overlook a little damage done by a government that provided amusement copiously. That was the kind of government he undertook to establish in Florence, with the damage nicely proportioned to the amusement. He also counted on the support, unofficial but important in times of real danger, of those thousands of workers who did not have rights of citizenship but were just as eager for amusement.

With the Pazzi, the Alessandri and others away on their foreign missions, Lorenzo had no immediate opposition. Tomasso Soderini, finding himself alone, shrugged his shoulders and gave up all idea of being the power behind the throne. He was rewarded for his unassuming allegiance. Alone among the men of his generation who had sat in Piero's inner council, Soderini continued to hold an important place among Lorenzo's advisers. Perhaps his advice was ignored more often than pleased his vanity, but he was there.

Around him at the conference table he saw quite young faces. The elders trained by Cosimo were being ousted from all positions of genuine power. Bernardo del Nero, Antonio Pucci, Bernardo Buon-girolami, Pier Filippo Pandolfini—inexperienced youngsters all—were the men on whose counsels Lorenzo relied. He believed that their dependence on his favor and their devotion to his person were ample compensation for any faults which might be implied in their lack of years. Besides, they agreed with him. They shared his faith in the value of living splendidly, and at the same time amusingly. Their fathers demanded some substantial return when they patronized an artist. The old men were concerned with what they called the realities—a painting or a statue or a book or a palace. Lorenzo and his friends were content if the artist left them with the memory of beauty—a glimpse of splendid pageantry, an im-provised tune, a witty discourse.

Because that was so, their city became at once an altered place. It would have been hard to say just how the difference first made itself apparent, but everyone felt it, the artists who had enjoyed Cosimo's bounty, the beggars who had taken his alms, the peasants who had gaped at the churches he built, the laborers who had applauded his pageants, the visitors from abroad. These last commented on the increased gayety of Florentine society and the cheerfulness of the people. They were inclined to explain it simply by the youth of the new ruler.

But the true reason lay deeper than that. The artists had been accustomed to winning their pay and their applause from men who believed patronage was a form of condescension to persons of inferior stamp, and they showed it. Now they had to do with men who believed the encouragement of art was a privilege, who took pains to understand what they were encouraging, who treated the artist as a friend rather than a servant or a strange new specimen of the race.

The beggars had always received their alms to the accompaniment of grave looks and pious exhorta/ tions. The doles had been passed out in such generous measure that not even Rome herself contained more mendicants than Florence. But now, though the generosity continued, the gravity and piety had de/ parted. Coins were tossed about with a smile and a jest. The recipient of sweet charity no longer needed to assume an expression of undeserved suffering. A grin went just as far.

The peasantry still came every Friday afternoon from the surrounding countryside to gape at the mangificence of city buildings. But more and more the architects were being employed in designing palaces. Cosimo's generation had done their work well. There were enough churches to accommo/ date many more than the half million people who acknowledged the sovereignty of the Florentine

Signoria. Most of the half million, if they had chosen to renounce the world, could have found living quarters in the existing convents and monasteries.

For years manners had been growing ever lighter in Florence, so the new spirit throve without check from moralists. Even those who mourned for that mythical golden age when beauty and virtue ruled together were not yet inclined to reject beauty just because they could not instil into their world the particular brand of virtue of which they happened to approve.

Idealists who had striven to weld the hot precocity of the new Italy into an alloy of Spartan severity, Athenian grandeur and Christian humility had given up the struggle and retired to nurse their resentment in impotent isolation. It had been many years since anyone tried to enforce the old, stern laws against frivolous adornment of the person. It would be many years before anyone thought of them again. All those desires and tastes which, the Church preached, were only the Vanities of this miserable world had become the serious business of mankind. Lorenzo proposed only to eliminate the seriousness, to revolutionize manners, not morals. He too would pursue the Vanities, but with an appropriate, urbane levity.

So with his new advisers he entered upon his reign with no higher ambition than to make Florence a paradise for polite worldlings. He dreamed of a

the Magnificent

city where all men would be devotees of love, learning and laughter, where good taste would count for more than good intentions, where men and women would hold perpetual carnival to the rollicking tune of

Fair is youth and void of sorrow,
But it hourly flies away.

IX

In those early years of Lorenzo's power, he might have believed that his dream was coming true. Florence had never been so peaceful or so prosperous, and the Medici Party took all the credit. Lorenzo was on gift-and-compliment-exchanging terms with every foreign court and was backing Florentine trading expeditions to the East. Venice and Genoa had long monopolized the profits from the Indies, but the enterprising merchants and adventurers of Florence were beginning to demand their share. Under Lorenzo's patronage they were getting it, and one of the young men most highly thought of among the sea-going Florentines was Amerigo Vespucci, cousin to the fair Simonetta.

The Medici Banks were making as large gains as if their nominal head had known how to run them. The managers Piero had trained were quite competent to carry on. All they asked was to be let alone. Only the London branch was giving cause for anxiety. One of Lorenzo's first major deals was a loan of 120,000 ducats to Edward IV to finance his civil wars. More money had been advanced since, and the King was repaying none of it. No other House in the world save the Medici could have survived such a blow, but they took the loss without disaster.

Lorenzo's domestic affairs were the least thriving of all. He had married solely to please his parents and to have children, and Clarice in this respect at least proved satisfactory. Fourteen months after their marriage she was safely delivered of a girl, whom the delighted father named Lucrezia—after his mother, not his mistress. He celebrated the event with a pageant which all the city admired, with a furious spree of alms-giving and with the customary donations to the Church.

But Clarice presumed too much upon her position as wife and mother. She made the mistake of attempting to influence her husband in the distribution of patronage. She did not really care a bit for the office seekers whose fortunes she urged, but her pride drove her to exhibit her power. Her mortification when she learned that she had no power embittered her married life and cut her off from her own family. For the Orsini did not understand. In their arrogance, they believed that one of their noble race had only to ask a favor and it would be granted. They were a large family, and every member commended to Clarice deserving dependents from their households. Lorenzo was to find all the Orsini hangers-on lucrative sinecures. Ashamed to admit that her recommendations were consistently ignored, Clarice took refuge in complete silence, and soon the Orsini, angered by her apparent indifference to their appeals, ceased to trouble her.

Any Florentine could have told them how such

requests were to be presented. If the prospective beneficiary was a man of learning or art, his own talents must plead for him. But all others would be well advised to leave Clarice alone. If they felt the need of feminine assistance, they should request the friendly intercession of Lucrezia de' Medici or Lucrezia Donati. The most circumspect of Florentine matrons advised their sons to win the favor of the younger woman before they confided their ambitions to her lover. Rarely fortunate indeed was the suppliant who had secured the good offices of his benefactor's mother and mistress too. To such a darling of the gods the road to political advancement or commercial prosperity was already as good as travelled.

Although Lorenzo was willing to base business and governmental appointments on the whims of the women he loved, his cultural conscience was in no one's keeping. Every contributor to the arts or scholarship had to prove to the patron himself that he deserved patronage. All kinds succeeded, and none in that day was at all bashful about expounding his own superlative deserts. So it was not an unusual letter that Lorenzo received one day early in 1470.

"Magnificent Lorenzo," it began, "to whom Heaven has given charge of the city and the state, first citizen of Florence, doubly crowned with bays lately for war in S. Croce amid the acclamations of the people and for poetry on account of the sweetness of your verses, give ear to me who, drinking at Greek sources, am striving to set Homer into Latin meter."

The writer went on to propose that Lorenzo should support him. In exchange he offered the dedication of his great opus. He begged to commend himself and signed the quite unknown name of Agnolo Poliziano. The missive was rewarded with a cloak and a pair of shoes, for the scholar had confessed to a shameful shabbiness. Lorenzo did not care much for dedications from the unknown—they were no novelty to him—and would never have thought of the Homeric translation again had he not received as thanks for his gift some charming Latin verses

See at my call Calliope appear,
Her lyre's shrill warbling strikes my listening ear,
She stood confessed, but gazed with wild surprise,
Nor knew the poet in his gay disguise.

He read and decided that the author would repay further consideration. The versifier proved to be a ragged youth of seventeen, even uglier than Lorenzo. Undersized, bandy-legged, with a leering squint, a huge, rapaciously curved beak of a nose and a wry neck, Agnolo surprised all who met him by his ability to converse beautifully and wittily. A few years before he had descended upon Florence from Monte Pulciano, famous for producing the best wine in Europe. He abandoned his family name for that of his birthplace and enrolled for study under some of the same masters who had taught Lorenzo.

They spoke highly of his talents, and the young ruler added another poet to his household. Poliziano was given a room in the palace on the Via Larga and was free forever from the fear that he would be forced by the demands of an empty stomach to exchange his studies for a mercantile career. He remained eternally grateful to his patron. Although his opinion of his own abilities was high, he never failed to acknowledge that Lorenzo had shown commendable perspicacity in showering favors upon him.

"Even in the Greek language I have contended with the Greeks themselves—a species of merit that I may boldly say has not been attained by any of my countrymen for a thousand years past," he once boasted to the King of Hungary, but in the same letter he added that it was the friendship of Lorenzo which had raised him to the heights of literary fame.

In the midst of Lorenzo's successes, there was one threat to the realization of his dream city. His comrades in the dissemination of the new spirit of fun thought their duty was done when they had spent money. But Lorenzo knew that the ostentatious rich could not excite admiration without exciting envy too. If his ideas were to be carried out, Florentine prosperity would be so obvious as to be a constant invitation to armed attack.

Already there had been one such attempt. Bernardo Nardi, an exile from Pitti conspiracy days, had gathered a little force of mercenaries for a raid on Prato. They were beaten off and Nardi was brought back to Florence to die, but the incident alarmed the new government. How could a State be gay if it must live in constant apprehension of invasion? The obvious answer was that war must be avoided, so at twenty-one Lorenzo adopted a peace policy to which he clung all his life.

Anywhere save Italy a young man who did not look upon war as offering the highest opportunities for acquiring honor would have been driven from polite society. Fighting, whether for public or private causes, was almost the only path to fame that the transalpine peoples knew. Some of these rude men from beyond the mountains travelled, and were horrified by the Italian disregard of all that in other countries was supposed to constitute a man's inviolable honor. But the Italians had their own notions of honor, and in their turn despised Englishmen, for example, because these northern islanders were crude in their cruelty, warlike and—worst of all—could never be trusted commercially. Business honesty was still outside the English code, while chivalry in Italy was already considered a relic of barbarism.

Lorenzo's pacifism, therefore, was a practicable political philosophy in his own land. His fellow citizens were never fighters themselves, and if peace could be realized they saw prospects of lower taxes. The condottieri could then be dispensed with and trade would still be secure.

Lorenzo's task was eased at first more by the struggle between Moslem and Christian than by the willingness of his people to abolish war. The Turks

in their perpetual feud against the infidels of the West
had been passing triumphantly from victory to victory
ever since the fall of Constantinople nearly twenty
years before. Venice, the chief bulwark of the Occi-
dent against the fierce troops of the Crescent, had
just sustained a terrible defeat at Negropont. The
Sultan, Mohammed II, already anticipating the
paradisiacal joys which awaited such an exterminator
of heresy as himself, had promised in the name of
Allah to carry a crusade of his own into the heart
of Christendom. Exalted by victory and the blood
of the thousands he had seen massacred, he swore to
wipe out forever the hated religion of the Cross. All
Europe would be made safe for the Faithful, he announced, the Vatican would be a mosque, the
followers of Christ slaves.

His threats, although bombastically phrased, were
by no means idle boasts. Mohammed had ships and
men and money too. What the Moor had done in
Spain, he might well repeat in Italy. In the heat of
the fear he inspired, the host of animosities which had
kept the peninsula hopelessly divided evaporated.
All the states, big and little, were ready to join with
Venice against the threatened invasion. For the first
time since the Empire, all Italy was united in a single
league.

Fortunately for the allies, their good faith was not
put to the blood test. Mohammed became prudent
and decided to turn his armies to more easily accessible conquests. But the peace which Lorenzo

wanted in Italy had been secured, at least for a little time. The young man, assured by his envoys in the East that the danger of a Turkish invasion was over, devoted himself to the further glorification of his aesthetic tastes.

It was too bad Pius was no longer Pope. The time was ripe for a crusade, but Paul was too busy amassing wealth, and only Ferrante of Naples was genuinely interested in Holy War. He had visions of military glory; he contended that the best way to prevent an attack was to keep Mohammed busy at home, and during the winter he made a great show of gathering troops. But his good friend Lorenzo, upon whom he relied for financial and diplomatic support, would have nothing to do with the scheme. Ferrante expressed his disappointment to Luigi Pulci, who was visiting Naples, and the poet wrote reproachfully to his patron, condemning such callous indifference to the cause of religion.

"I trust God may convert you during Lent and lead you to behave as a Christian," said Pulci.

But when Lent came, Lorenzo only gave still further proof of what many, even in gay Florence, considered a deplorable lack of respect to God and His representatives on earth. Galeazzo Maria had come to Florence with his Duchess, Bona of Savoy, to celebrate the alliance against the Turk, and to show Lorenzo that the noble Sforza were not to be outdone in magnificence by any banker in the world.

The visit coincided with a domestic tragedy which

at any other time would have plunged Lorenzo into the deepest mourning. Just before the Ducal party arrived, Clarice gave birth prematurely to twin boys, and the father grieved bitterly over the loss of male heirs.

"They lived long enough to be baptized," he recorded sadly in his reminiscences—his piety was displayed in rather unexpected places.

But not even this could permit him to ignore Galeazzo's challenge. Indeed, he rather welcomed the visit as a relief from his sorrow. He smiled a bit grimly when they told him that the Duke was spending two hundred thousand ducats in the effort to impress Florence with his elegance. But he felt better about it when this news was followed by word that Galeazzo was not evidencing much imagination in laying out the money.

Sforza relied solely upon mass to strike the beholder dumb with wonderment. Two thousand men rode with him across the hills to Florence, and as the immense cavalcade poured through the gate of the city under the festive banners hung out for the occasion, even Lorenzo's most fervent partisans were convinced that their hero could do nothing like this. Half of the visiting army were the personal retinue of the Duke and Duchess, all in splendid robes of silk and cloth of silver. The rest were the nobles of the Milanese court with their attendants in gaudy new liveries. The attention to detail was much admired. Even the kitchen scullions were quite inappropriately uniformed in silk and velvet.

A Carnival Scene in Florence

The two thousand were quartered about the city at the public expense, but the Duke and Duchess were entertained privately in the Medici Palace. Galeazzo had pleasant memories of his stay there a few years before, and he was in a very good humor as he greeted his host. He had heard with immense satisfaction the murmurs of delight and awe which attended the passage of his suite through the streets. He was quite happy in the certainty that the Medici could never match his display. There would be an end now to those adulatory dedications and speeches in which this young man of Florence was flattered as the most splendid product of his age.

He did not know Lorenzo. It was not by such simple devices as the reckless scattering of wealth that he had achieved his reputation. He used his brains as well as his money, and he was quite prepared to match his wits and his taste against all the revenues of Milan. He had the sense not to try to excel his guest in the number and splendor of his attendants. But he showed that he too could impress the multitude. He ordered a series of the new mystery plays to be performed in honor of the visitor. His engineers and artists worked out such ornately effective settings, such ingenious mechanical contrivances, such terrifyingly beautiful fireworks that the audience quite forgot, as they witnessed the first play, "The Annunciation of the Virgin," the procession which had ridden so proudly through the town a few days ago.

Not content with working his wonders upon the popular mind, Lorenzo went on to overpower the Duke himself. As they wandered through the palace and the gardens, he casually pointed out to Galeazzo the finest collection of paintings, the best examples of ancient and modern sculpture, the most complete library, the most cleverly carved jewels and cameos, the loveliest tapestries and vases that Sforza had ever seen. A great deal more than two hundred thousand ducats had gone into the gathering of these beauties, and the Duke was sufficiently the child of his time to appreciate what he had seen.

"In comparison with these," he confessed, waving a hand towards the Medicean treasures, "gold and silver lose their value."

Lorenzo had won. Never again would any Italian challenge his right to the first place among the "Magnificent." In his twenty-third year he had made that claim good beyond all dispute.

The scandal was only incidental to this splendid victory. The season was Lent, but the godless Milanese openly flouted religion by consuming animal flesh. Indeed, it was whispered that Lorenzo and other reckless young devils had joined their guests in this insult to the Lord. But the punishment for thus sinning was not long delayed. The performance of the "Ascension of Christ," the second of the trilogy of mystery plays, was suffered to pass amid universal applause without any evidence of divine wrath. The last of the series, "The Descent of the

Holy Spirit," which was produced aptly enough in the Church of Santo Spirito, was to have been the most gorgeous, and those orthodox folk who had been shocked by the highly improper proceedings of the last few days were gloomily triumphant over the result. "The Descent of the Holy Spirit" was accompanied by more flames than had ever been attempted in a theatrical performance before, and by more than the old Church could stand. The building caught fire and was completely destroyed. Galeazzo's generous contribution to a rebuilding fund failed to restore his popularity or check the grumbling of the superstitious.

Good churchmen had much to think about that year besides scandal. For in the summer Pope Paul ended his miserly career, and the Sacred College was convened to select his successor. Francesco della Rovere, a Franciscan monk possessed of a large family, ample means and no scruples, secured the tiara at an enormous price in bribes and promises. He was widely known as an eminent theologian, but just as widely known for other qualities.

A handsome man of ascetic appearance, which belied his tastes and habits, he was a devoted father and a famous hater. His vindictive, hasty temper, cruel disposition, incorrigible sensuality and un-ashamed greed had already been plentifully displayed in his rise from obscurity to a place of power in the Church. He was so unpopular that the Roman mobs, seldom disposed to express disapproval of moral turpitude, broke forth into fierce rioting which disrupted the elaborate ceremonies and almost necessitated another election. But the mobs were dispersed, and della Rovere ascended the throne of St. Peter as Sixtus IV.

Florence was not much interested in the moral character of the new Pontiff. But she did want to be on good terms with him. Lorenzo himself headed the embassy of six which was sent to Rome to congratulate Sixtus on his accession. They arrived in time to hear some queer stories. Officially it had been announced that the Papal treasury had been found empty, that Paul must have dissipated in unaccountable ways the wealth he was known to have amassed. But, oddly enough, just after this announcement, the new Pope's horde of nephews blossomed out in a splendor that hardly accorded with their known means.

Lorenzo cared nothing for all this. He preferred a venal Pope; such a man could be bought. He had a most satisfactory interview with His Holiness. The Medici Bank was to keep the Papal account, the alum monopoly was continued and Uncle Giovanni Tornabuoni was entrusted with the profitable task of selling Paul's jewels—Sixtus needed the money.

After these matters had been settled, Lorenzo ventured to hint at a hope which he had been nursing for months. The great rulers of Christendom were as a matter of course represented in the Sacred College. Lorenzo felt that the Medici too had reached a point which entitled them to a man in the inner council of the Church, and he had in his own mind selected Giuliano for the post. The youngster was only eighteen, untrained for holy orders, but such an exalted rank as that of Cardinal required no preliminary training.

To Lorenzo's great delight, Sixtus did not protest. He indicated that the matter might be arranged, and with considerable shrewdness selected a gift which, quite as much as the prospect of future favor, sent his visitor away happy. The present was a pair of antique marble busts withdrawn from the sale which Giovanni was to conduct.

With these and a quantity of other artistic treasures bought from the Papal storehouses at bargain prices, Lorenzo returned home exulting. He felt that his mission had been a complete success, that he had set the financial stability of the House of Medici above all possibility of harm, that he had won a Red Hat for Giuliano, that the new Pope was a friend and an ally.

An unpleasant surprise was waiting for him. The alum monopoly had led to a quarrel with the commune of Volterra, never a very submissive portion of the Florentine state. The Volterrans set up a ridiculous claim to the profits from their own alum mine, but of course this could not be allowed. It had been permissible when the mine was supposed to be of little value, but now that it was producing richly, other arrangements were necessary. The in-

dignant commune promptly declared its independence, ejected the Florentine commissary and hired a
thousand soldiers to defend the city.

There were anxious councils in the Palazzo
Publico while the Signoria waited to learn from
its rulers what orders it should give. Tomasso
Soderini spoke for conciliation. He proposed to
allow the Volterrans part of the mine earnings. But
once again Lorenzo ignored his advice. Four times
within living memory the stubborn dependency
had revolted. Lorenzo thought it was time to end
that. He wanted peace, but on his own terms, and
he settled the argument at last in one of the parables
of which he was so fond.

"That physician is often most cruel who appears
most compassionate," he declared.

The Signoria understood. Federigo d'Urbino was
hired to bring the rebels to their senses, and the
soldiers were given Lorenzo's words to ponder.
There was no fighting. At the approach of Federigo's
overwhelming force, Volterra surrendered without
a blow and the mercenary troops swept through the
city, burning, plundering, ravishing and killing with
a ferocity rare even in the terrible records of Italian
civil war. Federigo, whose reputation as the only
humane military man of his generation had encouraged the rebels to give themselves up uncondi-
tionally, was unable to restrain his followers. He
tried, but the work of destruction proceeded furiously.
The soldiers hired to defend the city were even more

savage in rending their employers than were the conquerors.

When the flames died down and the army had departed with everything of value that could be saved, Lorenzo paid a visit to the ruined city. The desolation was even more complete than he had believed possible, and he tried to make amends. But Volterra never forgave him. The fortress which he built to overawe the citizens was a constant reminder to them of the horrors which even in that age of senseless cruelty were looked upon as a little excessive.

In the midst of the excitement over Volterra, the introduction of a new German invention into Florence attracted little attention. Bernardo Cennini, the goldsmith, brought into the city a queer mechanical contraption for the making of books. Cennini was an enterprising man, the first Italian to cast his own type, but he received little encouragement from the literary celebrities of his native city. Even Lorenzo was cold.

His Magnificence did not altogether approve of printing. In the first place, the products of Cennini's press were uglier than the flowing script, the brightly illuminated margins of Lorenzo's literary treasures. Furthermore the press was a menace to the value of every library in town. Lorenzo was spending thirty thousand ducats a year for manuscripts, and his agents were sniffing through old monasteries like bloodhounds on the scent of forgotten masterpieces of antiquity. What would this collection be worth and what would his friends the copyists do for a living if every ignoramus could possess books at a couple of scudi apiece?

Lorenzo altogether neglected Cennini, and the goldsmith printed only one book. But he had made a start and within a year John of Mainz came down from Germany to set up another press. Still Lorenzo refused to become excited, although some of his friends patronized the new discovery "made among the barbarians in some German city" so well that several more printers were attracted.

X

No one had yet thought to ballyhoo the press as a disseminator of knowledge and bulwark of education. Perhaps such an appeal might have earned for Lorenzo the honor of patronizing a new art, for education was one of his hobbies. The taste for pedagogy, noticeable in the nursery and cropping out perennially in his correspondence, grew upon him. Like every true pedagogue he revelled in study so much himself that the urge to force similar pleasures upon others was irresistible.

In the midst of a severe famine, which for Florence was alleviated by the munificence of her ruler, Clarice had presented him with a son. Called from his work of distributing the produce of his farms among the people, the father celebrated the day, February 15, 1472, with an enthusiasm rare even for him. No one would have suspected that a famine was raging. He named the infant after his father, and called upon all Florence to pray that the little Piero would grow up into such a wise and good man as his grandfather had been.

When the first transports of his joy had subsided, he began to take thought for his child's education. The problem of tutors for the first years was easy; his own preceptors were still available and ready to regard the task of teaching his son as an honor. But the question of higher education interested him. For himself he had never considered any university; his superiority to most of the professors of that day was too marked, and anyway he had never had time for it. However, he did not purpose that his son should follow altogether in his footsteps. The boy should have all that his father had missed.

The University of Florence had never attained the high rank among European institutions of learning which might have been expected from the wealth of the city, the fame of her scholars and the eagerness of her people for knowledge. Lorenzo decided that it needed his attention. He soon discovered why it had not fulfilled the hopes entertained by its founders more than a century before. The University had opened its doors in the midst of a plague and had been sickly ever since. Florence was the most expensive city in Europe. Students from abroad were discouraged by the high cost of living, while the native population was too small to support a first class academy, especially as the wealthiest youths were educated almost entirely by tutors.

Lorenzo had another objection to his own city as the seat of an institution of learning. He knew from his own experience that life in Florence offered so many pleasures, a young man's mind might easily be seduced from his books. How often, he sighed, had his own quiet evenings of study been interrupted by the irresistible call of revellers dancing down the

Via Larga! Even today, mature man of family and respected head of the state though he was, he could never be safe from friends who would drag him out into the night to help serenade a lady or try his luck with the dice or make the circle of babblers around the wine flask complete. Not only could they try to inveigle him away from his books, but they could all too often succeed. If at his age—he was twenty-three—a man was not immune to these temptations, what could be expected of young students?

But Lorenzo had taken up the idea of a university and he could not let any project drop. He would revive the ancient glories of the academy at Pisa. Since she had passed under Florentine rule early in the century, Pisa had declined to an almost deserted city, peopled by the feeble, dejected remnants of a once pushing citizenry, living on her memories and losing her best blood to livelier places. But in the days of her independence, the fame of her school had been proclaimed throughout Europe.

What had once been, said Lorenzo, could be again. Besides, he owned a good deal of property in Pisa. The re-establishment of the University would increase the value of that property wonderfully. Aside from that, Pisa was an ideal spot for his purposes. It was very dull, very cheap and there were enough empty houses lining the forlorn streets to accommodate more students than were likely to come. He decided to leave two departments of the university in Florence—the schools of philosophy and philology. Most of the philosophers were his intimates, and he could not bear to part with them. So at Pisa were established only the schools of law, theology and medicine.

By December, 1472, all the preliminary arrangements were complete. Lorenzo himself had spent some months in Pisa preparing the ground, outlining his plans to the inhabitants and gathering information about the town. That done, he endowed the new school handsomely, secured a state subsidy of six thousand florins a year and persuaded Sixtus to permit the clergy to be taxed locally for part of the faculty payroll.

The salaries of the professors ran into much money. The most famous lecturers in Italy would alone satisfy Lorenzo, and they had to be rewarded with incomes that were envied by prosperous merchants. A man had to rise high in the Church to receive the compensation which a professor of note could command, for the competition was keen. Venice, Siena, Bologna and other universities were ready to bid high for the services of instructors. It was the golden age of the teaching profession, the only genuinely golden age it ever knew.

The entire direction of the University was confided to Lorenzo. He had four fellow trustees, but they left everything to him. Every year he had to meet a big deficit, and did it gladly. Every year he spent more time than he could really spare in Pisa. And every year he was called away from the business of his home city to soothe or discipline the turbulent spirits who occupied the chairs of law and theology. Fortunately the hunting was good. Lorenzo was fond of the chase and of hawking, and these sports pleasantly beguiled visits that were otherwise chiefly devoted to accommodating disputes or planning scholarly improvements.

Professors of that day were not at all bound by any traditions of aloofness from the world. They were not cloistered scholars poring over books or elucidating their nebulous theories in comfortable seclusion while the world roared by them unheard and undesired. They were not even very respectable members of society, little as respectability was accounted and low as its standards were. They were much more likely to be quarrelsome, swashbuckling fellows, as ready with the sword as with the pen. Indeed, they often knew more about the management of weapons than soldiers. They needed to; they were much more belligerent. They were as keen politicians as the lawyers or the churchmen. Though their lectures frequently explored the most profound depths of abstract philosophy, their conduct was based on very practical, cold blooded, calculating principles. They taught their students to enjoy the excitement of inquiry rather than the repose of study. Of all the learned men who flocked around Lorenzo and looked to him for protection, they were easily the most arrogant, unmanageable and troublesome. They pressed fiercely for ever higher salaries; they intrigued bitterly; they fought rancorously and with a wealth of vulgar invective; they were not even honest.

At the very top of his profession was Bartolommeo Soccini, engaged at great expense to teach civil and canon law. The offer of a higher wage from the Venetian university soon led the learned jurist to break his contract. Without notice and quite secretly, he set out for his new position, taking with him some of the most valuable books that had been entrusted to his care. He was caught before he could reach Venetian territory, and brought back to Florence to stand trial as a thief. Soccini's biting tongue had given great offence to many of the city's leading citizens, and the Signoria lost little time in sentencing the professor to death. But his talents were too useful and famous to be wasted.

"So accomplished a scholar should not suffer so ignominious a death," said Lorenzo.

He procured pardon for Soccini, and, to assuage his injured feelings and soothe his vindictive spirit, gave the graceless professor a very substantial in-crease in salary and sent him back to Pisa. There for three years he was suffered to teach the law, rob his students and his employers and insult anyone who disagreed with him. At last his peculations and his insolence became so notorious that Lorenzo lost patience. He had Soccini flung into the Stinche, but even that foul prison could not break the jurist's spirit.

"It is an outrage that so distinguished a man should

be confined in so vile a place," he complained in-
dignantly to his erstwhile patron.

But this time Lorenzo was firm in his determination to discipline the culprit.

"It is neither the place nor the punishment that
makes a man infamous, but the crime that brings on
the punishment," he retorted.

At last, however, the Pope intervened for the
prisoner and Soccini was released. He retired, fuming, to Siena where his vanity was gratified by a
quarrel between rival universities that claimed his
services. This reached such an intensity that the
Sienese Republic was preparing actually to go to war
on his behalf. The rivals gave way, and Soccini was
able to devote the rest of his life to urging the Pisans,
from a distance, to rebel against their Florentine
masters who had so grossly insulted him.

One of Soccini's colleagues on the law faculty,
Filippo Tristano, gave Lorenzo almost as much
trouble. He, too, refused to recognize the sanctity of
contract, and was constantly cutting his classes to
engage in verbal warfare with his professorial rivals.

"Neither gifts nor kindness can soften the
man's wrath, rashness and inconstancy," Lorenzo
mourned, but he could not bear to allow the escape
of one who brought so much honor to his darling
university.

Besides, he had a genuine respect for the instructors
of youth. He was often reproached for the favor he
showed them—the envious were constantly criticiz-

ing him for his support of unworthy men—but he replied with characteristic loftiness:

"If we esteem those who contribute to the prosperity of the state, we ought to place in the first rank our children's tutors whose labors are to influence posterity and on whose precepts and exertions the dignity of our family and of our country in a great measure depends."

Ordinary men hesitated to offend so formidable a band of antagonists as university faculties by making any of the rather more obvious retorts.

Meanwhile, in 1473, the new academy at Pisa was formally opened. Lorenzo was so determined to make a success of it that he resisted all importunities to return to Florence for All Saints Day. A very superior festival had been arranged, but Lorenzo regretfully declined. He wanted to see that the Pisan ceremonies came off well, even if they were not much fun.

The Medici patronage had won for the institution a student body worthy of the young founder's ambitions. The very violence of the instructors also attracted pupils, a reputation for professorial pugnacity serving the same purpose that future homes of learning were to find in a reputation for athletic prowess. Lorenzo even sent his own brother to attend some of the first sessions, and Giuliano sat docilely at the feet of the eminent theologians and lawyers at Pisa as he had once sat before Lorenzo. He did not, however, have a brilliant university career. He was a little too old for the place—nineteen—and he had left too many interests in Florence. He could not concentrate on his studies. He wished to get back to his jousting, his football and his friends.

The university offered splendid opportunities for the professors to make names for themselves, but it furnished no scope at all for a young man like Giuliano. He could not spend his money in the style to which he was accustomed; he could not exploit his fame as one of the leading athletes of Italy; he could no longer enjoy the elevated conversation of artists and poets, and he did not like the ladies of Pisa.

Giuliano, therefore, soon tired of college life, and returned to Florence where his generosity, beauty and skill at sports earned for him a popularity rivalling that of his brother. He did not remain to see Lorenzo's university acquire even greater fame than it had known in the most glorious days of Pisan independence. But Lorenzo watched with delight as this work of his own brain and efforts developed into the favorite seminary for the heirs to the mighty, a training school for the most splendid of Italy's future Popes and Princes.

XI

Europe had ceased to look upon Lorenzo de' Medici as a promising young man. He was only twenty-four, but the magnificence of his embassies abroad, the success of his administration at home, the mature works of his pen and the praises of other scholars had in the last four years endowed him with such fame that it was impossible to patronize him simply because of the small number of his years.

His advice and material assistance were sought with equal eagerness by writers, painters, students, wives, statesmen and even kings. Poliziano would bring forward a new poem for criticism, and bear suggestions with patience. Ficino was willing to adopt his pupil's ideas on moot points of Platonic doctrine. Botticelli listened with awe and gratitude while the great man discoursed on the ideal of painting and proposed subjects for canvases. Sandro had recently left Pollajuolo to set up his own studio, and Lorenzo was backing him against the cruel witticisms of elder brushmen. They were sneering, with a good deal of jealous apprehension behind the sneers, at the innovations which this rather crude practical joker and sensitive idealist was bringing into their well systematized art.

Stung by the taunts of his elders, Botticelli came to

Lorenzo for comfort. He was rewarded by commissions, and in the Medicean circle he found both
money for his purse and models for his pictures. He
also learned something of polite society and was
privileged to listen to the wits and poets as they contended for the applause of their patrons.

Apart from this group, Sandro was seeing a great
deal of Verrochio's pupil, Leonardo, who had been
admitted to the painters' guild, that of the Physicians
and Apothecaries, about the time Botticelli opened
his own *bottega*. The two, each recognizing the
other's genius, held long, amicable disputes on the
theory of their art. Sometimes young da Vinci would
show his older friend designs for the most amazing
projects, feats of engineering at which the simple,
rather ignorant Sandro marvelled without the slightest understanding. There were plans for canalizing
the Arno, for new, improved mills, for tunnelling
through mountains by means of machinery such as
had never before been imagined, for storing water in
such quantities that there would be plenty available
even for quite poor people.

In spite of these schemes, Leonardo was doing so
well at his work that Andrea Verrochio had sworn
never to attempt colors again since a mere pupil could
surpass him. Da Vinci had been entrusted with the
execution of one angel off in the corner of one of his
master's large paintings. When it was finished,
Verrochio was enraged to see that the one corner
overshadowed all the rest of the piece. He was so

angry that although he was Lorenzo's favorite artist, next to Botticelli, he refrained from commending Leonardo to the patron.

One of the reasons for the respect entertained for Lorenzo abroad was that he had never allowed his friendship for the Neapolitan royal family to decline. With Ippolita, Duchess of Calabria, he had long maintained a correspondence nicely balanced between ardor and philosophy. They discoursed of books and love for the most part, but at times more mundane considerations intruded. For despite Ferrante's cruel exactions—perhaps because of them— the Kingdom of Naples was not prosperous. Taxes came in slowly and the nobility were usually either hostile to the court or too poor to be of much help. So when Ippolita was pressed for funds, she would write such letters as this to her banker friend in Florence:

"Illustrious and mighty and paternally respected lord:

"The old existing kindness and intimate friendship between the family of Your Magnificence and our late illustrious parents and your especial affection for our most illustrious brother, the Duke of Milan, assure us and fill us with the certain hope that you will support us in our great embarrassment, for which we shall ever owe you gratitude. We beg you, therefore, to lend us two thousand ducats gratis for a time to be fixed by yourself, we promising its punctual repayment on the word of an honorable woman."

Banking under such circumstances was a pleasure. Ippolita got her loan, even though the terms were a little unusual. The Medici Bank was not accustomed to forego its interest. The custom of the day was to limit the rate only by the borrower's need, but Lorenzo had learned from his father's experience that bad business is sometimes very good politics.

Naples from a purely commercial point of view was not a very sound place in which to sink money. Ferrante had daughters growing up, and he was under the necessity of providing them with dowries suitable to their rank. In a way it was worth it, for he was enjoying the game of matrimonial alliances and was planning to relate himself to all the important princely families of Italy. The Este were one of the greatest. Ferrara, by virtue of a little expansion and some fame as a centre of culture, had raised itself to the status of a dukedom, and Ferrante had promised his daughter, Eleanora, to Ercole, the new head of the House. The final negotiations ended early in 1473, and the Duke sent his brother, Sigismondo, to bring home the bride.

The young nobleman shared with the rest of his family a passion for beauty that made Ferrara second only to Florence as a haven for artists. He travelled in becoming state, and flattering orations resounded all along the route he took. The whole party stopped at Florence on the way back, and were elaborately entertained by the Medici.

Clarice was again fulfilling her wifely duty. She

was carrying a child whose name was to be Maddalena in honor of her maternal grandmother, but
Lorenzo's wife was almost the only person in Florence who did not take a tremendous interest in the
preparations for receiving the guests. The city was
in a ferment because a new favorite was rising to
rival Simonetta Vespucci. Marco's wife had for
several years reigned alone in the hearts of men. She
had been the Queen of a tournament Giuliano de'
Medici gave to rival that of his brother, and all
Florence had cheered madly as, before mounting her
throne, Simonetta impulsively bound her own scarf
around her cavalier's arm. They had applauded still
more madly when Giuliano vindicated her taste by
unseating every one of his six opponents and placed
the first prize at his lady's feet.

But now another beauty had grown up. Albiera
degli Albizzi was only fifteen, but her superior
charms were being extolled by some of the very men
who had only a year ago been ready to fight to prove
that Simonetta was the modern Venus. By the time
Eleanora reached Florence, these men were in the
majority, and the young daughter of the Albizzi was
easily the belle of the ball. During the dancing in the
banner-hung squares every afternoon, the watchers
shouted to each other that Albiera was even more
beautiful than Simonetta and more graceful than
Bianca, Lorenzo's sister, hitherto the most acclaimed
dancer in the city. The new favorite's triumph was
short. She fell ill a few days after the visitors departed,

and died amid the loud lamentations of the poets. There was no one now to dispute Simonetta's reign.

The general mourning for Albiera was so great that it distracted popular attention from a grave scandal which Sigismondo d'Este had aroused. The much admired, liberal patron of the arts had repaid the most splendid hospitality Florence could shower upon him by putting into circulation huge sums of counterfeit Florentine money. The recipients of his bounty and merchants who had been proud to serve him were furious when they discovered that the coins which they had taken with so many humiliating expressions of gratitude were worthless. The courts promptly convicted Sigismondo of forgery, but any attempt to execute the sentence must have been attended by an inconvenient war with a friendly neighbor, so the matter was hushed up.

With one daughter safely married, Ferrante turned with renewed energy to disposing of the others. He opened negotiations with the Duke of Savoy, and immediately entangled himself in major international politics. Anything that might seem to strengthen Savoy was frowned upon by the King of France. Louis had a son himself, not very bright and remarkably ugly, but available for the creation of a diversion which might disrupt the plans of others.

Besides a wife for his son, he wanted a watch dog for his bedchamber, and as a matter of course he looked to his banker to get him both. The diplomats

of Florence were famous all over Europe; many of
the exiles from successive civil storms had found
pleasant, profitable service in foreign courts where
they had justified the proverb which credited all
Florentines with "keen eyes and sharp tongues."
Louis was sure he could not find a better agent than
the man who had held Florence peacefully for four
years, was still keeping the balance even in the teeter-
ing scale of Italian politics and was bound to France
by the strongest financial ties that the Medici Bank
of Lyons could forge.

Louis dictated a flattering letter asking Lorenzo
to correspond with Ferrante; object, matrimony. He
professed a desire to see the Dauphin married to a
Neapolitan princess—apparently he was not particular which one—and he begged his good friend to do
his best. As for the dog, the suspicious monarch, who
feared with all too good reason that the men around
him were no more trustworthy than himself, hoped
that a dog with a savage disposition would insure the
safety of his slumbers.

The dog was easy; the Florentines had developed
a peculiarly ferocious breed especially for the guarding of treasures. The marriage presented more difficulty. Lorenzo dutifully wrote to Ferrante, but his
heart was not in it. He knew the King of Naples
better than Louis did, and realized that the South-
erner was no fool. The conditions on which the
French monarch was prepared to welcome a
daughter-in-law from Italy were such that Ferrante

would find himself the avowed enemy of Spain, Savoy, Burgundy and anybody else with whom the unpredictable Frenchman might find himself at odds.

Ferrante returned a nobly negative answer, glad of the opportunity to rid himself of some lofty sentiments that must have been rather uneasy in his company. The proposal was allowed to lapse, but Lorenzo was very proud of having been entrusted with it. Hitherto the relations between the Medici and the Capets had been purely financial in an era when a banker was very much the servant of a royal client. Now Louis had shown that when he addressed the Florentine as "cousin" he really meant it. The Medici had risen from the status of middle class merchants to terms of equality with kings, were admitted to the inner circle of family councils. It was the rank of his client that flattered Lorenzo, for he was no despiser of titles. As a human being, he regarded Louis rather unfavorably, not altogether a civilized person as Italy understood the term, but still a King.

Encouraged by this evidence of his importance in the international scheme of things, Lorenzo renewed his efforts to have Giuliano made a Cardinal. He corresponded eagerly with men known to possess the confidence of the Pope. He had been able to do a few trifling favors for Giuliano della Rovere, Sixtus's warlike young nephew who had been raised to the Cardinalate in the first year of his uncle's reign. Lorenzo counted on the good will of this young man when the time should come.

Even more he counted upon Cardinal Ammanti, a veteran of Vatican politics, who undertook to engineer the appointment. But though Lorenzo was prepared to spend more money than a seat in the Sacred College was considered to be worth, there were difficulties. The handicap of youth, it appeared, could only be overcome in the case of members of the Pope's immediate family or personal favorites. Cardinal Ammanti suggested that it might be well to groom a second candidate in the event of failure. He proposed Lorenzo's cousin, Filippo de' Medici, Archbishop of Pisa, "or anyone else who would suit you."

"Choose anyone," he repeated emphatically, "so he is not a person to be ashamed of."

But Lorenzo would hear of no one but his brother. He brushed aside the argument of youth. All Italy was still snickering discreetly over the recent creation of a Cardinal who was only twenty and had previously been valet to His Holiness. The boy had only his personal beauty and his homosexual habits to recommend him, but Lorenzo refused to admit that in the Vatican of that day these were the best qualifications, next to near relationship to the Holy Father, that a young man could possess for a Red Hat.

He had set his heart on the appointment, and he was not used to being disappointed. Ammanti reluctantly ceased to urge the advisability of having another candidate in reserve. He continued to work for Giuliano's interest, but he warned Lorenzo that the younger brother would have to serve a certain apprenticeship. It would be necessary for him to become a protonotary "for at least a month, for none of us would venture to suggest that from a layman he should at once be promoted to so high a position."

Soon it appeared that Lorenzo had been right in persisting, for Sixtus had lavished so much money on his children that the price of a Cardinalate would be a powerful bait. Giuliano himself took far less interest in his proposed career than Lorenzo. The younger brother was not ambitious, but he was ready to do anything Lorenzo asked. Giuliano had a very proper respect for the head of the House, and never once dreamed of asserting any claims to a share in the direction of those mysterious affairs of state which were Lorenzo's province.

The elder was well content as the months rolled placidly by, no flaw as yet marring his enjoyment of success. Ahead lay a succession of ever higher honors, and Florence had become all that he once dreamed. A few years of perfect peace, a few years of admirable example from above, a few years of education in the art of having a good time had lifted Florentine taste and prosperity to new heights. Every citizen was on the way to becoming a connoisseur of the arts, a literary critic, a sportsman and a rollicking good fellow withal.

Lorenzo's palace was being beautified with the

brilliant silks which represented his own triumphs in his favorite sport of horse racing. As regularly as race day came round, one of the Medici entrants earned for his master a banner which he valued as much as if it had been a relic of antiquity. Between meetings he superintended the training, exercising and feeding of his racers, and even when he was out of Florence he wrote home instructions about the conditioning of the horses he planned to run the next time the Borgo degl' Albizzi was cleared for the fray.

Without any appearance of restlessness or haste, Lorenzo passed with immense energy from one field of pleasure to another. It pleased him to hear men marvel that he could find time for so much business, so much politics, so much diplomacy, and yet devote himself to beauty in all its forms.

But indeed, his affairs were running so smoothly that they required less attention than people thought. His bank managers might complain that he violated all the known principles of finance, but the institution still flourished. Government and diplomacy seemed to be all the better for his apparent neglect. He was quite carefree as he wandered from palace to villa, abandoning his energies and his talents to song, conversation and love. He travelled almost constantly, moving from one villa to another, visiting friends all over Tuscany and stopping occasionally to enjoy the mineral water baths which were being widely exploited throughout the country. His mother found her skin troubles greatly helped by these waters, and was spending her life in making the spas worthy of Roman traditions. But her son did not yet need them, although he enjoyed them.

Everywhere he went he was entertained delight-fully. He always travelled in some state, his minimum retinue consisting, aside from those friends and ad-visers who shared his pleasures, of a chaplain, a house steward, two secretaries, two singers, a sculptor, a barber, two valets, a butler, five crossbowmen, ten grooms, an equerry, a cook and a kitchen boy. But his suite did not tax the accommodations of his hosts as much as might have been expected for fourteen beds sufficed for the whole party.

Almost always the master of this entourage was back in Florence every two months to supervise the drawing of the names for the new Signoria and Priory. Every sixty days another set of petty trades-men listened with rapturous delight while the splen-did Lorenzo de' Medici addressed them respectfully as "Magnificent and Illustrious." Naturally they could do no less after that than just exactly what he told them.

It never occurred to them to question what happened to the taxes they levied. They all had confidence in Lorenzo's ability to spend money, and if some of the public funds found their way into private pockets, it was no more than right. The recipients deserved well of their country. They kept it amused. Lorenzo had proved his theory of government, and the city was so serene that the Ferrarese Ambassador had difficulty filling up his dispatches.

"There are no politics here," he was obliged to report. "The only news is that Lorenzo lost two falcons."

XII

The Ambassador was able before much longer to tell of greater losses. At twenty-six Lorenzo began to learn that the griefs of which he had on occasion sung so well but with so little understanding are not to be avoided by any man who seeks to explore all possible human experience.

The first blow was the death of a baby born to Clarice only a few months earlier. This, however, was soon compensated by the birth of another son, and as the second male child, the infant Giovanni was dedicated from the beginning to the Church.

Lorenzo was still in mourning when he received word that the fair Simonetta was dangerously ill. He was in Pisa when the news reached him and, greatly alarmed, he ordered his own physician to attend the sick woman. This man and the Vespucci doctor could not agree on a diagnosis but fortunately they were as one in the treatment to be followed so their dissension made little difference in the progress of the patient's ailment. Couriers mounted on the fastest horses from the Medici stables galloped daily from Florence to Pisa with bulletins reporting the lady's health.

Her husband and Giuliano watched anxiously together at the bedside. They could spare no time to write, so the task of keeping Lorenzo informed fell to Marco's brother, Piero. In one jubilant letter, tempered by a few expressions of hope that the doctor's bill would not be larger than the Vespucci could afford, Piero announced that by charms and spells and medicines the fever had been exorcised. But while Lorenzo was rejoicing over the prospect of the fair one's imminent recovery, there came a relapse, and a few days later all Florence was plunged into mourning by the announcement that Simonetta was dead.

The pleasures of Pisa turned bitter. For several days Lorenzo lost his power to enjoy. He hurried back to Florence, talking gloomily of the sorrows that fall to every man's lot in this empty world. His grief found outlet in a sonnet with a sentiment four and a half centuries younger than it is today, but still not new:

> *Bright shining star! Thy radiance in the sky*
> *Dost rob the neighboring stars of all their light.*
> *Why art thou with unwonted splendor bright?*
> *Why with great Phoebus dost thou dare to vie?*
> *Perchance those eyes which Death so cruelly—*
> *Too daring Death!—has ravished from our sight,*
> *Have given to thee the glory of that light*
> *Which can the chariot of the Sun defy.*
> *Oh new-created star, if star thou art,*
> *That Heaven with new-born splendors dost adorn,*
> *I call on thee! Oh Goddess, quickly hear!*

Of thine own glory grant me now a part
To fire these eyes, with endless weeping worn,
With something of thy light that they may bear.

The poet reached Florence in time for the funeral. Seldom had the city worn such a mournful aspect as when she who had queened it there so long was carried in solemn, tearful procession through the reverently hushed streets. The calm lovely face which all susceptible youths had worshipped was uncovered so that they might gaze once more upon perfect beauty.

Behind the flower-covered bier marched Lorenzo and Giuliano de' Medici, arm in arm, heads bowed, eyes streaming. They were the chief mourners, for they had loved the dead woman dearly and she had returned their love. Certainly no one, least of all her husband, who walked modestly at their heels, disputed their right to head the ranks of prominent citizens who were proud to give the belle of Florence such homage as generals and statesmen seldom received from them. Indeed, everyone agreed that the brothers had displayed to great advantage the delicacy of their affection. It was even said that Giuliano had in the excess of his emotion committed to paper some mournful verses that were as good as anything Lorenzo had ever done, but if written these lines were never very widely distributed.

One ardent admirer had been absent from the lamenting crowds. Botticelli, for whom his patron's mistress had deigned to pose, spent the entire day, alone in his studio, in an agony of grief that so much beauty should be lost to a world that needed beauty badly. Yet not altogether lost, for the world would have the loveliness that had dazzled Sandro perpetuated in his "Birth of Venus."

It was while Lorenzo was still grieving over the death of Simonetta that his own health began to fail. He had been almost vulgarly robust, but now he fell a victim to an hereditary tendency towards gout. He was young to be so afflicted, but he had crowded into his twenty-six years enough good living to account for his pains.

Although not a gluttonous eater, he indulged himself with a rather richer diet than was usual in that day. He was also fond of wines, the heavy vintages that are the despair of the gouty. These alone would have explained his ailment, but the very few moralists who wrote in the fifteenth century were inclined to blame his physical sufferings on his sexual excesses. The relation between diet and gout was not appreciated, nor did these men take into consideration the fact that Piero had first been attacked when he was only fifteen. They only knew that the number of Lorenzo's loves was large, and they declared that gout was a just punishment for his sins.

Certainly it helped destroy his happiness. Never again could he go hunting or enter a learned dispute or undertake a delicately diplomatic conversation or indulge in an amorous intrigue without the fear

The Fair Simonetta as She Posed for Botticelli

"The glory which can the chariot of the sun defy"

that a sudden twinge of intolerable pain would spoil his pleasure. Of course he never dreamed of giving up the chase or study or business or revelry, but the once keen edge of unalloyed enjoyment was gone. Lorenzo had become prematurely middle-aged, and the joyous exaltation which some few men have been able, by virtue of a naturally perennial youthfulness, to carry into old age was no longer possible for him.

The loss of his child, his mistress and his health did not complete the sum of his disillusionment. While he was still suffering from all of these, he saw his rosiest dreams for the future disappearing before the onslaughts of over-harsh realities. The high honors which he had thought were waiting to fall to him freely—or at a cost of only money—were receding beyond the realms of practical politics. The peace that meant so much to Florence's prosperity, and to the Medici rule, was wearing thin. The Bank was developing a limit to its resources, yet some restraint had still to be exercised in appropriating public funds. And finally, powerful and greedy men were gazing rather longingly upon the magnificence which they regarded as the perquisites of a Florentine governor.

These men were to be found both within and without the state. For the first time since Cosimo returned from exile, the family power was threatened by both foreign and domestic enemies of brains and influence. Lorenzo's diplomacy had been solely of the fair weather variety. He had bound no one to him by ties which self-interest would not find it easy to break. He had made the mistake of believing that pomp and eloquence were the sole uses of statesman-ship, and his young advisers had encouraged him. At home they had relied too securely upon the at-tachment of the masses. They had forgotten one of the major premises in Lorenzo's own theory of Government. He had set it up as a rule that the populace asked only prosperity and amusement. It followed that if someone other than the Medici would provide these indispensables, the people would hardly exert themselves very strenuously to prevent a change.

With a lack of foresight which was the last ex-pression of his youth, Lorenzo had permitted one family to attain to an importance which would not easily be overwhelmed. At the same time he had given them some reason to resent his rule. The Pazzi had grown almost as rich as the Medici, and for that very reason Lorenzo had kept them from obtaining a share in the administration proportioned to their wealth and numbers.

Cosimo had hoped that by marrying Bianca to Guglielmo de' Pazzi, he would check the inevitable rivalry. But though the arrangement worked out well enough for Guglielmo himself, his kinsmen, who were bankers too and competed with the Medici all over the world, could not see that it much benefited them. However, they were not hot-headed fools, and they knew that without foreign support they would stand little chance of displacing Lorenzo. So they were waiting patiently until he should lose some of that foreign friendship which it had always been the aim of the Medici to cultivate.

The Pazzi found the help they needed in Rome. The revenues of all the Catholic world could not satisfy the greed and ambition of the Pope's family. As a matter of fact, Sixtus had two families, the della Rovere and the Riario, and for the moment the Riario had the greater share of his favor. One of these sons, Pietro, had set himself the task of surpassing all previous records for expensive vice. Unbalanced by the unexpected good fortune of being raised suddenly from obscurity to the Cardinalate, he spent so much money rioting through Italy that His Holiness was obliged to adopt one of Ferrante's expedients. He created an artificial famine and proclaimed a monopoly of bread in the Papal states. By extorting a huge price from his subjects for inferior grain and selling the better grades abroad, Sixtus managed to gratify Pietro's tastes. The young Eminence could not stand the pace, however, and after two years of dissipation which was the wonder of all Italy he died. The Papal affections were transferred to the only one of Sixtus's sons who had remained a layman.

This was Girolamo Riario, who had supported himself in genteel penury as a customs clerk until his father could rise far enough in the Church to rescue his family from poverty. Girolamo had princely ambitions but few princely acquirements. He was a more temperate man than his younger brother, but he was just as expensive a favorite. For he would have nothing less than a principality, and the fond Sixtus could not bear to refuse him.

As a preliminary step Girolamo was created a Papal count and married Caterina Sforza, the bastard daughter of the old condottiere and the only one of his children to inherit both his shrewdness and his courage. To support the young couple in a style befitting their titles, Sixtus bought from the Manfredi the little state of Imola, paying forty thousand ducats for it and transferring it to his son. The city of Forli was also for sale, but after the purchase of Imola there was for the moment no more money in the Papal treasury. Sixtus had recourse to his bankers.

He soon found that there was some inconvenience in having a financial agent who was also a statesman. Lorenzo had been observing the rise of Count Riario without enthusiasm. To his mind there were too many independent rulers already in Italy. Another, especially one who could command the unquestioned backing of Rome for all projects of expansion, would inevitably add to the dangers of that general war which Lorenzo wished to avoid. The Medici Bank at Rome received instructions that no money was to be advanced to the Pope if it was to be used to swell the property of Girolamo.

Sixtus was furious, and in his balked paternal rage the Pazzi saw their opportunity. Of all the family, the most ambitious, the most intolerant and the most resourceful was Francesco, brother of Guglielmo and manager of the Pazzi Bank in Rome. Francesco promptly offered to lend His Holiness all the money he needed and within a few weeks Girolamo Riario was proclaimed lord of Forli. It was Lorenzo's turn to rage, but such an ordinary financial transaction afforded no pretext for inflicting the punishment he considered appropriate. The Pazzi wisely refrained from pressing their advantage as yet. They continued to exchange compliments and dinners with the Medici, took their turn in public office and obeyed orders as before.

But the breach with the Pope widened. Sixtus had no opportunity to forget his wrongs, even if he had been of the forgetting kind. For Girolamo now had his heart set on the town of Castello, and it had been promised to him. The Papal treasury was again empty, but there was a Papal army led by a perfectly trustworthy and accomplished general. Cardinal Giuliano della Rovere was having his military tastes gratified without stint. He had been given charge of the war which the Popes seemed to be constantly waging against their refractory subjects. The young Churchman had recently distinguished himself by a brilliant attack on Spoleto and a cruelty towards the conquered which was reminiscent of Volterra. If his nephew could win his son's principality, Sixtus felt, it would be sound economy.

The Cardinal joyfully undertook the conquest of Castello for the Count. But the place was a stronghold on the borders of Florence. In the hands of an enemy it would be a perpetual threat, and for years it had been in the hands of a life-long friend, Niccolo Vitelli. Castello exhibited a surprising resistance to the Papal army, surprising, that is, until it was learned that Lorenzo de' Medici was financing the defense. In the privacy of the Vatican Sixtus used some rather worldly language about the presumption of these Florentines.

He took what revenge he could. He deprived the Medici Bank of the Church's business, and gave the account to his friends, the Pazzi. The financial loss was a heavy one, but Lorenzo was much more concerned about another aspect of the quarrel with the Vatican. There could be no hope now of obtaining a Red Hat for Giuliano until a new Pope was elected, and Sixtus was an unusually robust old man.

Furthermore that short era of peace over which Lorenzo had presided so happily was obviously nearing its end. Sooner or later Girolamo's greed and Sixtus's partiality would give the condottieri a chance to earn their pay. When such a moment arrived, it would be well for Florence to have allies, and Lorenzo reluctantly began preparations for the war he dreaded.

In such an emergency, he found, his friendship with Naples would be worthless. Ferrante could forget neither the slenderness of his own rights to his throne nor the Papal claim to dispose of it. His policy was obviously to find Girolamo a lordship in the north left Sixtus should be tempted to offer his beloved son the crown of Naples. His Majefty had approved and assifted the attack on Caftello, and he shared the Pope's anger when the attempt failed.

Eftranged from Ferrante, Lorenzo had no choice save to seek alliances with Milan and Venice. The three banded together in a league for mutual defense, but it was not the ftrongeft protection Florentines could imagine. Venice was a notoriously unftable ally, and her interefts ftill lay outside Italy. If she were occupied in the Eaft, she would give no affif tance until both Florence and Milan were over run and her own territory on the mainland was threatened.

Milan at any other time might have been a mighty bulwark, but while Lorenzo was fearfully awaiting the outbreak of hoftilities, the Duchy was weakened by domeftic difficulties. Galeazzo Maria, surrounded by flatterers and courtesans, had grown careless. His cruelty had made him many enemies; his lufts had outraged the honor of some high spirited nobles; his crushing taxation had alienated the affections of his people. Three young men with very different motives determined to rid their country of the tyrant. One of them had seen his family butchered to provide amusement for the Duke; another sought to avenge a fifter's loft virtue; the third had been reading Roman hiftory and wanted to play Brutus.

The firft part of their conspiracy was successfully carried out. As Galeazzo marched at the head of his usual gorgeous procession into the Church of San Stefano to hear mass, the three young men crowded forward as petitioners. They had rehearsed the scene over and over again, and all three daggers found their proper sheath. But the army remained loyal to the Sforza, and as the Duke lay dying on the Church pavement, two of his assassins were cut to pieces. The third was soon caught and the four quarters of his tortured body exhibited about the city as a warning.

The murdered Duke's heir was only five years old. The child's mother, although aided by the advice of a shrewd secretary, Cecco Simonetta, was not strong enough to suppress her husband's ambitious brothers. The assassination of Simonetta opened the way for the ablest of these men, and before long Ludovico Sforza, Duke of Bari, had displaced the Duchess Bona as regent. He hastened to assure Lorenzo that the alliance was unimpaired, but it was obvious that he would be too busy bolstering up his own position at home to lend much aid abroad. Besides, no man in his right senses would have banked very heavily on Ludovico's word. The Duke of Bari was an incorrigible liar. He preferred deception, even when the truth would have served him as well.

He was an unpleasant person in every way. So dark that he was nicknamed "Il Moro," he possessed all the sly cruelty, treachery and pride which good Christians attributed to the Moors. It was whispered fearfully that he could actually command the services of demons and knew the formulae for strange, sinister spells. He took no chances of suffering his brother's fate, and all strangers who approached him were stopped at a bar so far removed from the Duke that they had to shout to make themselves heard.

With such allies, Lorenzo's public life could not be easy or amusing. Privately, too, everything seemed to go wrong. He had undertaken in the interest of literature to bring Dante's ashes back to the city from which in life the great poet had been exiled. But the Venetian Republic, suzerains of Ravenna, where Dante was buried, refused to hear of it.

And to cap the climax, Lorenzo was pained and horrified to discover that there were limits even to the largest private fortune in the world. Ever since he could remember, he had been accustomed to regard his resources as inexhaustible. Now his bank managers were telling him that such was not the case. Shocked as he was by the news, he could not learn to economize. He would not even try. Suggestions that he turn some of his income back into the business, as his cousin Pier Francesco did, were greeted with contempt. Lorenzo still had higher ideals than the success of the Bank.

Overwhelmed by anxiety about the approaching war, by his own ill health, by disappointed ambition and by financial troubles, he refused to relax for a moment his pursuit of beauty and pleasure. While he waited for the deluge, he planned carnivals with all the usual splendor of frivolity, sent out his expeditions in search of rare manuscripts, sang love songs to his mistresses, watched with discriminating admiration while his painters produced their immortal canvases, jested with the wits, disputed with the philosophers.

Nevertheless, there was a grimness about it all which had been lacking hitherto. Much of the spontaneity had departed from the fun; he embraced gayety seriously. The reform of manners in Florence, the education of the people to take their amusements with a light-hearted disregard of anything unpleasant that might be waiting in the future, remained his aim. But he could no longer catch the same spirit himself, and he had to watch his people distance him in the acquirement of insouciance.

XIII

Everyone agreed that war was inevitable, but as usual no one really wanted it to happen. The members of the League were not prepared to fight, and Sixtus still hoped without a general war to punish the impertinent Lorenzo while securing to Girolamo the greatness he deserved. His Holiness had a great respect for the power of money as embodied in the Medici, and for the remnants of old Francesco Sforza's army, which Ludovico could still command. Force on a large scale seemed so crude; it might end disastrously. He proposed to try strategy.

The Count Riario and Francesco de' Pazzi were much together. They were seen strolling about the corridors of the Vatican, arm in arm, deep in conversation that absorbed them completely. During the Christmas festivities of 1477 they became such close friends that shrewd observers told each other the pair had obviously reached a mutually satisfactory agreement of importance.

The observers were right, and the first fruits of the understanding were seen in an attempt to open amicable negotiations with Lorenzo. Hints were conveyed to the ruler of Florence that Sixtus, though hasty in his anger was equally quick to forgive, a rather unique interpretation of the Pope's well known implacable vindictiveness. It was suggested that if Lorenzo would only come to Rome for a free, full, frank discussion, his recent differences with the Holy See would evaporate. Sixtus would, no doubt, relent handsomely and all would be as before. By January the discussion of these differences had proceeded so far in correspondence that Girolamo was writing to Lorenzo with what he considered consummate guile:

"I do not in the least doubt that the Holy Father would receive you with joy, while I, with the affection which I owe you from our mutual friendly relations, would behave so as fully to satisfy Your Magnificence, and all considerations of grievance which may have arisen from the afore-named events would vanish."

The Count and his banker friend flattered themselves that the sweet tones of this letter would lure Lorenzo to Rome to make his peace with the Pope. It would, of course, be the peace of the tomb. Once Lorenzo was disposed of, his enemies would have Giuliano killed, and Florence would be at their mercy. The Pazzi would step easily, and quite naturally, into the place so suddenly vacated by the Medici. The Pope and his son would have their revenge.

The rest of the plan was not confided to Francesco. Count Girolamo had designs which looked far beyond mere vengeance. As he envisaged the future, the Pazzi would govern as his tools. Soon he would be able to work without tools. Then the Pazzi could be eliminated as the Medici had been, and the former customs clerk would become, say, Duke of Tuscany. With such power, and with the paternal benevolence of the Vatican to support him, it should not be difficult to add the whole of the Romagna to his dominions. And then—well, there was no limit to his ambition.

But the Medici still stood in the way. Riario had counted too much on his own eloquence. His sugared phrases had not imposed at all on Lorenzo, would hardly have deceived a much simpler man, for the double meanings in those phrases were thinly veiled. His Magnificence saw in the missive only a death threat. He politely regretted that business detained him. At the same time he welcomed with a proper show of gratitude the hope of a reconciliation.

Girolamo and Francesco were disappointed, but not discouraged. If the intended victim could not be brought to the butcher, the butcher would be sent to him. The assassins employed to put Giuliano out of the way would have a double task; that was all. So while the rest of Italy was preparing to celebrate Holy Week, the Pope's banker and the Pope's son were elaborating a murder.

There was no great difficulty in finding the butchers. Francesco himself was not averse to wielding a knife or mixing a judicious dose of poison. There were plenty of bravos and adventurers hanging around the Vatican to help him. From among these idlers, the heads of the plot selected three. Bernardo Bandini was a comparatively young man of good family, ready for anything. Dissipation had bankrupted him without depleting his energies, and the promise of another fortune would induce him to take any risk. Antonio Maffei, a priest from Volterra, felt an irresistible call to avenge the miseries of his native place. Stefano da Bagnone, an apostolic scribe, hoped to win with the dagger ecclesiastical preferment which he was not likely to obtain in any other way. These three men guaranteed to pick up enough like-minded fellows to insure a quick, clean job.

Meanwhile Girolamo and Pazzi had been joined by Francesco Salviati, Archbishop of Pisa. He had been appointed to this See on the death of Filippo de' Medici, but he had quarrelled with his predecessor's family, and they thought it hard that their recommendations for a post so important to them had been ignored. In the then existing state of his relations with the Vatican Lorenzo could do nothing to prevent the nomination, but he could—and did— keep the new Archbishop from taking possession of his office.

Salviati had been nursing his grievance in Rome, and was able to make several valuable suggestions. One of these was that the bloody end of the plot should be entrusted to a man whose business was blood. A soldier, he thought, should take charge of these priests and ruined gamblers. The right man was drafted from the Papal army. Giovanni Battista Monteseco had earned an excellent professional reputation as a captain under Cardinal della Rovere, which meant that he was loyal to his employer and ruthless to anyone else. He was quite ready to obey any orders, but when he was told what his orders were, he looked grave. He had friends in Florence and thought that perhaps these Romans did not know quite what they were doing.

"Have a care, gentlemen," he warned them. "Florence is no small matter, and Lorenzo, I hear, is very popular."

With a great show of mystery, his employers informed him that a greater than themselves was behind all this, that not even Lorenzo was to be compared with the Pope. Monteseco expressed some polite doubts that Christ's vicar on earth would deign to be mixed up in such a business—the Captain was a rather simple soul. Girolamo offered to produce evidence that would quiet all Christian scruples. Together the four—Riario, Salviati, Pazzi and Monteseco—came into the august presence. The Count opened the discussion by asking his father just what he thought about Florence.

"I will have no bloodshed," His Holiness began loftily. "It is not consistent with my office to cause the death of any man. Lorenzo has behaved shamefully and iniquitously towards us, but I do not desire his death, although I do desire a change of government."

This was not quite what the conspirators wanted. Riario broke in with a request that the Pope issue in advance a blanket pardon, valid before God and man, for anyone who was obliged to commit a murder in effecting the change.

"You are a stupid fool," was the retort, but the speaker's calm, indulgent expression and kindly tone did not fit the angry words. "I tell you I will have no man killed, although I desire the government to be changed."

Sixtus leaned back reflectively, considering the probable effect of his next words, and then turned confidentially towards his Captain.

"To you, Giovan' Battista," he said slowly, "I repeat that I wish the government of Florence to be changed and Lorenzo to be overthrown, for he is an undutiful and a bad man, who defies us. When he is out of the way we can deal with the Republic as we choose and as will be most convenient for us."

The conspirators looked triumphantly at Monteseco, but he still seemed to be a little puzzled. A great many words had been spoken, but the Pope's real meaning remained obscure. Did he or did he not want Lorenzo killed? He said not, but what else could he mean by that phrase "out of the way" when speaking to men steeped in the traditions of the Renaissance? Salviati saw the soldier's embarrassment and came to the rescue.

"Holy Father," the Archbishop inquired per-

suasively, "are you content that we steer this boat?
We will guide it well."

"I am," replied Sixtus, "but see to it that the
honor of the Holy See and of the Count does not
suffer."

The audience was over. Monteseco was taken
back to Riario's apartments and convinced that the
Pope would approve of the murder. Of course he
could not say so openly, they told the Captain. But
surely it was a dutiful service to the Church to remove a man so obnoxious to her head. And no one
would consider a killing, especially if successfully
executed, reflected on the honor of the Holy See.
They begged Monteseco not to be a child, and at
length he consented to join them.

They themselves were not content with a Papal
blessing and absolution. They wanted more definite
safeguards. They knew as well as Monteseco that
Lorenzo was popular in Florence, and they did not
have much faith that a pardon from Sixtus would
of itself avail them much in this world, however
effective it might prove in the next. All their possible
strength must be mustered to take instant advantage
of the blow when it fell. Lorenzo and Giuliano were
to die together. In the brief period of confusion before
the leaders of the Medici Party could rally their
forces, the Pazzi must seize the city.

They knew their own friends would not be
enough for this. They would have to be reinforced
by mercenaries. Two thousand soldiers were hired

and ordered to drift inconspicuously in small groups and by different routes towards Florence. They were to wait outside the walls for a signal from their employers.

Although inadequate for the work in hand, the Pazzi forces inside the city were formidable. Their palaces along the Borgo degl' Albizzi contained many loyal armed retainers. Each one was assigned a task and well drilled in it. Only Guglielmo was left out of the conspiracy. He was too closely related to the Medici to be trusted, although he might prove useful after the deed was done. All the other members of the family, even the least ambitious, were enthusiastic for a change, for they all knew something that was a profound secret to the rest of Florence but could not be kept a secret long. The Pazzi Banks were greatly over-extended, and must fail with terrible loss unless they could be supported through the crisis by the public treasury.

The head of the family was Giacopo, long notorious as one of the most daring gamblers in Florence. The sums he staked at play were repeated with awe by common mortals, and his private fortune had been repeatedly squandered and recouped in the most startling speculations. He was an old man now, but after a few preliminary scruples had been argued away, he embarked on the scheme with the ardor of a boy. He was childless himself, but he longed to see his ten nephews well provided for. The prospect of one last glorious gamble with life, fortune, reputation and affections to be won or lost in an hour inspired him to great exertions, although he was proverbially lazy. His generosity, when he was winning, had made him popular, and he scurried about the city reinforcing that popularity with kind words and kinder promises. The plotters hoped to start a stampede for him as soon as the Medici brothers were dead.

As a further aid to the conspiracy, Girolamo's young nephew, Raffaello Riario, was placed under the orders of Salviati. Raffaello, who at seventeen had recently been created a Cardinal, was studying at the University of Pisa. He was not told anything about the plot, for he was to serve only as a decoy.

All this time the Pazzi had been careful to remain on their old friendly terms with the Medici. The pretence was so well kept that Lorenzo cordially welcomed Francesco home for Easter, and the two families mingled with delightful amity throughout Holy Week. These festivities, the conspirators had determined, were to be the last at which the Medici would dazzle the spectators with their magnificence. It was even decided that the assassination should take place during one of the splendid celebrations when the brothers could easily be trapped together and their enemies could assemble their full strength without attracting much attention.

To insure a continuation of the gayety after Holy Week, so that their mercenaries would have time to arrive, Raffaello was ordered down from Pisa to see the wonders of the Cathedral. The conspirators knew that a visiting dignitary of such exalted rank would always be entertained elaborately in Florence for just as long as he cared to stay. In this case, Lorenzo was only too eager to do the boy well, for he still had hopes of propitiating the Pope and averting war. The improbability of an attempt to murder him in his own city, surrounded by his most beloved friends, seemed so great that he never dreamed of taking any precautions.

With supreme disregard of all the unpleasant events of recent months, he greeted his guests with his usual hospitality. His artistic treasures were displayed before them; his musicians regaled them with the jauntiest airs while they feasted on the rare delicacies of far countries; his literary friends taxed their famous wits to amuse the visitors.

There was something almost feverish about the gayety of these beautiful spring days. Everybody was trying just a little too hard to be the life of the party as they wandered from the flower-filled gardens on the slopes of Fiesole down to the more artificially decorated churches and palaces of the city. The conspirators, always tensely on the alert, despite their attitude of merry carelessness, were anxiously awaiting the proper time to strike. The Medici were having one last fling before settling down to the task of fighting for their dominion and their wealth.

XIV

A very animated party was in progress at Lorenzo's new Fiesole villa. Laughter and the unrestrained boisterous talk of men whose tongues have been loosened by wine and good fellowship echoed through the rooms and out over the garden where tables were being laid for the feast.

The host was standing on the terrace with his guest of honor, the Cardinal Riario, pointing out to him the particular beauties of the landscape. Fiesole swept down from their feet in a brilliant kaleidoscope of color to the grim brown walls of Florence, enclosing the domes and spires and parks of the city. Through this jewel-box of a town the Arno curved languorously, glowing golden in the sunlight, and beyond lay the green bulk of San Miniato.

Raffaello exclaimed with pleasure as he gazed, and turned to invite the appreciation of the men grouped about him. There was Francesco de' Pazzi, his admiration of the scene enhanced by the belief that all that met his eye would soon be his. Beside him stood Archbishop Salviati, benevolently ignoring the fact that he was still kept out of his See by his host's orders. Somewhere in the background

[165]

Captain Monteseco fingered the hilt of his sword and swore with amazement and awe at the lavish display of beauty around him. Bernardo Bandini was there, too, and in the Cardinal's train two priests were always conscious of the daggers concealed beneath their robes.

Monteseco, when he was not marvelling at the rich plate and furnishings of the villa, was keeping a sharp eye on Lorenzo. He had undertaken to dispose of the elder brother single-handed. Bandini was keeping as close as he could to Francesco, for they had rehearsed together the murder of Giuliano. But where was Giuliano? No one had seen him all day.

"My brother is ill," Lorenzo explained in answer to Francesco's anxious question. "It is nothing, a slight fever, but he will be unable to attend today."

The conspirators stared at each other in surprise and fear. Could their plot have been betrayed? Was this elaborate entertainment a counter-plot, a trick to collect them all together for their undoing? If so, they might strike first; it would be easy at this moment to rush upon Lorenzo and cut him to pieces. But that would be a useless exhibition of fury while Giuliano lived to add his brother's popularity to his own. Gradually, however, their fears quieted. Messengers came pelting up the hill to report that Giuliano really was sick, and it was plain to men whose consciences were not too greatly burdened by a sense of guilt that Lorenzo had no suspicions.

The party continued, but at a less hilarious pace.

A good many of the guests were so busy wondering how the Medici brothers could be caught together that they failed to enjoy to the full the amusements that their host had provided. At last it was over, and the conspirators could meet in the seclusion of the Pazzi Palace to rearrange their plans.

They could not delay much longer. Their mercenaries were close to Florence and could not be kept under cover indefinitely. The longer they waited, the greater was the danger of discovery. But how could they be certain of finding both victims together and unprotected? There was only one answer —in church. The boys had been reared piously. They could be trusted to go to mass, but all too often they heard it in their own chapel on the Via Larga or in the parish church of San Lorenzo around the corner. However, a pretext for getting them into the Cathedral, where all the conspirators could go too, was easily found. Cardinal Riario, it was announced, would celebrate mass at Santa Maria del Fiore the next Sunday. Lorenzo and Giuliano, for very decency, would have to attend.

All the conspirators save one thought very highly of this plan. The one was Monteseco. He had no objections to the murder of a man whose hospitality he was enjoying, but he drew the line at committing the murder in church. Like most of the soldiers of his day he was as pious as he was greedy and cruel. He had listened with horror while his superiors arranged the details, and when they fixed upon a signal for the double assassination—the elevation of the sacred host—he could contain himself no longer.

"I can have no further part in this affair," he cried. "It would be in the very presence of God! I cannot do it."

They argued with him in vain. Not even with an Archbishop to soothe him, no, not even with the Holy Father himself to urge him on, would he commit such a sacrilege. Murder? Yes, and gladly. But not sacrilege. And with God actually looking on, too! He reverted again and again to this exclamation, and could not be moved by argument. He was willing to take any other part in the conspiracy, to help raise the city, to overpower the Priors in the Palazzo Publico, to lead the mercenaries. But he would kill no man in church. At last his employers had to give over all attempts at persuasion. The murder of Lorenzo was entrusted to less scrupulous souls.

The priests Maffei and Bagnone had none of the alarming superstition which frightened the soldier. Presumably they were too inured to the presence of God and too accustomed to the solemn, holy atmosphere of Cathedrals to shrink from a killing. So with all the arrangements made, they told the young Cardinal that he wanted to celebrate mass next Sunday, and he duly repeated the desire to Lorenzo.

On Sunday—it was the twenty-sixth of April— His Eminence's entire retinue dined in the Via Larga before proceeding to mass. All the leading citizens of Florence were there, except Giuliano. That young

man was sick again! The conspirators were con-
founded, but only for a moment. Lorenzo was heard
assuring the Cardinal that his brother, although too
ill for feasting, would be present at church.

They were all in good spirits as they walked the
few hundred yards from the Medici Palace to the
Cathedral. Giuliano had not yet arrived. The service
began, and still there was no sign of him. In great
alarm Francesco de' Pazzi and Bandini ran to the
young man's house, and found him just ready to
start. With the familiarity of an old friend, Francesco
threw his arms around the convalescent and con-
gratulated him on his improvement. As he clasped
Giuliano to his heart, he signed over the victim's
shoulder to Bandini that all was well. Giuliano was
wearing no chain mail under his tunic. He had even
left the dagger, an almost indispensable article of
Florentine attire, in his room.

Exchanging compliments and jests, the three
hurried back to the Cathedral. Inside they joined the
fashionable promenade around the choir where the
notables of Florence were accustomed to stroll, offering each other bits of the latest gossip, during the
protracted services of their church. The newcomers
were just in time. Pazzi had only a moment to see
that Maffei and Bagnone were close behind Lorenzo
when the sacrament was raised and the words "*missa
est*" were echoing under the great dome.

Before they had died away, the Volterran Maffei
was leaping forward, his dagger in his fist. But though

his rage, nursed through years of brooding on the brutality which had destroyed his home, had made him fierce, the dexterity of his hand was not proportioned to the fury of his hate. He found himself shaking with anxiety and eagerness even as he raised his arm and heard the hissing of Bagnone's breath behind him. To steady himself for the blow he placed his left hand on his victim's shoulder and aimed for the throat.

At the touch Lorenzo naturally glanced behind him. The knife, glittering wickedly in that dim, religious light, flashed before his eyes as he threw himself impetuously to one side. The blade just grazed his neck, and before the stroke could be repeated, before Bagnone could push forward to complete the work, Lorenzo's sword was in his hand, his cloak was wound around his left arm as a shield. He parried Bagnone's timid thrust and then ran for shelter, while the two priests, in a panic of fear after their failure, were flying in the opposite direction.

The hands lifted against Giuliano had not shaken. As Maffei placed his hand on Lorenzo's shoulder, Bandini on the other side of the choir, without giving any preliminary warnings, stabbed the younger brother in the breast. Giuliano staggered back, but before he could cry out, Francesco de' Pazzi had borne him to the floor and was venting the accumulated envy and rage of years by plunging his dagger again and again into the limp body. He struck with such blind hate that one blow slipped, and wounded Francesco himself in the thigh. Even this did not calm him, and he continued to hack at his enemy until the madness of rage gave way to a madness of terror, for he learned that Lorenzo was still alive.

Bandini, the only one of the conspirators who kept his head, had seen even as he launched Giuliano's death blow, that the priests had failed. Without waiting to observe the result of his own thrust, he sprang in pursuit of the flying Lorenzo, but Francesco Nori, a staunch Medicean, blocked his way. Nori, though unarmed, flung himself forward to grapple with the assassin, and his death took just long enough for Lorenzo's friends to gather around him in a ring which Bandini could not hope to pierce. He turned away, thinking only of his own safety, as the little knot of badly frightened men around their leader dashed into the sacristy and bolted the heavy brass doors behind them.

Dull and muffled, they could hear the screams and curses resounding through the church as choir boys, priests and worshippers fought to escape from what they all believed to be a massacre. The young Cardinal, speechless and pale with fright, stood immovably at his post, gazing in horror at the armed retainers of the Pazzi who were scurrying aimlessly about the Cathedral seeking victims who were not there and adding to the panic of those whose only desire was to get out into the open air.

"The uproar was great," Filippo Strozzi wrote

with conscious restraint. "I was there talking with Messer Bongianni and the other gentlemen, and we were all struck with astonishment, people flying now here, now there, while the church resounded with loud shouts and arms were seen in the hands of the Pazzi, who had joined in this matter. The Cardinal was left all alone by the side of the altar until some priests came and led him into the old sacristy."

In the new sacristy, Lorenzo stormed up and down, careless of the wound on his neck, and crying over and over again:

"Is Giuliano safe? Is Giuliano safe?"

No one answered him, as he looked at them each in turn. Antonio Ridolfi, Sigismondo della Stufa, Poliziano, some young men of the Pandolfini and Neri, they all avoided his eye. Ridolfi created a diversion by suggesting that Maffei's dagger had been poisoned. He insisted on sucking the wound before binding it up.

Meanwhile the tumult in the church subsided as the vast nave emptied, leaving only two bodies lying in their blood upon the pavement. But the silence did not reassure the anxious prisoners in the sacristy, for now they could hear sounds as of rioting in the city. Men rushed, yelling incoherently, past the Cathedral; bells were tolling furiously; the hooves of galloping horses rang on the stones. The men locked behind the brass doors were all afraid to express their thoughts, for they were wondering how far the conspiracy had spread. Were the volatile Florentines al-

Courtyard of the Medici Palace

ready acclaiming new masters? Was a foreign army already marching through the gates? Only Lorenzo spoke, and he was still demanding:

"Is Giuliano safe?"

Suddenly a clanging knock shook the big brass doors, and the men inside drew their swords.

"We are friends, we are relations," impatient voices called. "Let Lorenzo come out before the enemy gain a foothold in the city."

"Enemies or friends, is Giuliano safe?" Lorenzo shouted back, and there was a sudden silence outside as the newcomers gazed at the corpse huddled so forlornly alone in the pillared immensity of the gray Cathedral.

Before Lorenzo could repeat his question, della Stufa had clambered up into the organ loft. Looking down into the body of the church he could see the faces of loyal Mediceans grouped about the sacristy doors.

"Open, they are friends," he called.

The whole party crowded closely around Lorenzo, talking fast and with many gestures lest he see his brother's body as they hurried through the church.

They had much to tell him. As the first knives were drawn in Santa Maria del Fiore, the Arch-bishop Salviati, followed by about thirty armed horsemen, rode into the Piazza della Signoria. While most of the troop waited in the courtyard and lower apartments of the Palazzo Publico, Salviati hurried upstairs with a few men to seize the titular heads of the government. His followers waited in one room on the floor where the magistrates lived while the Archbishop tried the effect of eloquence in the next, for he had an exaggerated notion of his own powers of speech.

He was disconcerted to find that the Gonfaloniere of the day was Cesare Petrucci, the man who had frustrated the attack on Prato a few years before. Petrucci was known throughout Tuscany for his singular courage and his devotion to the Medici.

Faced by such a person, the Archbishop began to temporize, but he did not have his words ready and talked rather confusedly about the Pope's desire to confer some favor upon Petrucci's son. Meanwhile Salviati signalled for his men to come to his help, but they were themselves helpless. No Florentine official ever felt safe from treachery, even in the most peaceful days of Lorenzo's reign, and it was the custom for each incoming set of magistrates to put new locks on the doors. Petrucci had devised a spring lock which on the closing of the door had automatically imprisoned the bravos in the next room.

His visitor's uneasy glances towards the door through which no one came, quickly aroused the Gonfaloniere's suspicions. He suddenly interrupted the Archbishop's rambling sentences to shout for the guard, and Salviati betrayed himself by running away. He never got outside the Palace. On the way downstairs he met the rest of his troop coming up, and they agreed to storm the magistrates in their chambers. But the officials and their servants, seizing spits and knives from the kitchen, defended themselves until a strong party of Mediceans came to the rescue. Effectively trapped in the Palace between the magistrates and the rescuers, Salviati and his entire band, with one exception who was not found for several days, were captured on the spot.

A few minutes later Francesco de' Pazzi was brought in, naked and crying aloud from the pain of his wounded leg, which had been none too gently treated by his captors. He had fled straight from the Cathedral to his uncle's home. There he was speedily found, cowering under the bedclothes. His captors brought to the magistrates their first news of Giuliano's death and Lorenzo's escape. Petrucci thought that this was no time for any protracted judicial proceedings, and the other members of the government agreed with him.

Without a moment's respite for trial, confession or prayer, the prisoners were butchered. Most of them were beheaded in the Palace courtyard, but half a dozen of the chiefs were hung out of the upper windows by the neck and left to strangle slowly in the sight of the people. Pazzi, naked as he was caught, was suspended beside the Archbishop, who was still clad in his rich prelate's robes. Swinging side by side, hearing as long as they could hear anything the bloodthirsty, gleeful shouts of the mob that watched their agonies, the bodies swayed against each other and apart again until in a last paroxysm of rage the

[*175*]

Archbishop clenched his teeth in Pazzi's bare breast. The two jerked once convulsively, and then hung without further movement, but Salviati had not relaxed his grip. Even those watchers who had seen only comedy in the contorted sufferings of the dying men were silenced for a moment by this last exhibition of what they all took to be implacable hate.

Of all the conspirators except Bandini, who was already beyond the gates and travelling fast, Giacopo de' Pazzi showed the most enterprise. While his nephew was cutting ferociously at Giuliano's dead body, while Salviati was blundering at the Palazzo Publico, the old man was mounted at the head of some hundred armed retainers riding through the most populous quarters of Florence, attempting to raise the city.

"Liberty! Liberty!" he shouted as he trotted slowly along, waving his sword.

But there was no magic left in the word. Even at the very beginning, when no one knew the fate of the Medici or what strength the Pazzi commanded, there was no response to his cries. Men on the streets pressed back against the walls to let the cavalcade go by, but they did not fall in behind to swell the rebel force. No cheers came from the faces at the windows. Soon the silence which had greeted the troop's passage was actually giving way to hostile replies.

"Liberty! Liberty!" Giacopo cried, but now there was more of despair than enthusiasm in his voice.

The answer, starting with a few muttered groans and curses, swelled rapidly to a mighty roar as the news spread that the handsome, generous, beloved young Giuliano was dead, but that the Palazzo Publico still was holding out for the Medici.

"Palle! Palle! Death to the traitors!" the crowd was yelling, and the old gambler knew that once more and for the last time, he had played for too high stakes and lost.

His own devoted hundred were breaking ranks to seek an inconspicuous asylum among the increasingly angry mob. The people of Florence had forgotten the old man's generosity in the days of his prosperity, and he knew them too well to think that he could be safe with any of them. He ceased to shout his slogan, and the cry of "Liberty!" heard no more that day, was not uttered aloud again in Florence while Lorenzo de' Medici lived. The last man to raise it spurred dejectedly through a crowd not yet strong enough to stop him and passed safely beyond the walls. The mercenaries who had been waiting there to help him were already retreating as rapidly as they could travel towards their homes.

Within the walls the storm of popular fury was rising fast. The riot which began in a burst of sincere indignation was continuing in a lust for blood and plunder. Heads and quarters, multilated and bleeding, were paraded on lances through the city to the ever louder roar of "Palle! Palle!" The yelling mobs that followed these horrible trophies broke into the

Pazzi palaces, looted the rich furnishings and passed on. Here and there a stripped corpse lay on the cobblestones to be kicked by every passer-by. Among those thus massacred were most of the innocent attendants of the Cardinal Riario. Even Guglielmo de' Pazzi was not safe, but he had the good sense to take refuge in Lorenzo's own palace, and he was well protected there.

He was concealed in an inner room when the mob, diverted for a few moments from its bloody hunt swarmed into the Via Larga to see their ruler. He appeared at a window, his neck swathed in bandages, his eyes filled with tears. The multitude went into a frenzy of delight, loudly and incoherently protesting their everlasting devotion.

Lorenzo seized the occasion to make a speech. Even in the depths of his grief for Giuliano and the heat of his rage against those who had betrayed his hospitality, he was thinking hard. He was in the right before the world, and he meant to stay that way. He did not propose to allow his enemies to evade his accusations by pleading that their brutality was more than matched by his.

With rare artistry he avoided all attempts at eloquence. He faltered as he spoke of his dear younger brother, and soon the crowd was not only sharing his grief but losing its own thirst for vengeance. With conscious, politic magnanimity, he urged his friends to allow the law to take its course. Enough innocent blood, he reminded them, had already been shed.

As he concluded his remarks, after a rather tearful appreciation of the kindness which his fellow citizens had shown him in his bereavement, he retired out of sight but not out of hearing of his partisans, who were raising a deafening yell of affection under his windows.

The next day there was some indiscriminate killing, but after that the lynchings stopped. Only one more victim was given to the mobs. Old Giacopo was captured a few days after the murder by Tuscan peasants who were afraid to accept his bribes, and would not even take pay to kill him. The head of the House of Pazzi was dragged with ignominy back to Florence. Order had so far been restored that his execution, preceded by torture, was allowed to take place according to due legal forms.

He was quietly buried in the Church of Santa Croce, but was not permitted to remain there. Rains, unusually heavy even for Tuscany in spring, gave rise to a superstition that God was angry because so great a sinner had been interred in consecrated ground. With great solemnity the Signoria ordered the body removed to an unmarked grave outside the city walls.

The next morning the grave was empty. The street urchins of Florence, with a ferocity which they had had ample opportunity of learning from their elders in the last few days, dug up the corpse and were dragging it with whoops of delight through the approving town. The body, already mutilated by the tortures devised in the Bargello, was hung to trees and whipped in all the four quarters of the city, cut down, dragged further, and at last, an unrecognizable lump of flesh, was thrown into the swift, swollen Arno. Rolled along on the torrent which this peaceful stream had become, the gambler's remains passed under the bridges from which watchers of these childish antics were gazing in silence, and disappeared towards the sea.

The rains now stopped, and the people were content, for the insult to God had been expiated.

XV

But if God had forgotten, men had not. Giuliano was buried in San Lorenzo with a pomp exceeding even that on the occasion of Simonetta Vespucci's death, and there were threats of vengeance heard in the church. Every young man of fashion who, after the conspiracy, was still alive and in possession of his estate, went into mourning.

A young girl named Fioretta Gorini, daughter of a tradesman, also went into mourning, for she had replaced the fair Simonetta in Giuliano's affections and a few months before his death had borne her lover a son. While concealing his amour and its result from his family, the young father had taken some of his friends into his confidence, and they now undertook to intercede for the mother and the baby. Lorenzo was genuinely pleased that Giuliano had left an heir. He sought out Fioretta and persuaded her, without much difficulty, to let him have the rearing of the child.

The boy had already been baptized as Giulio de' Medici, and he now took his place on an equal footing with his uncle's own five children—Luigia, another daughter, had been born the year before. Clarice's views on this latest addition to her family are not recorded, but the child was soon sent off to live with Antonio da San Gallo, his godfather, until he was seven, when he returned to Lorenzo's house and was dedicated, like his cousin, Giovanni, to the Church.

Meanwhile a few more examples were being made, always after due process of law, among the Pazzi, the Salviati and their adherents. The last of the Arch-bishop's followers, found starving and mad with thirst in the Palazzo Publico, was pardoned because of his insignificance and his sufferings. The name and arms of the Pazzi were ordered erased from every private palace and public hall, but in the case of such a huge family this was more easily ordered than executed. Guglielmo was technically banished to his villa in the country, as much to protect him from violence as because his name was Pazzi.

In unguarded moments while the conspiracy was hatching, some men whose names were not Pazzi had let slip remarks that were now remembered against them. They went either into exile or to the cells of the Bargello. Among them was Piero Vespucci, and not even the memory of the fair Simonetta, his relation, nor of more recent favors conferred by his daughter, Ginevra, could save him. Ginevra did her best. She sought a personal inter-view with her former lover, but he refused to see her. She then resorted to the pen.

"Beloved," she wrote reproachfully, "I had hoped to recall to you the love and good will you bore to this house, the words spoken and the promises made to me and the kindness shown to me."

But even if this was not to be, surely he would still grant her father's release. He could not be so cruel to her now, she told him, and she begged that he would restore the head of the family to his loved ones.

"Surely this should be so," she concluded, "were I with you, for then should you suffer my persistence even thereunto."

However, she was not with him, and Vespucci left his prison only to go into exile. Nor would too great clemency have been safe for the suspects themselves. The people were still remembering their rage, and Lorenzo did not want them to forget.

He found himself in a position of power which even he had never dreamed possible. The affection which Florence had held for Giuliano was transferred to the surviving brother, and went to swell the admiration which the people had always had for him. He had only to name his desires, and they would be granted. While the memories of April twenty-sixth remained fresh, he was able to take from the public treasury as from his own purse, to dispose of public offices with even greater freedom than ever, to acquire a despotism that no longer needed the periodic, farcial summoning of the citizenry for approval.

His friends were just the men to keep the popular fury alive. On the outer walls of the Palazzo Publico, Botticelli painted the figures of the chief conspirators, hanging by head and foot. The extravagant price of forty florins which he was allowed by a generous Republic would not, except for his love of Lorenzo, have tempted him to execute the commission. For the fickle populace was wont to indulge in sarcasms at the expense of painters who took such liberties with the dead. Andrea del Castagno was never able to shake off the title of "Andrea of the Gallows" after producing a similar work to celebrate Cosimo's return from exile.

To commemorate the fortunate failure of the plot, medals were struck, sermons were preached, figures of wax to be placed in churches were modelled under the direction of Andrea Verrochio.

More effective than pictures or medals or sermons or figures in keeping public excitement hot was the war of words that broke out between Rome and Florence. That too went well, for Lorenzo had at his command the best writers in the world. Poliziano, Ficino, the Pulci brothers, Matteo Franco, the masters of invective at the University, all made his quarrel their own.

Even Filelfo, eighty years old, but still renowned for that biting turn of phrase which had once infuriated old Cosimo, offered his services. It had been more than forty years since fear of Medici assassins had driven him from Florence, and he had forgotten this incident in the heat of a much more recent dispute with the Pope, who had refused him the rewards which he believed due his talents. With such men to plead his cause and abuse his enemies, Lorenzo emerged easily victorious over the Roman scribes.

Unfortunately more than words was needed now. Sixtus, who did not need the careful goading of Girolamo Riario, lashed himself into an apoplectic frenzy when the news of the failure came to Rome. Monteseco had been captured, and before he died had dictated a confession which showed just what part the Count and the Pope had played. Lorenzo wisely decided to avail himself of the despised press, and had the confession printed. It was even said that no torture had been applied in obtaining the Captain's story.

In the Vatican His Holiness raged so violently that it was not safe to approach him. Lorenzo, his enemy, still lived, and the very means used to destroy him had made him more powerful than ever. Florence would never fall to Girolamo.

Suddenly, in the midst of his imprecations, the Holy Father remembered the insult to the Church, and he mounted his best dignity. An Archbishop, he thundered, had been infamously murdered; a Cardinal, his own relative at that, had been foully imprisoned; harmless priests had been brutally cut to pieces. But Lorenzo and Florence would soon find that Christ's Vicar could look after his own. It was in vain that the Florentine Ambassador expostulated. In vain he protested that the Archbishop had been guilty of a vile crime, that the priests had been his accomplices, that the Cardinal had only been protected from the mob and had been treated with every courtesy befitting his rank.

Donato Acciajuoli had been sent as special ambassador to make these representations, and he carried a letter from Raffaello expressing his gratitude to Lorenzo for preserving him from the righteous indignation of the people. But Sixtus refused to listen to anything. He talked wildly of confiscating property and imprisoning all the Florentines he could lay hands on, including the Ambassador. He had actually given orders to take Acciajuoli to the Castle of San Angelo when the envoys of Milan and Venice declared they would share their colleague's punishment and trust their governments to avenge them. Sixtus, thus threatened, reluctantly decided to observe the elementary forms of international law, and Acciajuoli was sent unharmed back to Florence.

However, the Pope lost no time in venting his wrath. He launched a bull of excommunication against Lorenzo de' Medici and all the magistrates of Florence. He placed the entire State under an interdict. Theoretically the Church ceased to function in Florentine territory, but the clergy were pro-Medici and obtained legal advice that the bull was without effect.

Most of it was directed against Lorenzo, that "son of perdition and child of iniquity." His Holiness related the wrongs he had endured with humility "according to the example of our Saviour" from the time of the attack on Castello. Speaking with great detachment in the third person, he declared:

"He had long suffered in peace the insults and injuries of his enemies, and he should still have continued to exercise his forbearance had not Lo-renzo de' Medici, with the magistrates of Florence and their abettors, discarding the fear of God, in-flamed with fury and instigated by diabolical sug-gestions laid violent hands on ecclesiastical persons, hung up the Archbishop, imprisoned the Cardinal and by various means destroyed and slaughtered their followers."

Upon the offenders Sixtus heaped all the anath-ema which centuries of theological controversy had been able to develop. He aroused an even more violent answer, for his opponents did not confine themselves to theological terms. Lorenzo's old tutor, Gentile Becchi, now Bishop of Arezzo, convoked a synod of the Florentine clergy. They drew up an impassioned missive in which Sixtus was addressed in his own language and was called murderer, swindler, traitor and false pope besides.

A more reasoned document was prepared by Bartolomeo Scala, Chancellor of the Republic. Scala was an eminent lawyer, but by no means the literary stylist he fancied himself to be. Lorenzo had his composition revised by Poliziano, to the Chan-cellor's great disgust. The whole history of the con-spiracy was neatly summed up, the confession of Monteseco quoted copiously, the Pope condemned for his nepotism and bellicosity. The paper closed with appeals for help to the Emperor and the Kings of France and Spain. These were reinforced by private letters from Lorenzo.

Louis of France had already taken his banker's part without being asked, and was prepared to go as far as mere expenditure of words would take him to aid the Florentine against his enemies. In the beginning he saw in the affair only a bit of a feud between two powerful financial houses. Giuliano had been murdered, he remarked, "by those of the Pazzi Bank and their dependents." He wrote a letter of condolence to bereaved Florence, condemning "the great and inhuman outrage, opprobrium and injury."

But soon His Majesty learned that politics were involved too. The Pope, secure in the support of Naples, was likely to adopt temporal as well as spiritual measures of coercion. The whole story was given Louis by the Florentine envoys and lost nothing in the telling. News of the excommunication followed, and then came a letter from Lorenzo himself.

"I well know and God is my witness," said the writer after imploring the King's help, "that I have committed no crime against the Pope save that I am alive and, having been protected by the grace of Almighty God, have not allowed myself to be murdered. This is my sin; for this alone have I been excommunicated."

The pious, humble tone of the letter was well

calculated to win the King's favor. It was such a tone as he might have used himself, and he bestirred himself to join in the war of words. Louis, abjectly superstitious and devoted to the most arduous religious exercises, always drew a neat distinction between his Faith and the earthly head of that Faith. He was very much afraid of graven images, but not at all afraid of a living Pope.

To this particular Pope he addressed some very high language. He actually named Girolamo Riario as guilty with others of having "killed, murdered and assassinated" Giuliano. He, Louis, as an ally of Florence and the cousin of Lorenzo, came close to accusing Sixtus of complicity too. He threatened to convoke a general council, the one legal means of disciplining a Pope and one which generally frightened the occupant of the Vatican.

"Amends shall be made for this crime," Louis demanded, "by punishing the delinquents and all who may have aided or participated, in such a way that it may be an example for all men to remember and that greater ills shall not arise."

Lest this be capable of misinterpretation, the King proceeded to almost open threats against the Holy See if the reparation asked were not made. Speaking as one sovereign to another, and as the stronger to the weaker, he went on:

"Otherwise, by virtue of the alliance and confederation existing between us and the Florentines and on account of the love we bear to our cousin, we have determined to declare against all those who are implicated and not allow this thing to go unpunished."

It was as close to promising material aid as was possible for a man who did not intend to give any such aid. But he was not through. The end of his letter contained one of those suave, keen thrusts of polite irony which Louis could give at will.

"We pray the blessed son of God," was his humbly reverent conclusion to a threatening letter, "that Your Holiness may long be spared to rule over Holy Mother Church."

Unfortunately for Lorenzo, his ally and cousin was too well known. Sixtus was no novice in international politics, and it would have taken a very young diplomat indeed to be frightened when King Louis only threatened. A French army to back these threats would have alarmed Rome tremendously, but no one believed Louis would ever be induced to send it. It was not his way. For the rest, the Pope was willing to let France do her worst.

He was wise. Louis's worst was to forbid the French clergy to transmit money to Rome. He also sent the diligent diarist, Philippe de Commines, to represent him in Florence, and the envoy recorded with complacency that it was a most profitable embassy for him. The Medici were generous. The only other result of the French interference was that Lorenzo was kept informed concerning Roman doings by Cardinal d'Estouteville, who entertained a broad contempt for Papal edicts which proclaimed his friends as lost souls unfit for human society.

Words, and not much more, also came from Venice to help Lorenzo. The Republic of the canals was accustomed to speak arrogantly, and did not moderate its tone for any Pope. Only a few years ago the Venetians had seized some Papal galleys proceeding on the Pope's warlike business against one of their friends. In answer to the indignant protests from Rome, the Council had airily explained that they were only keeping the seas free of pirates. Now they haughtily advised Sixtus:

"The Holy Father must not flatter himself that he can conceal the purpose of his evil thoughts."

Weeks passed in this exchange of compliments. The amenities of diplomacy must be observed. Insults always preceded blows, and there had been almost enough insults now to warrant the Pope and his ally, Ferrante, in launching an attack that might really hurt. Lorenzo prepared to gather the sinews of war. The few months that followed the crushing of the plot had sufficed to put the Medici Banks firmly on their feet again. A judicious distribution of the public funds had eased the strain in all branches, but now other expedients must be sought, for the public funds would be needed at home.

In looking about for other resources, Lorenzo discovered that for a banker there is no aid like diplomacy. He used his new powers in the State to employ Florentine envoys as agents for the Medici Banks, and they served him at least as well as they served their government. Frequently they did not know which master they were representing in a given transaction, but they were satisfied that it would all redound to the glory of Florence in the end. One day in July, 1478, Girolamo Morelli, the Ambassador to Milan, was told to look around for thirty or forty thousand ducats to be produced at a moment's notice. He never learned whether he had deposited the amount in the Medici Bank to the credit of the government or to swell Lorenzo's private account. He was much too discreet to inquire very closely.

Years later Alessandro de' Pazzi, Bianca's son, declared that if only his uncle had been left alone he would have ruined himself. Given just a little more patience, and his rivals might have stepped into his place quietly without wiles or bloodshed. Alessandro knew that the Medici Banks had been on the verge of collapse in the spring of 1478, and must have fallen but for the conspiracy. As it was, the judicious manipulation of new war taxes revived the finances of the House.

XVI

The popular verdict in the war of words had gone to the Florentines by a wide margin. In the scramble for money they were also well out in front. It remained to see how they would fare in the actual battle to which these other activities were preliminaries. The summer was wearing on, and the generals could not waste much more fighting weather. The diplomats were retiring, well pleased with themselves for having forgotten no possible insult in the heat of argument; the troops were mustering, and Poliziano was singing

> Strong in our cause and in our friends,
> Our righteous battle Jove defends.

Jove was almost the only ally Florence could depend upon, and the only one she did not need to subsidize. France had never been expected to take an active part in hostilities once they reached a material stage, and now Venice found an excuse for keeping out. Sixtus had declared he was fighting only against Lorenzo as an outlaw, and Venice virtuously protested that her honor would not permit her to engage in a private quarrel. Milan, sincerely concerned in keeping a friend in Florence, was willing to help, but Ludovico had troubles at home with ill-conditioned rebels who remained strangely loyal to his brother's wife. The army he could send was much smaller than had been hoped.

Formal declaration of war was postponed only until Ferrante could send an embassy to Florence and troops to join the condottieri the Pope was hiring. The diplomats were charged to demand the surrender of Lorenzo de' Medici to the Pope. Refusal was to be interpreted as a desire for war. The refusal was promptly given, although Lorenzo offered himself as a sacrifice. In a speech to the Signoria he said he would give himself up if they thought it would serve the public interest, but he did not neglect to remind his hearers that he, his father and his grandfather had given their lives to the State. In conclusion he worked upon every patriot's emotions by recalling his brother's death.

"Where parricides and assassins are secure," he cried, "the Medici find their murderers."

The Signoria would not hear of the sacrifice. With tumultuous shouts of affection, they assured Lorenzo of their support—they were all his men— and appointed a guard of honor to protect him from any further attempts on his life. The Neapolitan envoys were dismissed with a short answer, and the rival armies began to move a little faster.

Of all the soldiers of Italy, the most dreaded were those of Naples. They were not mercenaries; they actually fought to kill, and they fully came up to the general standard of cruelty to non-combatants. Their leader, the Duke of Calabria, had acquired a quite unmerited reputation for military science solely because his followers fought for patriotism instead of pay. The Pope had hired Federigo d'Urbino, the foremost general of the peninsula, to lead his troops.

Against this combination Lorenzo employed a number of condottieri with Duke Ercole of Ferrara at their head. All the military chieftains had by this time won tiny states of their own to which they and their armies could retire between campaigns, and their prices had risen to match the new titles they had assumed.

The war was waged with far less vigor than the penmen had displayed in their combats. The Duke of Calabria wandered, looting extensively, through the country until he reached Arezzo to which he laid siege. Ercole, also making free of the property of the people he was defending, wandered south to meet him. He was in no hurry, for he had consulted the stars in Florence. They had told him that the afternoon of September twenty-seventh was a good day for a battle. However, when September twenty-seventh came, no enemy was in sight, and Ercole did not catch up with him until it was much too cold and wet to fight. There was just time to sign a truce and retire into winter quarters.

Through the summer and early autumn Florence lived in fear that her general's tardiness would permit the enemy to advance to the walls of the city. Lorenzo took it upon himself to prepare for a siege, and laid in huge stores of provisions. To add to the horrors of war, the plague made its visitation, and all gayety departed from the city. The dead could not be buried; the living crept about in terror, avoiding each other instinctively; trade was at an end.

The wealthy sent their families out of town, and among the first to go was Clarice with her five children and in expectation of another. Her husband thought he owed his people an explanation so to a gathering of notables he reported:

"I now remove from you these objects of my affection whom I would, if necessary, willingly devote to your welfare; that whatever may be the result of this contest, the resentment of my enemies may be appeased by my blood alone."

Poliziano, as tutor to Piero, went with the family to visit friends at Pistoia, and he enlivened the journey with sarcasms at Clarice's expense. It was very dull for the great scholar. There was nothing to do except teach a couple of small children, a most uncongenial task. There was no one worth talking to in the place. He wrote resignedly that he would have liked to serve his patron in some greater manner, "but since this has fallen to my lot I will do it gladly."

He was bored and fell easily into the habit of speaking to Clarice with an irony which she was not too stupid to understand but with which she could not cope. She soon hated him cordially—she had always distrusted these overly clever Florentines —but she said she would try to put up with his impertinence for her husband's sake. She was herself in an unpleasant frame of mind, for she was in mortal fear of a miscarriage. Lorenzo dispatched the family physician to her and he reported that "your Madonna Clarice has more the symptoms of serious trouble than the trouble itself." A few days later he was able to announce proudly the birth of another daughter, Contessina.

Meanwhile, in a day when such a privilege was not accorded to her condition, Clarice was becoming querulous. She wanted company, and when she got it she did not like it. She thought she would like to see her husband, and while he was worrying about battles, subsidies to lukewarm allies, provisions against siege and the plague, she was demanding his presence at her bedside.

"I wish for many reasons that you would come and spend an evening here," she wrote, "especially as I cannot believe your business keeps you so tied there as you would like to have me think."

Lorenzo sighed and went on with his work. He did not even bother to dictate a reply, and his wife grew increasingly plaintive because she heard about him only through others. She finally ceased her complaints about his absence when told that he would be in danger of capture on the journey, but she did not change her opinion of his business responsibilities. Indeed, although he worked long and worried much, life still held some attractions. The best of his companions, Poliziano, was considering himself an exile, but there were other wits to take his place and not all the handsome women had left Florence.

Hardly had his family returned from Pistoia to the villa on Fiesole than he sent them back again to the country. This time he selected Cafaggiuolo because it was half a fortress, easily defended in case of a sudden raid by his enemies. As winter approached, Poliziano and Clarice railed at each other with increasing bitterness. It was frightfully cold and the villa had been built as a summer house. All day long the family sat, wrapped in furs and cloaks, shivering and bickering. There was even less company than at Pistoia, and they had plenty of time to write long letters to Florence bemoaning their discomforts, the lack of news, the dreariness of life in general.

Poliziano protested that Clarice actually had the effrontery to suggest that he should teach her children. He reported proudly that he had managed to save Piero from her, but he was obliged to add:

"As to Giovanni (who was three) you will see. His mother has changed his reading to the psalter, of which I do not approve. When she did not interfere, it is incredible what progress he made. He could already find all the letters and some words in the book by himself."

Lorenzo, again immersed in diplomacy, brushed all such letters aside. He was trying to make peace before spring, but his embassies to Rome failed. Sixtus had just sanctioned the establishment of the

Spanish Inquisition and he was in no mood to show mercy to heretics like the Medici. There was nothing for it but to levy more taxes and hire more troops. It kept Lorenzo too busy to interfere in his wife's quarrel with his friend. Clarice's dissatisfaction was increased by his indifference and aggravated by still another pregnancy, her last. But even after the child, named Giuliano for his murdered uncle, was born, her temper failed to improve. She became more irritable than ever, and at last ordered Poliziano to leave the house.

He was not sorry to go. Cafaggiuolo was an insupportable place, but he did not know just how Lorenzo would regard the dispute. Prudently he paused at Careggi to await some hint as to the reception he was likely to receive. He sent ahead a request for a personal interview.

"I beg you," he wrote, "to allow me to tell you the reason and the way of my departure by word of mouth, for it is a long story. I think that when you have heard my tale, you will agree that I was not wholly in the wrong."

He did not overestimate the effect of his eloquence. Lorenzo assured him he was not to blame. The poet was sent up to the Fiesole villa and told to occupy the master's room. Clarice was furious. The Orsini never suffered so much as in their pride, and she felt she had been humiliated by her husband's obvious preference for a man whom she considered no more than a servant. She neither expected nor particularly desired Lorenzo's faithfulness, love or confidence, but she did demand his respect. That, she felt, he had publicly denied her by refusing to cast Poliziano from him.

"Though he has called me a thousand names," she said, "if it is with your approval I will endure it, but I cannot believe that is true."

She could not bear, she cried, "that Messer Agnolo can say that he will stay in your house against my will and that you have given him your own room at Fiesole." But she had to bear it, although Poliziano did not boast of his victory. She was always afraid of her husband's clever friends; the Orsini could not abide ridicule, and she had been an apprehensive witness of what such men could do.

Lorenzo told his friend to stay right where he was at Fiesole, but he found the quarrel very trying. Just when the Florentine armies were ready to take the field, when there were prospects that Venice might be cajoled into lending assistance, when the citizens at home needed careful handling to prevent grumbling about hard times and high taxes, in the midst of all this Clarice had to be unreasonable. Her husband, fuming, rode up to Cafaggiuolo to show her the error of her ways. He never doubted that she would yield to his authority, so he was greatly chagrined to find that where her stubborn pride was concerned he could do nothing. Then when he got back to Florence and his troubles, he learned that she

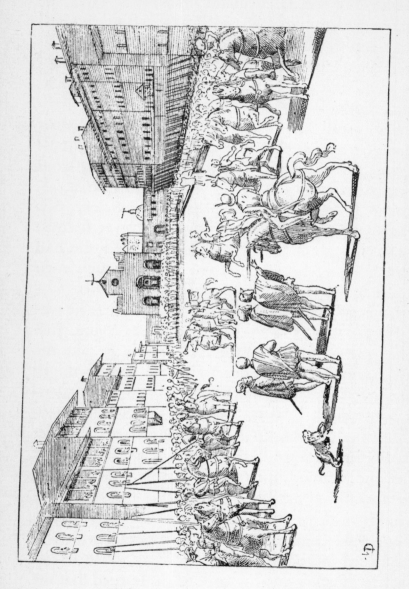

A Tournament in the Piazza Santa Croce

had spitefully sequestered Poliziano's treasured library.

"Monna Clarice," he wrote sharply, "I have been much annoyed that the books have not been handed to Messer Agnolo as I requested you. Send them on receipt of this, for I wish him to have them all. Let them be sent here this evening without fail."

He was so angry he did not add the polite formal plaint that it seemed a thousand years until he saw her. He did not subscribe himself as hers, he sent no loving messages, he brusquely signed himself "Lorenzo."

He was gloomy all summer. The gout was bothering him again. Financial worries had returned, and he was obliged to borrow from his cousins. The war was going badly and in their misfortune the people were beginning to forget those hysterical vows of undying loyalty made under his windows more than a year ago.

Their troops, at last supported by a small Venetian contingent, had achieved some early success over the Papal mercenaries, and had then turned to the more congenial work of looting. There were too many generals, quarrelling over precedence and the division of the spoils. At last the Duke of Ferrara resigned his command in a fit of pique, the Neapolitan army fell upon their demoralized foes and the road to Florence was open. Calabria was too much the soldier of his time to follow up such an advantage, however, and Lorenzo secured a truce which would last until the season was far enough advanced for the armies to hibernate.

Relieved of their immediate fears, the citizens of Florence grumbled more than ever. Even loyal Medici officials were saying they had supported one man's quarrel long enough. They would not wait to be completely ruined by him; he should make peace instead of trying to wring from a reluctant people the means to go on fighting. Lorenzo became sensitive to this feeling long before it was widely expressed. He could no longer enjoy society, for he felt that his best friends were reproaching him. In this sad extremity, worried by his family, in bad health, harrassed by financial troubles, faced with a defeat that would mean his ignominious death, he wrote some poetry. He felt called upon to apologize for it. He knew this was no time to be singing love songs, but he explained his seeming levity by saying:

"Persecuted as I have been from my youth, some indulgence may perhaps be allowed me for having sought consolation in these pursuits."

He derived a mournful satisfaction from regarding himself as the butt of all the fates. He had for the moment forgotten the joys of his youth; he told himself that he was a predestined martyr. He would write a poem about it, a sad love poem, but it was in the prose preface—he always introduced his lighter verses with serious philosophical disquisitions—that he revelled most expansively.

"I had intended," he wrote, "in my exposition

of this sonnet to have related the persecutions which I have undergone, but an apprehension that I may be thought arrogant and ostentatious induces me to pass lightly over them. In relating our own transactions it is not indeed easy to avoid these imputations.

"When the navigator informs us of the perils which his ship has escaped, he means rather to give us an idea of his own exertions and prudence than of the obligations which he owes to his good fortune and perhaps enhances the danger beyond the fact in order to increase our admiration. In the same manner physicians frequently represent the state of their patient as more dangerous than it is in reality, so that if he happen to die the cause may be supposed to be in the disorder and not in their want of skill, and if he recover the greater is the merit of the cure.

"I shall, therefore, only say that my sufferings have been very severe, the authors of them having been men of great authority and talents and fully determined to accomplish by every means in their power my total ruin. Whilst I, on the other hand, having nothing to oppose to these formidable enemies but youth and inexperience, saving indeed the assistance which I derived from divine goodness, was reduced to such an extreme of misfortune that I had at the same time to labor under the excommunication of my soul and the dispersion of my property, to contend with endeavors to divest me of my authority in the state and to introduce discord into my family and with frequent attempts to deprive me of my life, insomuch that I should have thought death itself a much less evil than those which I had to combat.

"In this unfortunate situation it is surely not to be wondered at if I endeavored to alleviate my anxiety by turning to more agreeable subjects of meditation and in celebrating the charms of my mistress sought a temporary refuge from my cares."

So far as the present was concerned he did not exaggerate the dangers, for he discovered several plots to ruin him by wilier means than force of arms. A priest came to him with a rather tempting offer to poison Girolamo Riario, the most uncompromising of his enemies, but the would-be assassin was so eager that suspicion was aroused. Only a little torture was needed to extort a confession that the Count himself had hired the priest to make the offer and then expose Lorenzo to the world as a murderer.

However, the burden of the cares he lamented was greatly lightened as soon as he had written about them. Admiration for his own powers of composition restored his faith in his ability to meet all difficulties. Once more he was able to preside over learned debates, listen to his favorite music, greet people cheerfully as if he did not know they were looking upon him as the cause of all their troubles. He even bestirred himself to grant his sister Nannina's plea that the war might wait while he procured a place for a tutor her husband had unjustly dismissed.

"Whoso wants to do as they wish should not be

born a woman," she complained in lamenting that she had no money to pension the man, and her brother was always touched by such an appeal to his munificence.

His own eloquence had not only revived his generosity, it had calmed him sufficiently that he could for hours at a time forget all the problems of state in the delights of study. But again he felt obliged to apologize.

"When my mind is disturbed with the tumults of public business, and my ears are stunned with the clamors of turbulent citizens," he said, "how would it be possible for me to support such contention unless I found a relaxation in science?"

XVII

With both science and poetry to relieve his anxieties and soothe his pains, Lorenzo once more felt fit to grapple with any problem that politics could present. Since he had expended his feelings in verse and prose, he could watch with more interest than emotion as public discontent grew to proportions that must soon become dangerous. When that happened he would step in and calm his people. He knew now just how he would do it, but he wanted their fears to reach the highest possible pitch before he dissipated them. Only then would Florence be properly grateful.

He took very few of his party into his confidence, waiting and elaborating his plan carefully in private. He did not want many to know that what he proposed was, while the armies were still inactive, to start a diplomatic offensive that would detach Ferrante from his ally, Sixtus, and thus force the Pope to make peace. Lorenzo would go alone to Naples, throw himself upon the mercy of a man renowned for his lack of that gentle quality and by bribes, promises and arguments save himself, and incidentally Florence, from destruction. He strained to the limit the credit of his banks but at last he raised the money he would need and by December all was ready.

There were two recent precedents for such an act
as he contemplated, both still fresh in public memory.
The minor poets had not yet stopped singing of how
Alfonso of Naples, despairing of success in battle,
had ridden alone into old Francesco Sforza's camp,
trusting to the chivalry of a man who despised
chivalry and was not accustomed to such marks of
confidence. But Alfonso had guessed right. The
benevolent ruler and the rude soldier managed to
find grounds for friendship and the Kingdom of
Naples was saved.

The other precedent, while never the subject of
heroic verse, was even more recent and much more
pertinent since it concerned the man with whom
Lorenzo would have to deal. Ferrante had early in
his reign quarrelled with Giacopo Piccinini, who in
his day was the Sforza's only rival as a condottiere
chief. He had contended with rather more honor
than most of his class could boast on all the important
battlefields of a third of a century. He had won for
himself a principality and Sforza's daughter. His
growing prosperity was his only fault, for it aroused
Ferrante's jealousy. The King suggested peaceful
negotiations of their imaginary differences since they
were too fast friends to fight.

Armed with a safe conduct signed by the King's
own hand, Piccinini came to Naples and was immensely pleased by the kindness with which his
enemy received him. For twenty-seven days he was
feasted and fêted; the nobles of the court crowded

around to do him honor; his business seemed to prosper marvellously. But on the twenty-eighth day he was murdered in one of the dungeons which abounded in Ferrante's palace. The King sanctioned a rumor that Piccinini in trying to escape from his unexplained imprisonment fell out of a window and broke his neck. However, few pains were taken to conceal the truth, and the story was known all over Italy.

Lorenzo too had a safe conduct. He had been secretly corresponding with old friends in Naples and was assured of a friendly reception. He did not overestimate the value of that assurance. Men said that Piccinini's bleeding ghost never left his murderer's side, but if that were true the King gave no indication that he was bothered by the supernatural visitation. A certain fearful expression clung to his plump features, but that was a tribute only to his living enemies, and Piccinini's spirit had never been able to dissuade him from any crime. Of course, Lorenzo was a more considerable personage than any condottiere, though the soldier might be a princeling in his own right, and it seemed probable that even Ferrante would respect his visitor's person. If not—well, it would be just as well to die in a Neapolitan dungeon as be burned by the Pope.

While he considered these precedents, Lorenzo's only other problem was to calm the grumbling citizenry he would leave behind so that there would be no rising against the Medici while he was gone.

For this too he trusted to his eloquence. By December the alarm of his people was ripe; there was still plenty of time for talk before the spring offensives began, and Ferrante was expecting him.

Quietly, almost secretly, Lorenzo rode out of town with his secretaries, valets, barber, artists, cooks, men at arms, equerries and the rest. He stopped at San Miniato to send back a carefully prepared letter, and then the whole group trotted off towards Pisa. While he travelled, the Signoria read his farewell, and soon had spread the news to all the city that their magnificent Lorenzo was trying to save them all at terrible personal risk. The popularity which he had purposely allowed to ebb rushed back in a flood of gratitude as the people repeated to each other the noble phrases in which their hero expressed his intention to save them or to die.

"Most illustrious my lords," he began, and the men enjoying for a few weeks the position which could bring such a salutation from a Medici expanded with pride and gratitude. They were equally pleased as the writer apologized for not having consulted their wisdom before embarking on this adventure. Now that he was on his way, he asked permission to go in search of that peace which Florence needed.

"Seeing that all other endeavors have been fruitless," he went on, knowing that his audience was now in the best of humors, "I have determined to run some peril in my own person rather than expose the city to disaster. Being the one most hated and persecuted by our enemies, I may by placing myself in their hands be the means of restoring peace to our city."

Shrewdly he pointed out that his visit would also test the sincerity of the claim that Naples was not making war on Florence but on the Medici for Florence's own good. He was willing to make the test because as her leading citizen "I am more bound than any other man to give up all, even my life, to my country." He continued in strains of swelling patriotism and piety that were widely, admiringly quoted:

"Perchance our lord God desires that this war, which began with the blood of my brother and my own, should be put to an end by me. My ardent wish is that either my life or my death, my misfortune or my well-being should contribute to the good of our city. I am certain that our citizens will unite to protect their liberty so that by the grace of God it will be defended as was always done by our fathers. I go full of hope and with no other object than the good of our city, and I pray God to give me grace to perform what is the duty of every man towards his country."

There never has been a public opinion which could remain cold to such words from those in positions of power. The mercurial citizens of Florence, peculiarly susceptible to any emotional appeal, responded as Lorenzo had known they would respond to his confidences. They might at that moment almost have been persuaded to an enthusiasm for this inglorious, expensive war. However, their master was too prudent to put their recrudescence of loyalty to such a test.

While he was at Pisa, arranging for the ship that was to take him to Naples, the last of the Pazzi conspirators was brought into Florence. It was bad luck for Bernardo Bandini that the moment of his arrival should coincide with the new flare of Medici popularity.

As he had been prompt and skillful in executing his share of the plot, so he had been diligent in making his escape. He had posted tirelessly to the Adriatic, outriding the swiftest couriers bearing news of his crime, and had found a ship sailing for the Orient. He deluded himself with the belief that in the domains of the Sultan he would be safe from all vengeance. He had hoped, indeed, that the news of the conspiracy would never reach so far as Constantinople.

He did not realize the full extent of Lorenzo's influence. Florentine trade with the Levant was increasingly profitable and Lorenzo, as was his custom, had allied diplomacy to commerce. Of all the rulers of the West he was esteemed the most at the Mohammedan court. No sooner did the Sultan learn that his friend's enemy had taken refuge in his new capital than Bandini was seized and put into chains. They were not knocked off until he had been delivered in Florence along with a letter from his captor saying that out of the great respect the eastern conqueror bore Lorenzo, Mohammed was surrendering the fugitive to justice.

Botticelli's painting of the assassin with its inscription

Bernardo Bandini, new Judas, am I,
In Church a murderous traitor,
Awaiting the day when more cruelly I die

had not yet faded from the walls of the Palazzo Publico, and the promise of the lines was elaborately fulfilled with all the barbarity of which Italian torturers were masters. The ceremonies ended with Bandini being hung from the window in just the position he occupied in Botticelli's painting, while from the square below young da Vinci, his universal curiosity attracted by the prospect of studying a strangling man's contortions, hastily sketched the scene. Lorenzo was very pleased when news of the execution reached him, for it justified the boast that his influence at the Porte was great.

He needed all the encouragement he could get. The Bay of Naples as he sailed into it was bright with sunshine and the gayly decorated galleys of his royal host. Behind the beflagged vessels which moved slowly out to meet him, Vesuvius smoked grimly, and Lorenzo shivered. He was remembering those twenty-seven days of festivity which preceded Piccinini's death.

However, there was some reassurance in the

presence on the leading galley of Federigo. Their mutual admiration had not been interrupted by the war, and the visitor knew that in the young prince he had a friend. The two disembarked together into the midst of a holiday crowd come to stare at the man from the north who had been reviled as the cause of all this trouble. They were curious but silent as Federigo escorted the guest to his father.

Ferrante was kind, courteous, almost cordial. Again Lorenzo thought of Piccinini, but his thoughts were not reflected in his face as he answered protestations of admiration and delight with even more fulsome flattery. He accepted with dignified thanks the use of a magnificent apartment in the palace and a guard that made the palace a prison. Everywhere he went he was attended by a retinue so splendid that no one except Lorenzo himself could tell that it was a retinue of jailers.

He did not delay in opening his campaign of bribes, promises and arguments. Gorgeous, judicious presents were distributed among the courtiers; the people of Naples were prodded out of their curious silence by showers of coins which drew shouts of heartfelt applause. Beggars found themselves suddenly opulent; scholars were delighted with pensions and books; poor peasant girls obtained husbands thanks to dowries furnished by Lorenzo; galley slaves whose freedom he purchased shouted his praises in the streets. The whole capital was invited to wonder at entertainments which rivalled anything he had ever devised for the delectation of Florence.

The real business of his mission did not go so well or so quickly as the winning of popularity with the mob. Ferrante was readily accessible, always willing to listen. He showed a very genuine interest in Lorenzo's promises of help in securing the throne of Naples to the present dynasty. He was receptive of arguments designed to prove that Florence could be his most useful friend in Italy, that the Pope's success against Lorenzo would be followed by the assertion of Papal sovereignty over Naples, that the humane generosity of a great monarch was hardly compatible with his present alliance with murderers. The King's replies were just as long as the arguments, but contained much less substance. He evaded, procrastinated, postponed decisions.

Weeks passed, and still nothing was settled. Every courier from Florence brought Lorenzo warnings that if he did not come back with a peace, it would be better not to come back at all. Messengers were also arriving from Rome, and Lorenzo knew that they bore bids from Sixtus for sending the common enemy north for the execution of the sentence of excommunication. That, the Pope pointed out, was the best way of securing the general peace which Lorenzo talked about so much. Ferrante enjoyed the sense of importance he derived from being the object of persuasion by the rivals, and his guest's anxiety increased.

He was so worried and occupied with business that he could neither eat nor sleep. He could not even enjoy the amusements organized for him. It was the harder because he had to wear the semblance of gayety; his conversation had to be witty and care-free; his smile had to be frozen on his face; his laugh must always be ready. That was when he was in public, or walking in the gardens with the Duchess Ippolita and other ladies of the court. He joked with them, flattered them, talked of love and beauty and art. But when he could escape to the relative privacy of his own apartments, he brooded un-happily. Already the negotiations had taken longer than he expected. The Duke of Calabria was ready to take the field again. Still there was no sign that Ferrante had made up his mind.

At times Lorenzo despaired; at times his hopes were high. When he had been with Ippolita dis-cussing the Greek and Latin poets or with Federigo in talk about painting and Italian verse, he was sure he would win. Ippolita was using all the influence of a beautiful and talented woman to hurry her father-in-law's decision. She was so eloquent on her friend's behalf—the two thousand ducats had been well invested four years ago—that the King rallied her with the greeting, "How do you stand with your confederate today?"

Of even more importance than any woman or prince in the counsels of the King was Diomeda Carafa, Ferrante's chief adviser and the greatest connoisseur of art among the Neapolitan nobility. From the beginning of his visit Lorenzo had exerted him﹒ self to secure Carafa's good offices. At laſt he suc﹒ ceeded; Diomeda joined his influence to that of Ippolita and Federigo, and soon a treaty of peace was being drafted.

The Neapolitans were to retire from the towns they had captured in Ferrante's own good time. Mean﹒ while Florence was to pay a heavy indemnity and release such survivors of the Pazzi conspiracy as were ſtill in prison. Lorenzo accepted these terms as soon as they were offered, and hurried on his homeward journey. Ferrante in token of their new alliance had given him a race horse, and the speeding gueſt thanked him with:

"The messenger of joyful news ought to be well mounted."

He had been in Naples three months, and was glad to get away. To Ferrante he spoke of his eager﹒ ness to see his family, of his anxiety to be the bearer of good tidings, of his fear that he might become so enamoured of Naples that he never could leave. Aĉtually he was in conſtant terror leſt the King should change his mind. It was with a feeling of intense relief that after protraĉted speeches of eſteem had been exchanged he watched the beautiful bay disappear behind him.

The successful diplomat had never enjoyed a voyage so much. In the end everything had happened juſt as he planned. His munificence and his argu﹒

ments had saved his life and his position. If his fortune was still to be retrieved after the immense expense of Naples, there was always the treasury of Florence to work with, and his cousins, thrifty souls, could be depended upon to rally round the head of the family with all their enormous savings. The main point to bear in mind was that he had escaped. He sang merrily to the waves as his ship leaped forward under a fair breeze towards Pisa.

His escape was narrow. While his vessel was still in sight from the headlands of Capri, Ferrante repented of his generosity and sent a swift galley after the guest urging in dulcet phrases an immediate return. New proposals had just arrived from Rome, so attractive that Lorenzo could never have competed with them. But they included the delivery of Lorenzo to the Pope's vengeance, and that was possible only if the Florentine could be persuaded to come back. Ferrante wrote most seductively, too seductively. The Papal embassy, he said, was ready to sign terms of general peace at last. But Lorenzo knew too well the dangers from which he had been preserved. He held on for the haven of Pisa, and it was now his turn to make evasive answers to direct questions.

He hardly paused in his university town to accept the congratulations of his friends. He wanted to reap the harvest that was waiting for him in Florence, and it was a bountiful crop. It was spring in the City of Flowers, and the spirits of the people rose to harmonize with the season. With garlands and bright banners, music and dancing, tears and laughter, speeches and cheers they welcomed Lorenzo home, a conqueror such as Italy loved, his victories the peaceful triumphs of brains and artifice over brute force.

Smiling, he rode in splendid procession through the gate while the Florentine mob stormed around him to pay homage such as had never been accorded to any man within those walls since the haughty nobles had been ruined two centuries before. They fought for the privilege of kissing his hand. They threw flowers at him, shouted themselves hoarse in his praise, drank his health in rivers of wine.

"Young and old, men and women flocked together to see him," wrote his friend, Niccolo Valori, the historian. "The people and notables rejoiced together to see him return safely. To all he gave his hand kindly and gratefully. The people embraced each other for joy."

Of course it could not last. Such ecstasies of enthusiasm never do. In this case the Florentines were disgusted because the tax rate, which had been raised oppressively to meet the burden of war, was retained in peace to pay the indemnity and to maintain the strained credit of the Medici Banks. The second item was the larger of the two. One hundred thousand gold florins went from the treasury to the branch at Bruges, and the other branches required similar support.

Nor were the Neapolitans in any hurry to vacate

the places they had captured. The Duke of Calabria, encouraged by Sixtus, who still hoped that hostili- ties might be resumed, stayed on with his troops at the expense of the surrounding country, and he was an extortionate visitor. Venice was also troublesome. She had contributed almost nothing to the war, but she thought it monstrous that peace should be ar- ranged without her approval. She was minded to throw in her lot with the Pope, whose fury was so great that his attendants feared for his life. Once more he had been balked of his revenge. But, he swore, he would have it yet, if not with the aid of Naples, then with that of Venice.

Florence was beginning to think she had bought her way out of one evil only to fall before another when she was saved by an incident so timely that none of his enemies could ever be persuaded that Lorenzo did not instigate it. A Turkish army landed on the Adriatic coast and occupied Otranto with the utmost brutality. Mohammed had ordered his troops to ravage the entire peninsula, and in the face of this danger not even Sixtus could afford to indulge private feuds. The Neapolitans evacuated Florentine territory and hurried south to defend their own coun- try. Venetian clamors were silenced as the common foe threatened more dangerously than ever before. Sixtus in the interests of Christian unity announced that he would be satisfied with as little as an apology from the men he had been denouncing for two years past as heretics fit only for the flames.

The diversion at Otranto was so opportune that the grocer-diarist Landucci referred to it as "pleasing God" and as one of "His consummate miracles." Less friendly reporters recalled Lorenzo's recent boasts about his influence at Constantinople. But Landucci was the more nearly correct. Even Ferrante absolved Lorenzo of all blame in the interests of their new alliance. Indeed, the Florentine was almost as greatly alarmed by the invasion as anyone in Naples. Despite his friendship with Mohammed, he threw Florence into the campaign against what he called "the Turkish dogs," and Otranto was re-taken. The aversion to Islam on religious grounds proved so slight that Naples gladly enlisted the captive invaders in her own army.

The peace of Italy, it appeared, now required only the conciliation of the Pope. If an apology would satisfy him, Florence was willing. Words were never cheaper than in those glorious days of the revival of learning. An embassy of twelve notables, headed by the Bishop of Volterra, proceeded to Rome to have the interdict lifted and the excommunication of Lorenzo cancelled. Sixtus received them ungra-ciously, railed at them bitterly, but at last consented to hear them. When they had finished he signified his approval, for the Christians were still skirmishing around Otranto and Italy was not yet safe. But his approval must have been a most insincere gesture. There was little to gratify His Holiness in Florence's formal submission to his will. The Republic was far from humble; all Sixtus had gained from his hatred, his intrigues and his wars was the acknowledgment:

"We know that in public and private we have committed various errors from human weakness which the Holy Father has perceived better than we."

XVIII

In spite of apologies and Turks and taxes and general weariness, peace was still elusive. To Lorenzo's horror the powers of Italy shifted into new combinations, slid into new patterns and got themselves ready for more fighting. His profound distaste for another war could not keep him out of this one. It was very discouraging.

The new struggle, too, was preceded by an assassination plot. The apology of the Florentine embassy may have satisfied Sixtus, but it hardly mollified his son. There were always plenty of exiles in Rome, and the Count Riario was most obligingly friendly to all of them. As he had once encouraged the Pazzi with fair words and promises, so now he sympathized with lesser malcontents.

A new band of assassins was hired, but this time there was little real danger. The active head of the conspiracy was a madman, Battista Frescobaldi, who had been a counsul at Pera, had been favored by the Medici and had seen Bandini taken in chains aboard a ship for Italy. All that Frescobaldi had learned from Bandini's example was that assassinations could be carried out in church, and he went about boasting insanely of what he would soon accomplish.

He talked so much that warnings of his project reached Florence far ahead of him, and the friends of the Medici were waiting. The assassins were arrested and put to the torture as soon as they entered the city. They confessed quickly, but the magistrates were puzzled. Lorenzo insisted on proceeding against the conspirators through strictly legal forms, and there was in Italian law no provision for punishing men who had only planned a killing but had not yet done it. At last a judgment was rendered which solved the problem. Any plot against Lorenzo de' Medici, the courts ruled, was equivalent to treason against the State and punishable accordingly. Frescobaldi and his accomplices were dashed to pieces on the pavement before the Palazzo Publico, and once again Lorenzo was attended by a guard of his own friends whenever he walked abroad.

Meanwhile the new pattern of states was taking shape. No sooner were the Turks ousted from Otranto, less by the power of Italy's united arms than by the demoralization of Islam following the conqueror Mohammed's death, than unity departed from the Christian ranks. Venice decided she had a claim on Ferrara better than that of the Este and believed this would be a good time to assert it. She persuaded Sixtus to agree, but privately the Pope thought that the Holy See could show better rights than either temporal claimants. He planned, once the present rulers were driven from Ferrara, to steal the spoils from Venice and confer them upon

Girolamo Riario as compensation for his recent disappointments.

Naples and Milan were on the side of the Este. Florence felt she had to join them for her own protection. Lorenzo undertook to manage the finances and the commissary for the allies while Federigo d'Urbino commanded in the field. Many battles were fought, many deeds of heroism were recorded, the aid of God was invoked with the usual intensity, the normal amount of suffering was inflicted upon a bewildered peasantry, but the objects of the war were lost in a fog of intrigue, suspicions and betrayals.

Roberto Malatesta, Sigismondo's bastard son, who had inherited his father's military genius along with his domains, was employed to lead the Papal army. He defeated the Neapolitans in a fierce tussle which was fought with complete disregard of Italian traditions. Many men on both sides were killed. Roberto received as reward for his victory a magnificent reception from the Pope and a cup of poison from Girolamo Riario.

Sixtus generously raised a monument to his dead general's memory while the Count, completely ignoring the war with Naples, turned to the gratification of his own ambitions. At the head of Malatesta's victorious troops he hurried to snatch Rimini from Roberto's son, Pandolfo, who was left defenceless. Federigo d'Urbino had died on the same day as the lord of Rimini. Though they had fought against each other often, it had not interfered with their friendship, and each of the condottieri had bequeathed the care of his children to the other. However, Federigo's place as Pandolfo's guardian was promptly taken by Lorenzo de' Medici. The Malatesta were saved by their enemies from their friends, and once again Riario was unsuccessful.

The case of Rimini was a commonplace in that war. No man could know how soon his friends would be attacking him. Whole armies suddenly changed their allegiance because a general's greed or ambition momentarily got the best of him. The smaller states whirled crazily from one side to the other. The larger powers feared their allies at least as much as they feared their enemies.

In this maze of petty politics even Lorenzo was confused, but he cut through the tangle to execute a diplomatic triumph. He had been working for a general council of the Church to discipline Sixtus and the Emperor was almost persuaded to summon the gathering. His threats were more to be dreaded than those of Louis, and the Pope, suddenly frightened, put the blame for the latest war entirely on Venice. With remarkable haste he joined forces with his enemies, excommunicated his friends in Venice and said graciously to the Florentine ambassadors who were sent to congratulate him on his display of Christian virtue:

"We have always desired the friendship of Lorenzo on account of his singular virtues, but up to now our destinies have been averse and have separated and disjoined us. Now I shall see that proverb verified which says that wisdom conquers the influence and inclination of the stars."

Lorenzo accepted the offer of friendship in the spirit in which it was made. He could use the Pope in a new scheme for the general pacification of Italy. He dreamed now of being the head of a great coalition which would crush Venice and enable the members to live in harmony. He really hoped that with so much spoil to administer jointly, Italy would be afraid to fight. He had his plans all ready to submit to a great congress of the new allies at Cremona. He easily dominated the gathering, for his proposal appealed to the avarice of them all. Lorenzo even managed to be affable to Girolamo Riario, who represented the Pope, at the same time taking care to be constantly and closely guarded. However, the Count attempted nothing, and Lorenzo could flatter himself that his project was on the way to fulfillment. With the Holy See, Naples, Milan, Florence, Ferrara and half a hundred smaller states all united, the Venetians were being driven hard and success seemed certain.

But Venice had diplomats almost as wily as Lorenzo, and the Pope was far from being the only ruler in Italy who could be bribed or frightened. Ludovico Sforza suddenly abandoned his allies. It was too much, even for the complicated treacheries of the peninsula; this last betrayal made everyone yearn for peace. The soldiers were so bewildered that they no longer knew their friends from their foes, and the last battle had been quite bloodless. The diplomats began to draw up a treaty which would leave everything as it was before, everything except the ruined farms, the sacked cities, the empty treasuries and the full graveyards.

As he contemplated these sole results of war, Lorenzo's pacifism swelled into the great passion of his life. The years of bloodshed had disgusted as well as frightened him. He mourned that the money which might have gone into books and buildings had been wasted on the condottieri. He realized at last that true peace is never won by war, and his policy changed once more. From now on he would devote himself to preventing such calamities as had almost destroyed him and Florence. He would have to be the greatest man in Europe to do it; he would have to be the acknowledged umpire of all Italian quarrels; his neighbors must understand that all his wealth, all the strength of the State he ruled, would be thrown against the first to refuse his arbitration.

He set himself to the working out of this policy with a grim determination which age had forced upon him and which he found extremely distasteful. Before the war of the Pazzi conspiracy he had never permitted public business to interfere with private pleasures. He had thought his odd moments would suffice to run any government. These last years had taught him that when he complained because statecraft took up too much time, he had spoken more truly than he knew. He had actually to sacrifice the delights of study to the dullness of diplomacy. The maintenance of peace had first call on his talents.

His old fine carelessness was gone forever. The enjoyment of a full life, he complained, is to be attained only by constant vigilance. Unmixed happiness is a dream. Every joy must be paid for in toil or suffering. For himself he preferred to pay in toil. He resigned himself to it, saying that after all his labor was more fruitful than that of most men in solid satisfactions.

There were, however, happier men around him, men more in harmony with the brutality of the time, but Lorenzo despised them for the smallness of their aspirations. He knew he lacked the cruelty which carried these others to power and happiness, but they were content with so little. All Alfonso of Calabria asked was the gratification of his taste for blood. Ludovico Sforza was happy only in intrigue and did not know that there was anything better in life than a successful lie. Rodrigo, Cardinal Borgia, whom Lorenzo considered only as a Spanish barbarian, sought at this time nothing beyond the satisfaction of his lusts and his affections. All of these men were quite indifferent to the sufferings of others and seemed never to have conceived of the blessings of peace. Yet all of them were appreciative of beauty and encouraged scholarship.

Lorenzo alone of those who aspired to rule knew that the pursuit of loveliness and of knowledge was much more fun than the substance of power. His contempt for the princes of Italy, spiritual and temporal, led him to take a very high tone in dealing with them. He set out to dominate them, not because triumphs over such men were worth the effort, but because he demanded peace for the enjoyment of his leisure. So, despising power, he sought it as eagerly as any of the men who believed in it as simpler folk believed in God.

In his search for peace and power, Lorenzo had to devise something new. His youthful policy of minding his own business had ended in disaster; his attempts to weld Italy into a single unit were defeated by the greed and treachery of his colleagues; he had no stomach for working for posterity, so there was no use trying to educate the world to higher ideals, even if he had believed in them. At last he hit upon a system which ever since his day has been alternately scorned and admired, but has always been used. Men called it the balance of power, and, once Lorenzo had showed the way, said it was a simple thing. Many of them have gone on to add that it is crude, unmanly, weak, dilatory, opportunist.

Lorenzo would have been amazed to hear them speak thus. Of course, he would have replied, there was no glory, no blatant heroism, no winning of empires in his policy. Great generals would never find honor and immortality in the blood and torment of their followers so long as the balance was kept. History might be very dull reading. Noble ideals, vaguely expressed so as to conceal the rather sordid ends war was designed to further, would be forgotten. Religion and morality would have to rely on stronger weapons than the sword. Principles, the companions of the ideals, would be ignored.

And what of it? All these things were mere words to Lorenzo. He craved no empire, no military glory, no spiritual crown. He scrutinized ideals and principles with the clear gaze of impartiality, and found them shams. All he wanted was peace, what the barbarians with their childish notions of chivalry might call a shameful peace. After that was attained he relied upon himself to procure the good things of this world, wealth and fun and art and love and learning.

He was perhaps a coward, a man of no principles and very little honor, inconstant, an opportunist, frivolous, and Epicurean. But he was neither a bloodthirsty brute nor a fanatical hypocrite nor a lecherous beast. These were the terms men came to apply to his contemporaries, not very justly, but they all called Lorenzo "the Magnificent," and those who had been young when he was in his prime looked back with longing upon the years of his dominion as the golden age of the Renaissance.

It was, said Guicciardini, the historian, with more than a touch of nostalgia, "prosperous beyond any other that Italy had experienced in the course of a thousand years." Lovingly he dwelt on the memory of those unique days when the soil of the entire peninsula was cultivated without interruption or fear, when the country "exulted not only in the number and riches of its inhabitants but in the magnificence of its princes, in the splendor of many superb and noble cities and in the residence and majesty of religion itself." Why, in that halcyon time, Guicciardini recorded with proud amazement, Italy was even respected abroad!

XIX

There was a curious parallel between Lorenzo's public and private lives. During the wars he was as much harassed by the family man's sorrows as by the statesman's cares. When peace descended upon the State after much suffering, happiness returned to the home, but it was too late.

In the midst of treacheries, defeats and disappointments which made up the struggle against Venice, Lucrezia Tornabuoni died and her son lost the only really companionable member of his family. Alone of the Medici, man or woman, Lucrezia had been competent to share his troubles and his joys. Whenever her health and the plague permitted her to be in Florence she had taken her part in the talk of the wits and scholars who surrounded Lorenzo. They never admitted their patron's wife to the bright discussions, nor did she care to join them, but they were all enthusiastic admirers of his mother.

Lorenzo adored her. She approved his poetry with more than maternal fondness, for she brought to it a critical appreciation which made her approval worth something. Her own verses, always pious, were much praised in their day, and even Poliziano listened to her advice and asked her opinion. The political sagacity and the friendships with which she

had helped her husband were of equal benefit to her
son, and she took as great a share in the government
of Florence as any man. Lorenzo had from his boyhood been accustomed to confide in her, and the
habit clung. He trusted her with secrets which he did
not tell even to his mistresses. His children were
taught to respect and obey her more implicitly than
their own mother, and her requests never were
ignored, as Clarice's usually were.

Lucrezia had never, however, attempted to abuse
her rights as a mother. She preferred to be regarded as
her son's friend. She wrote him gay little letters from
the baths to which her physicians were always sending her, and she never offered her counsel unless it
were asked. All his life she had shown him the respect
that was his due as head of the family. When she
dictated letters to him she used the second person
plural, the singular would have appeared disrespect-
ful in the hand of a secretary.

Lorenzo repaid her by asking her advice frequently. She could never complain, as did Clarice,
that he was a neglectful correspondent. He thought
so highly of her poetic talents that he made his
children learn by heart the Bible stories which she
put into verse.

All through her last illness he neglected his friends,
his business, his family and his political duties to sit
at her bedside. He read to her from new books which
had just arrived from his agents; he retailed the latest
bon mots of Franco and Pulci; he talked of public

affairs rapidly, as men do who strive to stave off anguish by sheer loquacity. When at last she died, in March, 1482, he still attempted to assuage his grief with words. It was the day of the Annunciation, and Lorenzo's sorrow found expression in the prayers and piety which his mother had taught him from babyhood, but which gave him little relief now.

He shut himself up alone and while the mournful, undignified details of death's aftermath upset the palace all around him, he spent the day in writing. He composed twenty-seven long letters, all copied in his own hand, pouring out to kings and princes, cardinals and canons, artists and philosophers the feelings which were overwhelming him.

"It is true that we ought to submit patiently to the will of God," he wrote to one, "but in this case my heart refuses to be comforted."

He found some relief in dwelling on his mother's virtues, her accomplishments, her abilities. But he sank back into gloom again as he contemplated the list of these talents which only emphasized the magnitude of his loss. There was but small consolation, even for one in his devout frame of mind, in the thought that "considering her blameless life," the repose of her soul was certain.

"I am as unhappy as I can say," he cried, "for besides losing my mother, the thought of which alone breaks my heart, I have also lost a helper who relieved me of many troubles."

He reverted again and again in the twenty-seven

Lucrezia Tornabuoni

"The Best Man Among Us"

letters to this same theme. He tried in each to display a proper humility in the face of what he had been taught to recognize as God's pleasure, but always the rebellious plaint recurred:

"You can imagine how disconsolate I am for I have lost not only my mother but my only refuge from my troubles and my relief in many labors."

He had to come out of his seclusion at last and walk with the rest of Florence's notables to the funeral ceremonies at San Lorenzo. The solemn beauties of the Church's last rites for its daughter rolled on with a soothing sonority while Lorenzo reflected that he had heard these ceremonies more than his fair share, for his parents, for his brother, for his mistress, for his children. And then it was all over, and he was back in the Via Larga struggling with the faithless-ness of men in wartime. In the heat of the struggle his grief moderated. His resilient spirit quickly recovered from sorrow, and the ceaseless activity of his life carried him rapidly past his memories.

When the war ended he was again able to enjoy his family. Clarice was more content than she had been at any time since her marriage. The management of their many households, which had been Lucrezia's duty, now devolved upon Clarice, and she was happy in the exercise of despotic power over house servants and slaves. She was so pleasantly busy with these affairs that she had little time to bother her husband about his. She did not even protest when she saw Poliziano's ugly face and crooked figure about the house. The poet was once more Piero's tutor and had nothing but praise for his pupil's intelligence.

Lorenzo took ever increasing pleasure in the accomplishments of his children. He exhibited them with paternal shamelessness, and the honor of dining in the Via Larga carried with it the penalty of listening to little Piero recite poetry. The father was extremely undignified at home. Ambassadors who came to see him on momentous affairs of state were horrified to discover the umpire of Italy rolling on the floor completely hidden under a swarm of screaming infants. The great man did not have the grace to be ashamed, nor did he make allowance for the embarrassment of those who intruded on him. He acted as if such conduct were quite natural. His visitors spread the scandal widely, and years later Machiavelli gravely deplored such lack of dignity in one who was in many other respects the model of a perfect ruler.

Lorenzo, however, was not self conscious. He did not care who knew he thought his children were most unusual specimens. As yet, he was glad to see, there was no trace of the Orsini heritage in any of them. The boys especially were most promising, their father said, Piero for his ability, Giovanni for his honesty (about which Martin Luther was one day to speak caustically) and Giuliano for the sweetness of his disposition.

Giovanni was a source of great pride in more ways

than this one. From the time he could crawl, the child seemed to realize that he was destined for Churchly honors. By the time he could walk he had adopted a suitable gravity of manner, a certain pompous, unsmiling dignity. He remained quietly, coldly aloof from those rowdy infantile games which his father promoted. When Lorenzo played with his second son, it was something unexciting like naughts and crosses.

Giovanni was seven years old when Lorenzo launched him upon his career. The solemn fat child was formally admitted to holy orders, and under the supervision of Gentile Becchi the curly head was tonsured, the round little body robed in priestly vestments and the shrill young voice abjured the world. The ceremonies took place in the chapel of the Medici palace, and Lorenzo nearly burst with joyful pride as he saw his son safely started on the road to greatness. He wrote ecstatically that Sixtus had not only confirmed the baby's elevation but had in recognition of the new friendship for the Medici declared him capable of holding benefices.

With such a hint from high places, ecclesiastical preferment was not long delayed. Louis of France "of his own free will"—Lorenzo stressed this point heavily—gave the new priest the Abbey of Fonte Dolce. This too was ratified by the Pope, who was kind enough to create the boy a protonotary, "and thereafter," wrote the overjoyed Lorenzo, "he was called Messer Giovanni."

[237]

It was a rare distinction. Few children of seven could be addressed by that title which alone was recognized as conferring distinction upon a Florentine. Lorenzo himself had had to wait until after his father's death to acquire it, and now he boasted to all the world. The diplomatic despatches of Florence were enlivened with the news of Giovanni's rise in the world, and there were special services to celebrate the consecration of God's new servant.

As yet he was only an Abbot, but it was a good start. As further proof of the good relations which now existed between Lorenzo and the seat of religion, Sixtus conferred upon the little priest the reversion to the Abbey of Pasignano, one of the richest in Italy. The present Abbot was very old, and the place must soon pass into the hands of the Medici. Messer Giovanni, it seems, was quite old enough to perform the duties of the office.

Even higher honors were near. The small Abbot was not quite eight years old when King Louis again became generous. He felt under deep obligations to his banker, for Lorenzo had secured for him the miraculous ring of Saint Zenobias, to which the superstitious King believed he owed his life. This wonderful relic, worn by the canonized Bishop of Florence nine hundred years before, was known to possess supernatural healing powers. Louis, ill and in abject terror of death, had asked for an opportunity to touch it. His banker had borrowed it for him from the Gherardini, whose chief treasure it was, and the talisman had proved its powers. Louis now showed his gratitude.

"On the eighth of June Jacopino, the courier from France, arrived about twelve of the clock with letters from the King, who has bestowed upon our Messer Giovanni the Archbishopric of Aix-en-Provence," Lorenzo wrote excitedly.

It was indeed a proud moment. Giovanni an Archbishop! And only seven years old at that! The happy father bragged to his favorite correspondents as if the boy had earned his honors by his own merit. They were certainly portents. What further heights might not this child reach. The Sacred College was only one step higher, and with the wealth which the boy would be able to command and with the influence which his elder brother would one day wield in Italy, the highest office in Christendom was not a vain hope.

Lorenzo hardly gave the French courier time to eat before sending him off with urgent letters to Churchmen of influence. The Pope's consent to Giovanni's elevation must be obtained. It could only be a question of price now that the Medici and the della Rovere were friends again, yet Lorenzo was a little worried. He condescended to despatch a begging letter to Girolamo Riario, who was at Forli, asking his old enemy's intercession. Then he sat down and wrote anxiously in his notebook: "God grant that all will go well."

Girolamo was friendly, or seemed so. He sent

back a recommendation to his father in Giovanni's favor, and this was hurried by swift messenger to Rome.

"God grant that all will go well," Lorenzo wrote again.

Of course there were obstacles. The bestowal of such high office was an important business transaction for the Church, but under Sixtus they were all for sale, although the purchase was usually attended by as much close bargaining as a wedding.

"At six in the evening," Lorenzo recorded what seemed the approach of concrete proposals, "came letters from Rome saying that the Pope raised difficulties about giving the archbishopric to Messer Giovanni on account of his youth, and the courier was at once sent on to the King of France."

In a way this was not discouraging. Sixtus could not be serious about barring the boy from a mitre just because he was seven years old. Obviously it was a ruse to make the Medici more eager, to raise the price. That would be all right; they were willing to pay. Negotiations, financial and otherwise, were under way to put the matter straight.

And then with the prize as good as in hand, the crushing blow fell without warning. There proved after all to be an insurmountable obstacle to Giovanni becoming Archbishop of Aix. Louis had been a little premature; the thing could not be, for His Majesty had given away what was not yet his to give.

"The old Archbishop is not yet dead," Lorenzo

wrote sadly, and one more dream was shattered by cruel realities.

He bore the shock philosophically. After the first burst of disappointment, he ceased to complain of the setback to a promising career in the Church and looked about for other opportunities rather than bewail those that had failed to materialize. When considered calmly, it was apparent that Giovanni still had a good deal of time to become an Archbishop.

It was during the excitement of war and domestic difficulties that Lorenzo was guilty of his only fumble as a patron of arts. In the horde of painters who competed for his favor he had hardly given a thought to Leonardo da Vinci. He had not heard that the arrogant young man was something quite unprecedented as an engineer, and the talents of Florence's most versatile genius were permitted to lie unused during the worst days of the war. However, in common with dozens of others, he had been given a few commissions and allowed to browse about the Medici art collections. He had aroused a very flattering jealousy among older painters, and these men guilefully refrained from either abusing or praising him. They simply did not mention him at all, and for once the patron's keen eye passed over genius without seeing it. Then, in the anxiety of Giovanni's lost archbishopric, he allowed the genius to escape him altogether.

Da Vinci had made the mistake—which he did not repeat with his later masters—of failing to bring himself to the attention of Florence's ruler. That was the one art which he had not yet mastered, and Lorenzo was susceptible to flattery. But Leonardo would not stoop, so he remained known to the universal patron only for a minor talent of which he did not brag much himself. The banker had noticed with approval that the artist was without a peer in the pleasant pastime of improvising on the lute. He enjoyed the young man's music as much as he would have admired the mature works of his genius.

It was not quite what da Vinci wanted from life. He knew himself to be the superior in every way of any artist in Florence, and he chafed under the neglect which was his portion as a lute player. He was very glad, therefore, when the chance to escape from his native city presented itself. Lorenzo was sending a lute to Ludovico Sforza, and he invited Leonardo to go with Atalanto Migliorotti to present it. The artist intimated a desire to remain and seek his fortune at the court of Milan. Lorenzo good naturedly wrote a letter of recommendation, and Leonardo had difficulty in restraining his resentment when he read it.

"I commend to you," it said mildly, "the best lute player in Italy."

When Sforza finally received this letter it was attached to a much longer one by Leonardo himself, for the adventurer did not want his genius overlooked. Besides being a musician, he said modestly, he had no equal in the world as a mechanic and inventor nor was there alive any man who could excel him as architect, painter or sculptor. His self-praise was not exaggerated, nor had Lorenzo been altogether wrong in recommending his lute playing. It was as a musician that Leonardo first endeared himself to the Duke, although he soon made himself indispensable as an engineer in wartime and as director of pageants in peace. In the latter capacity he displayed even more ingenuity than Lorenzo de' Medici and with less money to dispose of he made the shows of his adopted city rival in brilliance the best performances in Florence.

Lorenzo never knew what he had lost. There were plenty of others to take the place of the notary's son. The work of beautifying the city went on without pause, while in Milan the versatile Leonardo brought the wonders of his mind to bear upon the gratification of the Duke's pleasures, and in his spare time filled notebooks with calculations, theories and sketches. After all, his life was just beginning. He was thirty, and a full half century of splendid work was still ahead of him. He could afford to do without Lorenzo as easily as Lorenzo could do without him.

Perhaps the patron might not have cared just then if he had known how much genius had escaped him. He was again in love, this time with an intensity which he had never experienced before. He was even making himself a little ridiculous in the display of his new romantic attachment, and the people, always pleased to find their heroes subject to weaknesses of the flesh, snickered as they told each other, not without some tolerance to temper their ironical amusement:

"Lorenzo behaves himself in a way that would demean an inexperienced youth."

Like all his other mistresses, the lady was married, so an easy place of some public honor had to be found for her husband. This was quite in order. She was Bartolommea de' Nasi, wife of Donato Benci, and that was quite in order too. So far, no cause for laughter. But she was quite without charm for anyone save Lorenzo. She was plain, ungraceful and lacking in the homely woman's virtue of kindness, but she could talk well and listen better. She fascinated Lorenzo by the sharpness of her tongue and the sympathetic way in which she dulled the edge of her wit when they discussed his troubles.

Whenever some stupid ambassador kept him from his fun, whenever he had to check over the list of a new Signoria instead of taking part in a meeting of the Platonic Academy, whenever the day had been particularly unpleasant, he could rely on the consolation of Bartolommea's understanding tenderness at night. Regardless of the weather, he would ride out to her villa far beyond the gates while the rest of Florence slept. Always Luigi della Stufa and Andrea de' Medici rode with him, for they had devoted themselves since the last assassination plot to guarding Lorenzo.

They found these trysts extremely trying to their

loyalty, especially in winter when they trotted in chilly silence through the darkness, soaked by the rains, frozen by the icy winds, their horses stumbling over unseen stones and Lorenzo inappropriately singing love songs. At the Benci villa he would leave them on guard outside, and they crouched miserably with their horses in the inadequate shelter of walls and hedges, shivering despite their warmest clothing as the wind swept over the cold, sodden hills. While they waited, they exchanged curses and wondered why their chief had to select a mistress so far from town, so plain of feature, so caustic of wit, so inhospitable. At last Lorenzo would emerge, and the three would gallop back to the city, warming as they rode, just as the sky paled, giving barely light enough to see as they picked their way through the silent streets.

After a few of these more uncomfortable excursions, Luigi and Andrea could not resist repeating in society some of the sarcasms which they had elaborated during their cold vigils outside the Benci villa. Their hearers applauded and passed on the remarks. Soon the best of them reached Bartolommea by way of some of the beggars, rich or poor, who swarmed around her beseeching favors from her lover. The young matron was furious. Her position as mistress of the city's leading citizen was being made ridiculous.

One night while Lorenzo's two companions were freezing unhappily outside, she spoke of their impertinence. A few days later the Signoria ordered Luigi della Stufa on a special embassy to Cairo. The same order despatched Andrea de' Medici on a delicate mission to Constantinople. Lorenzo now rode alone through the darkness to see Bartolommea, and Florence roared with laughter while in their Eastern exiles the two young envoys cursed their own too ready tongues.

XX

Lorenzo had not forgotten his resolution to hold the balance of power in Italy so that other men might build in undisturbed peace the golden age of the Renaissance. He spent much more time and effort over the protracted treaty negotiations to end the last war than he did in romping with his children, intriguing for their advancement or seeking the consolations of love. He wrote more diplomatic despatches than sonnets. Only after he had finished penning cogent arguments for the preservation of Ferrara would he permit himself the luxury of versification. Politics influenced his style. He became quite wistful as he indited his poems, pouring out to Bartolommea his amorous longings, only to end with the cry:

> *But why these thoughts irrelevant and vain,*
> *If I, long since in Hymen's fetters tied,*
> *Am doomed to hear another call thee bride?*

The wistful mood passed with the sonnet. Love had never loosened his grasp of more important affairs, and he drove steadily towards his goal through the tangle of jealousies and greed with which his fellow rulers hobbled the progress of peace. He was thirty-five, in years the youngest of those who bargained at the conference table, but he had taken on many of the characteristics of an old man. He had the patience, the loquacity, the tendency to reminis- cense, the sudden fits of weariness, the desire to tender unsolicited, unwanted advice which come with age. His very ailments were those of a man past his prime. It was hard for him to get up in the mornings, even the mornings when he had not ridden out to the Benci villa. His colleagues rebuked him for his laziness, but he retorted:

"My morning's sleep is much better than your morning's business."

He had much more reason to complain of their lethargy than they of his, but at last the treaties were signed. The shock was too much for one of the parties to them. Five days after the conventions had been formally proclaimed, Sixtus died of an apoplec- tic stroke for which his many rages had well pre- pared him, and the wits of the Vatican were chuckling over some anonymous jokester's epitaph:

"Sixtus, who could not live in company with any treaty, died at the mere whisper of the word Peace."

None of the rulers of Italy, none of the princes of the Church save his own family mourned for the dead man. In Florence the magistrates with difficulty restrained public rejoicing until such a time as it could be made to appear the spontaneous celebration of a successor's election.

The choice of the Sacred College was one that

Lorenzo might have made himself. The new head of the Church was Giambattista Cibo, one of the stupidest of Cardinals (although the Florentine Ambassador described him as "not wholly ignorant"), proverbially good-natured, notoriously weak of will, quite free from prejudices. He took the rather appropriate name of Innocent, and his first act was to make some provision for the prosperity of his children. His next was to drop some words of praise for the ruler of Florence, whose attainments and munificence had long dazzled the rather simple Genoese.

Lorenzo saw in this man just the instrument he needed for preserving the peace. He lavished good advice on him, lent him money, made him presents. Soon the Pope was refusing to move in anything without consulting his friend. He furnished Lorenzo with a list of proposed Cardinals and conferred the Red Hat only on those whose names the Florentine approved. All Europe knew that the best road to Rome lay through Florence.

It was a promising start, but Innocent had the defects of his qualities. He was more difficult to handle than at first seemed likely. He was a child, but had a childish stubbornness as well as a childish simplicity. In the beginning only the simplicity was apparent. He was a father, fond of his family. He recognized his offspring openly, thereby setting a precedent for future Popes, and conferred high honors and lucrative places upon them. Only in the most formal documents, in which lip service had to be paid to the theory of clerical celibacy, was Franceschetto Cibo, Governor of Rome, Captain General of the Church, styled "nephew."

Innocent, like his predecessor, regarded the Papacy as very much a commercial enterprise, but unlike Sixtus he ran it according to business principles. Hitherto pardons for sins committed or about to be committed had been bought haphazard from almost anyone about the Vatican. No system had ever been introduced, although the sale of indulgences was a great source of revenue. The new Pope established a bank which dealt in divine mercy as the Medici dealt in promissory notes. It was highly successful. One hundred and fifty ducats of every purchase price went to the Pope; Franceschetto took the rest to pay his gambling debts. Even Boccaccio, who had written, "Send the most obstinate Jew to Rome and the profligacy of the Papal court will not fail to convert him to the faith which can resist such obloquy," had never dreamed of such corruption as had now been developed in the simple belief that this was what the Bishop of Rome was for. Penitents crowded to the bank to buy the forgiveness of Heaven at the market price. It was not even necessary that the applicant be a sinner; the intention of becoming one was enough, and many a client bought immunity for the crime he planned to commit next week.

But if he was simple, Innocent was no prude.

During his reign no attempt was made to enforce the edicts, which had been issued periodically from the Vatican, forbidding priests to keep brothels or act as panders. His Holiness was running a wide open town, and within a few years there were in Rome nearly seven thousand public prostitutes, "not counting," says a chronicler of the time, "nuns and concubines."

Pilgrims from all over Christendom, come to gaze in wonder upon the holy places and relics of their religion, were the best customers of the bawdy houses whose inmates swarmed in the narrow, filthy streets. Every woman of the town had her attendant bravos, mostly priests, ready to solicit or stab as opportunity offered. These things had always been, Innocent supposed, and he was not the man to inter-fere with tradition.

Nor would he allow others to do so. The Vicar of Rome, "watchful of his flock as befits an honorable man," says Infessura, issued on his own responsibility an edict threatening with excommunication any Churchman who kept a mistress, openly or in secret. The Pope was most indignant. He im-mediately cancelled the edict, informing the Vicar with a tartness quite foreign to his disposition that concubinage was not forbidden by the Church.

However, he was not altogether without religious feeling. He was extremely orthodox in his attitude towards witches, who apparently abounded in the Papal states as Poliziano said they did in Florence.

Practitioners of the black arts had been seen dancing to strange, obscene incantations on dark nights, and then somebody's cow died. Thanks to His Holiness's zeal, hundreds of dangerous sorcerers were tracked down, brought to Rome and burned with much ceremony.

These manifestations of Innocent's spiritual powers did not interest Lorenzo. But as months passed, the Pope proved altogether too tractable in temporal matters, and his mentor became alarmed. His Holiness obeyed almost anyone who obtained access to him, and sometimes he eluded Lorenzo's vigilance. On one of these occasions he was argued into a war with Naples, a few of Ferrante's enemies easily convincing him that the Kingdom really belonged to the Holy See and that he would be winning everlasting glory by asserting his rights. At most inconvenient moments during his pontificate this idea recurred to him, and each time threatened not only to involve all Italy in war but tempt French and Spanish invasions too. Lorenzo could not make the Pope see reason. The peace maker argued until he was tired, and then grew eloquently bitter about Innocent's stupidity and Ferrante's cruel folly in oppressing his people to such a degree that they looked to Rome for a liberator.

"This ecclesiastical state has always been the ruin of Italy," Lorenzo complained wearily, "because being ignorant and not knowing how to govern, the priests put the whole world in peril."

To the Ferrarese Ambassador he broke out an-
grily:

"I can believe anything of this Pope. I should like
to spend six months in some place where the affairs
of Italy would never be mentioned, and I hope to see
the day when the King of France will be lord over
all Italy."

"From which you can see," the Ambassador explained to his government, "how greatly His Magnificence is put out."

At last the quarrel was temporarily composed on
terms drawn up by Lorenzo, who perhaps appreciated better than either of the disputants how un-
satisfactory any terms would be. He had no illusions
about these men; he was not interested in abstract
justice; he wanted peace, not principle, and so he was
quite unconscious of any cynicism when he wrote:

"The King will hardly raise difficulties when he
has only to give promises. When it comes to keeping
them, they must just wink at each other, as all Popes
and all Kings have done."

While the Pope and the King were alternately
winking at each other and shaking their fists at each
other, their critic was engaged in a quarrel of his own.
Although it was a good deal more bloody than the
battles of the South, he did not dignify it with the
name of war, for it did not threaten the general peace.
He considered it a punitive expedition; outsiders
regarded it as a war between the two biggest banks
in the world, and it was remarked that the bankers,

one of them renowned for his pacifism even if it were
not an idealistic pacifism, were much more energetic
militarists than the condottieri.

The opposing financial house in this struggle was
the Bank of San Giorgio, a Genoese trading corpora-
tion which had swallowed not only the city of Genoa
but a dozen little principalities as well. Its fleets were
all over the seas; its agents bought and sold all over
the world; it was the only serious rival to the Medici
in the field of international banking.

This bank was always interested in buying cities,
and most of the free cities of Italy were for sale. At
the moment Sarzana was claiming to be free. Piero
de' Medici had bought it for Florence from its lord,
Ludovico Fregoso, but during the war of the Pazzi
conspiracy the seller's son, Agostino, had persuaded
the town to rebel and acknowledge his sovereignty.
When the war was over he saw he would never be
able to keep the city, so he offered it to the Bank of
San Giorgio. This institution was not averse to
fighting, and for two years battles raged around
Sarzana between Florence's hired men and the troops
of the Bank. Finally the conflict settled down to a
siege, but the place was so well supplied from Genoa
that it could not be starved out.

At last Lorenzo determined to try his own hand
at the game. His army was immensely flattered when
he rode into the camp, for the troops of Italy were not
accustomed to seeing men of his prestige among them.
They were as susceptible to eloquence as any of their

countrymen, and Lorenzo made them a speech. It aroused so much enthusiasm that the Sarzanans, hearing the commotion and fearing it would result in an outbreak of unsoldierly ardor when the fight-ing recommenced, surrendered without waiting to be attacked. The event was hailed as a great conquest in Florence. Lorenzo was welcomed as a military genius when he returned in triumph from the field of glory, and the minor poets who lived on his generosity sang his praises as a warrior.

He had not enjoyed it. The discomforts of camp life, the lack of cultured society in the army, the stupidity of soldiers bored him. The hero was quite confirmed in his distaste for battle, and he never tried it again. He attributed to the hardships of the field a particularly virulent attack of gout which for some months confined him at home or at the baths, unable to walk or ride. He suffered too from some obscure digestive disorder, and permitted himself a few gloomy reflections on the difficulties of keeping the peace. He did not trust Ludovico Sforza, the Pope and Naples were still at odds, petty princes were always bringing him their troubles and Clarice had taken it into her head to insist that he find a job for one of her friends. Her husband unexpectedly gave way, exclaiming:

"I long for peace at home since I see small reason to hope for it abroad."

The fit of depression which gave rise to such talk passed quickly. He was trying some interesting experiments in government and changing the entire policy of the Medici business enterprises, so there was little time to be despondent. In both his political system and his bank he was seeking greater wealth united to a greater security.

The government, with its everlasting rotation of inexperienced officials, was extremely inefficient, and it was always dangerous to appropriate public funds when almost every member of his party would have to know about it sooner or later. So to gain some stability for the administration and some permanent tool for his own purposes, he invited the people to sanction a sort of senate, called the Seventy—his creatures, of course—who inconspicuously took over the most important functions of government.

Through this machinery Lorenzo was able to dispose of his country's revenues with a freedom which almost obliterated any distinction between his bank and the treasury, even in peacetime. He grew more and more daring. He appointed his brother-in-law, Bernardo Rucellai, Commissioner of Coinage and Taxation, and by calling in old coins for new ones of slightly less intrinsic value they made a very handsome profit. An obsequious Seventy passed a decree for the payment by the State of all debts which Lorenzo de' Medici had contracted since 1478. He was thus enabled to return to his cousins the tremendous sums they had lent him during the wars, and the money was invested in the business which he controlled.

At last he grew so bold that he tampered with the Monte which insured dowries for girls of moderate means. For almost every female child born in Florence, the parents deposited something in the Monte dell' Dotte. The State guaranteed compound interest and payment of both principal and interest on the day of the girl's marriage. Lorenzo looted this fund so consistently that the Monte suspended payment, and the marriage rate fell off alarmingly. Almost every girl in the city had been deprived of her dowry, and no young man was so foolish as to take a portionless girl. If he had been, his parents would not have permitted it.

Lorenzo's anterooms were filled with fathers come to plead with him to release their money so their daughters might find husbands. Only the well disposed were accommodated, and even then Lorenzo's approval of the match was necessary. To the amusement of the childless and the indignation of all who had marriageable offspring, he insisted on being informed of every courtship. Marriage negotiations became three-cornered affairs with Lorenzo mediating authoritatively between the two families.

While he was thus grasping the government and the lives of the people more securely in his hands, he was revising the policy of the Medici Banks so that he could direct them himself without the heavy losses which he had sustained from time to time. As swiftly as possible he withdrew entirely from commercial banking. Ever since he had inherited control, he complained, he had been the victim of factors and agents who cheated him unmercifully, secure in his ignorance of commerce. The trading ventures which he financed had prospered but nearly always he lost money in them.

Lorenzo owned a half interest in the institution which half a dozen generations of his family had given their lives to build. The other half was in the hands of partners, mostly his cousins, and he ruled them completely. So there was no protest when the Medici Banks turned exclusively to international finance and pawnbroking on a princely scale. This was a field Lorenzo understood as well as any man alive. The union of diplomacy and business was congenial. As the ruler of Florence he had learned what countries he could trust as a banker. He was much more successful in bargaining with Kings and Popes than with the shrewd merchants of Italy. Once again he had charge of the Church's complicated finances, and it was extremely profitable. It also led him into one of the most unusual banking transactions, even of that day, the purchase of Prince Djem from the King of France.

Djem was one of the sons of the Sultan Mohammed. He had disputed the right of succession with his brother, Bajazet, had been defeated and fled into the West. He was passed from one refuge to another until he reached France. The victorious Sultan thought the best way of disposing of his rival was to keep him a captive, so he was paying forty thousand ducats a year to anyone who would take good care of the Prince.

The pay was tempting. The Vicar of Christ thought he would like to serve as jailer on these terms for the Caliph, and he instructed his banker to arrange it. The French treasury was in its usual state of depletion, and Lorenzo was able to manage the business to the satisfaction of all concerned. Through his influence, Bajazet consented to the change, France agreed to sell and the money was raised. The agent made a triple profit, a commission from the King, a commission from the Pope and interest on the money he found for His Holiness to complete the deal. In a few weeks Prince Djem came down to a new luxurious prison in the Vatican where he was to die.

Lorenzo's other great source of wealth was even more closely bound up with the preservation of peace than was his banking. As long as the condottieri roamed over Italy, pillaging while they tried to avoid decisive battles, agriculture was precarious. Where the armies passed, no crop was ever harvested, but when peace reigned in the land, the farmer could obtain good prices for his grain, his grapes and his olives in the crowded, prosperous cities to which the wealth of the world gravitated.

Among the first to see that much money could be derived from the soil in peacetime was Lorenzo, whose estates were already numerous and who now added to them extensively. He conferred with the best gardeners in Italy on how to make his land more productive. He actually called in such science as he knew to help with the farming. He had engineers to drain the marshes; he employed the head of his racing stable to improve the breed of cattle and hogs; he imported bulls and boars for breeding purposes. At Careggi, Poggio-a-Cajano, Cafaggiuolo, the Mugello, Agnana and Volterra his fields, orchards and vineyards stretched for miles.

His plantation of mulberry trees was so vast that he undermined the price of silk; all Florence was supplied with vegetables from the truck gardens at Careggi; his dairies were so productive that Tuscany no longer needed to import cheese from Lombardy. He was very much the banker as he boasted of his agricultural successes, and he took troops of his intellectual friends out to see how the soil was tilled. They were properly impressed, and in the contemporary poetry the ruler of Florence is compared *ad nauseam* to those noble stalwarts who, between harvests, were the backbone of the Roman Republic. Even Poliziano caught the spirit of his master's new pleasures and encouraged him to productive pursuits, crying from very far on the sidelines

Go on, Lorenzo, thou the Muse's pride,
Pierce the hard rock and scoop the mountain's side.

The statesman was assured that he would find all sorts of strange things awaiting him, and lest he might not recognize them the poet carefully summed them up

Lorenzo de' Medici
"The Muse's Pride"

Wide o'er thy downs extends thy fleecy charge.
There the Calabrian hog, obese and large,
Loud from his sty demands his constant food;
And Spain supplies thee with thy rabbit brood.
Where mulberry groves their length of shadow spread,
Secure the silkworm spins his lustrous thread;
And culled from every flower the plunderer meets,
The bee regales thee with her rifled sweets.
There birds of various plume and various note
Flutter their captive wings; with cackling throat
The Paduan fowl betrays her future breed,
And there the geese, once Rome's preservers, feed,
And ducks amusive sport amidst thy floods,
And doves, the pride of Venus, throng thy woods.

Lorenzo was indeed getting old. He actually preferred the pastoral joys, of which he sang much better and more correctly than Poliziano, to the once dear parade of foreign travel. He no longer enjoyed arraying himself in layers of gorgeous silks spangled with the finest jewels of his collection. He was no longer proud to ride, thus clad, at the head of a splendid troop to some foreign court. He was even a little tired of making and listening to interminable, sugar-coated, meaningless speeches. Such excursions had to be made. But now he resigned the opportunity to youth. He permitted Piero to represent him while he retired to repose and idle conversation to Poggio or Careggi.

Piero did this sort of thing very well. Tall and

slender with black curls, big brown eyes, a smooth
olive skin and a perpetual smile, his good looks set
off the beauty of his costumes. His share of the Orsini
pride was evident as yet only in a rather engaging
dignity of manner. By the time he was fourteen he was
quite experienced in the art of presenting an impres-
sively picturesque appearance, and he enjoyed foreign
travel. His father was much pleased, for it relieved
him of an unwelcome burden.

However, Piero was never trusted as Lorenzo had
been to speak for himself. Always he was provided
with the most minute instructions. He was sent to
Rome for no more important an object than to kiss
the Pope's hand and murmur a few polite phrases,
but he carried a letter of many pages telling him in
detail just how he was to act to everybody under all
circumstances. He was to be invariably civil, to talk
but little, not to presume upon his father's reputation,
to be chary of displaying his erudition, to visit the
family assiduously so the Orsini feelings would not
be hurt, to be very humble in the presence of the
Pope.

"After having recommended me to His Holiness
you will inform him," Lorenzo went on, "that your
affection for your brother induces you to speak a
word in his favor. You can here mention that I have
educated him for the priesthood, and shall closely
attend to his learning and his manners, so that he
may not disgrace his profession, that in this respect
I repose all my hopes on His Holiness, who, having

already given us proofs of his kindness and affection, will add to our obligations by any promotion which he may think proper to bestow upon him, endeavoring by these and similar expressions to recommend your brother to his favor as much as lies in your power."

XXI

In spite of gout and family cares and the increasing annoyances of business, Lorenzo saw that his work was good. The fruits of it were obvious wherever he went in Florence, and he could enjoy them to the full whenever he had time for a quiet evening at Fiesole.

New palaces built by merchants who were finding peace prosperous beyond their dreams, even if taxes did remain most outrageously high, were rising all over the city. Such men as Ghirlandaio, Botticelli, the Verrochios, Filippo Lippi, Pollajuolo, were decorating them. All these artists very flatteringly asked Lorenzo's approval of their sketches or his suggestions for subjects.

If he looked out of his own palace windows over the gardens of San Marco, he could see a host of earnest young men studying the antique models which he had collected there for their benefit. If he walked abroad he was free of any studio. All work stopped at once when the great man walked in. The head of the establishment hurried nervously from the inner sanctum where he had been painting proudly under the eyes of a few privileged friends and favored students to greet the distinguished visitor. The apprentices in the big, untidy outer hall were relieved from their tasks by the assistants so they might listen to the remarks of the patron.

Attended by the eager master of the studio, Lorenzo would wander around, praising, suggesting, criticizing. But he would listen, too, while the artists poured forth their theories, argued about colors, debated the value of anatomical research. The more advanced realists such as the Verrochios and Pollajuolo were almost sure to have the corpse of some poor wretch lying about for dissection. They would demonstrate eagerly the necessity of learning the play of every muscle, the hinging of every joint before the human figure could be reproduced on canvas. Botticelli would discourse dreamily of symbolism, of the artist's message concealed beneath the craftsman's skill.

Off to such a start, the debates were apt to be loud and long. The artists shouted at each other, seized pencils to sketch hurriedly some few lines to illustrate their arguments, flung taunts and insults with a freedom which was quite ignored in the heat of the dispute. Now and then they appealed to Lorenzo as a connoisseur. He would drop a few words into the discussion, but his opinion was never taken as final in the studios. He was no painter himself, so to the eager experimenters in color and line his views were inconsiderable except when they remembered that he could dispose of many commissions. For the most part he would sit among them, attentive but silent, while against the walls the students held their breaths and strained their eyes to miss nothing that the masters said or did.

At last after accepting a glass of wine from his hosts, Lorenzo would leave, and behind him the *bottega* would settle gradually back into its usual busy efficiency. The talk subsided to the usual buzz of instruction and comment. The master returned to his unfinished piece; the advanced pupils took up their brushes and pencils; the new apprentices went on stretching canvases, mixing colors and preparing the carved wooden chests to receive the paint.

If he continued his stroll, Lorenzo might cross the Piazza Santa Croce and come on the curious sign, a pile of torn, burning account books, outside the dark little shop where Niccolo Grosso wrought in iron ornaments whose delicacy was envied and admired by workers in bronze and silver. Niccolo's sign indicated that he worked for cash in advance only. Not even Lorenzo, his best customer, could obtain credit, and frequently the ruler of Florence, coming in to place a large, profitable order, was told he would have to wait until the artist had finished hammering out the iron pots for which he had been paid by the poor women of the neighborhood.

Lorenzo was comparatively silent in the studios, but he made up for it when the philosophers and poets gathered around a bottle and a new book. Among the most talkative of mankind, he easily dominated the conversation. No matter who might set the argument and assign the parts for the discussion, Lorenzo was sure to be one of the chief expounders. There was always a certain formality about the meetings. It was necessary, for all these men tended to talk at once. To restrain themselves they had fixed a few rules of procedure. One of the party gave the topic for the debate and assigned to each of the others his share in the conversation. Then, while the wine flask circulated rapidly, the evening would pass in a succession of impromptu orations, often very wide of the mark but always aimed at amusing the audience as well as displaying the speaker's scholastic attainments.

Around the Medici villa at Fiesole a colony of writers and scholars had clustered. Ficino, Poliziano, Landino, the Pulcis, Scala and the Greek Chalcondyles had their own places in the neighborhood. Matteo Bosso, superior of the Fiesole convent, an accomplished theologian, a prolific writer, was always welcome in the literary or learned discussions of the colony.

To judge by the poetry of these men, nymphs and dryads and fauns cavorted without shame or concealment in the woods and gardens of Fiesole. So frequently were these lovely, graceful creatures from the pagan golden age seen and interviewed by the poets that it was popularly believed that all the marble statues with which the walks around the villas were decorated came alive at night to dance in mad revelry among the trees with the godless artists who apostrophised them so tirelessly.

The little group of writers on the hillside overlooking Florence became famous throughout Europe. To them came one of those versatile young men who aspired to complete mastery of all knowledge, and who in that day were perilously close to achieving their ambition. Certainly this young man was well on the way. Giovanni Pico, younger son of the Prince of Mirandola, was only twenty-one but he had already aroused such professional jealousy among the ecclesiastical pundits of Rome that he was flying for his life when he found the haven of Fiesole, the congenial companionship of the world's most renowned thinkers and the powerful protection of Lorenzo.

Pico was a handsome youth—the hideous Poliziano was never tired of exclaiming that so much genius could be united to so much beauty. He had spent seven years in the leading universities of France and Italy. He had acquired twenty-two languages, dead and alive, and a taste for the most complicated, abstruse, long forgotten speculations of Greek, Hebrew and Arab philosophers. He had gone to Rome full of youthful enthusiasm with the laudable intention of proving his right to a place among much older and more respected scholars. As a start he published to a startled world a list of nine hundred theses ranging over the entire field of human learning —mathematical, philosophical, theological, magical, scientific. Pico challenged the scholars of Rome to debate with him on any or all of these points. It was the recognized method for a young man trying to get ahead in the learned world, but few had the temerity or the ability to propound such a long list of subjects.

Strangely enough the intellectual leaders of the Church read all through the newcomer's nine hundred theses. None of the men challenged cared to risk their reputations in public debate with a novice whose erudition was so obvious. Indeed, none of them could understand all the nine hundred theses. Yet it was impossible to ignore them. Rather than argue, the Roman scholars studied the publication once more in search of some excuse for avoiding the battle.

After grave consideration, they decided that in thirteen of the more profound, incomprehensible arguments, Pico had put forward heretical opinions. Obviously it was impossible for good churchmen to debate with such a man. To make quite sure that he would not bother them any more, they pointed out his heresies to the Pope. Innocent was always ready to believe that anything he was too stupid or too lazy to understand must be either of satanic or wilfully perverse origin. Without much persuasion he issued a bull against the young nobleman. Pico managed to escape to the more tolerant atmosphere of Florence, leaving his nine hundred theses to be cast solemnly into the flames by the Papal executioner.

He found able partisans in the colony at Fiesole. They encouraged him to reply to his clerical accusers, and he dedicated his defence to the patron of his new friends. Lorenzo read and was delighted with the talent displayed. He invited Pico to talk with him and was convinced that this man belonged among the leaders of thought. In any case he was a most amusing companion. The host was so cordial that Pico took up his residence among the literati.

Lorenzo undertook to manage Rome. He was quite indignant with Innocent, declaring Pico was an ornament to all scholarship and would never have been persecuted "if only His Holiness had the in-telligence to understand this." However, when Lo-renzo had explained it, the Pope withdrew his bull, although Pico was a long time in obtaining a full pardon. Meanwhile he endeared himself to Florence and astounded the gay citizenry of the place by the propriety of his conduct. They did not expect such scrupulosity from a good looking, rich young man.

Pico seemed to save all his enthusiasm for praising his protector. It was a never failing source of amaze-ment to the philosopher, who knew himself to be possessed of mental attainments inferior to none, that Lorenzo could find time to excel in so many various branches of study and yet maintain his reputation as the first statesman in Italy and the most influential banker in the world. He marvelled that Lorenzo could interrupt a dissertation on Plato to write a sonnet, pause in the sonnet to dictate a diplomatic despatch and then return to the argument as if nothing had intervened.

"So vigorous and yet so various is his genius that he seems equally formed for every pursuit," Pico wrote to Poliziano. "But what principally excites my wonder is that even when he is deeply engaged in the affairs of the republic, his conversation and his thoughts should be turned to subjects of literature, as if he were perfect master of his time."

Perhaps it was not so surprising as Pico seemed to think. Next to peace, literature was the great passion of Lorenzo's life. He was determined to place his native tongue, neglected and despised by artists for more than a century, in the literary firmament. He knew that he could do it. Patronage was not enough, however; he had to set the example too. Not since the days of Petrarch and Boccaccio had such brilliant Italian as Lorenzo's been produced. Not for as long again would his style be equalled.

It was the fashion among his friends, and dependents, to acclaim him as the superior of Dante, but they all knew that was flattery. Nevertheless in all seriousness Poliziano was able to find only three Tuscan poets worthy of lasting fame—Dante, Petrarch, Lorenzo—and he linked them all together in the lines

Be these thy boast, Oh Florence, these thy pride,
Thy sons, whose genius spreads thy glory wide!

Translations are odious, and it is hard to prove the justice of his verdict. However, it has been confirmed by later lovers of poetry who had no reason to care much for Lorenzo personally since they considered that he had enslaved his people through many future generations, and they had nothing to gain by praising him.

The critic Crescimbeni, describing the Renaissance of Tuscan verse admits that Lorenzo "preserved it from ruin, snatched it from the dangerous precipice which seemed to await it." The preserver's poetry, he adds, "exhibits a simplicity of style, a purity of language, a happiness of versification, a propriety of poetical ornament and a fulness of sentiment that recalled once more the grace and sweetness of Petrarch."

Muratori expressed the same degree of appreciation in more concise terms:

"It is gold from the mine, mixed with ruder materials indeed, but it is always gold."

The fact that most anthologies of Italian verse still contain specimens of Lorenzo's poetry is, perhaps, no additional recommendation.

He himself had no doubts about the value of his writing. He knew that it was good. He was so sure of it that he never bothered to brag, and no favors were ever won from him simply by praising his work. He did like to read his poems to the understanding circle at Fiesole. It was almost as much fun as listening to the recognized literary clowns, Franco and Luigi Pulci, abusing each other, their works and their most remote ancestors in ribald verse, outdoing each other in obscenity and scurrility for the entertainment of friends.

The writing men not only furnished Lorenzo with amusing talk, instructive discourses for himself, tutors for his children and scribes for his diplomatic correspondence. They also provided a new target for the ridicule of those scoffers who had not yet ceased to chuckle over their ruler's indiscreet passion for Bartolommea Benci. At last this incident was forgotten in the humor of the vastly more ludicrous spectacle of Poliziano in love.

The great poet took all the world into his confidence. The world learned with interested amusement that the object of his devotion, the inspiration of his Muse, was the beautiful Alessandra Scala, daughter of his old enemy, the Chancellor of the Republic. Poliziano first noticed her at a performance of Electra in which she played the leading rôle with such feeling that her admirer exclaimed:

"Thus would Electra's self have trod the stage!"

The ugly little man went home in a state of amorous exaltation which fed on his poetic fancies as much as on the memories of his beloved's appearance. Only the Greek tongue, he conceived, was worthy of expressing his emotion. A few days after her performance Alessandra received a bit of verse in which Poliziano confided to her, with appropriate preamble:

But when the fair, with love too well expressed,
Folds her Orestes to her heaving breast,
How I do long to fill the envied place
And wistful sigh to share that dear embrace.

Fortunately Alessandra could read Greek. Besides being one of the belles of Florence, she was unquestionably the most learned woman in the city. She had studied under Chalcondyles, and she was considered an authority on the newly discovered merits of Cicero's Latin prose. She was greatly pleased with the homage which Poliziano was wise enough to pay to her intelligence as well as her looks, and she answered him politely in Greek.

Her admirer was delighted beyond measure with the condescension of her reply. He felt himself encouraged by this gorgeous creature, and the ardor of his poetry increased. She answered with a few lines of appreciation for his genius and enclosed flowers. Then he was convinced that his love was returned with a passion approaching his own. He told her they two were destined to accomplish great things in literature, that he had dreamed of their works going down to a grateful posterity together. He believed in dreams, he said, and this one meant, among other pleasant things, that he would soon clasp her in his arms as he had seen Orestes do.

This was a little further than Alessandra cared to go. She had thought the affair was a purely intellectual friendship, a community of soul between two minds, embellished perhaps by tender images drawn from the classics, but without any real fleshly implications. She was a little disappointed in her learned correspondent. Anyway, her affections were engaged elsewhere. She decided to put the overly ambitious poet in his place. He should, she wrote him, interpret his dreams better. In a way she felt complimented, but he must know that her works were but the veriest trifles while his were immortal.

"Shall I," she concluded maliciously, "stand by your side because I have a little learning? Or—as the proverb says—should we not be as the gnat beside the elephant? Both have a proboscis."

The jibe at Poliziano's huge nose was pronounced very good indeed. All Florence roared with laughter at the discomfiture of this poor Cyrano who had no sword to defend himself and who could not even retaliate with his much feared wit upon the still beloved Alessandra. He suffered in shame and silence until the young woman furnished him with a public outlet for the venomous words he had been nursing in private.

She married Michael Marullus, a handsome Greek whose writings had brought him the patronage of Lorenzo and, in happier days, the praise of Poliziano as well. But now the poet turned on Marullus with a vindictive fury rare even in that age of unbridled invective. However, the Greek was well able to take care of himself, and for months the literate world was entertained by the epithets which the learned rivals for Alessandra's love exchanged.

The battle of words was so bitter, so well sustained on both sides, so attractive to all those who desired a touch of romance in their reading matter, that it almost obscured the saintly Pico's lamentable fall from grace. Lorenzo had at last secured for him the Pope's forgiveness, and the young nobleman was on his way to Rome to offer up formal thanks to his persecutor for relenting. He stopped at Arezzo overnight and as a friend of Lorenzo he was entertained by a poor relation of the family, Giuliano de' Medici. Giuliano had recently married a rich young widow of low degree, who had been attracted much more by the glamor of her husband's name than by the charms of his person. This couple dined Pico and his companions very elaborately and far into the night. When the husband woke he learned that his wife and his guest had departed together many hours before.

Armed with a warrant signed by the magistrates of Arezzo and accompanied by a troop of soldiers, Giuliano galloped in pursuit. The fugitives were travelling slowly, for Pico and the lady had to ride one horse. The husband overtook them, breathing threats of vengeance, and in the running fight that followed, his wife fell from the horse, Pico was captured and several of his servants killed.

Dragged back to Arezzo, both protesting their unsullied virtue, the two told extremely conflicting stories, neither of which found much credit from the scepticism of their light-hearted friends. The lady swore by all the saints that her guest had come upon her while she was taking an early morning walk in her garden and had kidnapped her by brute force which she had never ceased to resist, as witness her fall from the horse. Pico's version was that she had been waiting for him at the gate and leaped up behind him as he trotted by. Naturally, he said, a Pico of Mirandola could not be so ungentlemanly as to throw a woman to the ground, even if he could not requite her affection.

The magistrates were sorely puzzled, not so much by the conflicting evidence—they waved that aside with the amused smiles of worldly men—but by the fact that the outraged husband was Lorenzo's kins-man while the erring lover was Lorenzo's friend. It was one of those little dilemmas which wrung from one disillusioned foreign judge the bitter couplet

> *If there is a person whom you hate*
> *Send him to Florence as officer of State.*

At last, however, they referred the matter to Florence for advice. Lorenzo dictated a judgment which was duly passed. The wayward wife was sent back to her husband, for Giuliano could not afford to cast such a rich spouse from him, and Pico was permitted to continue, unaccompanied, to humble himself before the Pope for the heresy of his nine hundred theses.

XXII

The respite from appearing at public functions wreathed in smiles and gorgeous apparel was the only compensation Lorenzo derived from his children's increasing age. As they grew up he was not only deprived of those infantile amusements which he enjoyed, but he had to see that they married advantageously, a matter of wearisome discussion at home followed by protracted negotiations abroad. There was so much to confuse the issue, the maintenance of Lorenzo's dignity as the umpire of Italy, the strengthening of his position in the State, the financial strain of dowering four girls. Fortunately sentiment was left out; the introduction of mild emotion into marriage was left for softer people living in a less realistic age.

In the first place he wanted a Roman alliance, but the fact that he had himself been given a bride from the Eternal City did not enter into the reasoning. He thought only of his politics. The most unstable of the powers of Italy, the one most likely to disturb the balance, was Innocent. The man could not be depended upon for a moment. As his banker and confidential adviser, Lorenzo had won great influence, but the Pope was likely at any inconvenient time to go his own blundering way. Perhaps he would be more amenable if his guide were also a member of his family.

Negotiations were opened through the Florentine Ambassador for a match between Innocent's eldest son and Lorenzo's second daughter. Franceschetto was forty; Maddalena fourteen. But she was a sensible child; her dreams of romance were not built around a husband. It was well, for the Captain General of the Church possessed nothing glamorous except his title. He was a heavy man with a plain, dull face, no wit, a large indifference to beauty or books and one consuming passion—avarice.

"I hear he keeps aloof from frivolous people and those of evil report, and that he avoids play," Lorenzo wrote of him with approval.

He had been misinformed. Franceschetto did indeed neglect the lighter, more graceful vices, for which he had neither taste nor ability, but he was a notorious gambler, as famous for the recklessness of his wagers as for his consistent losses. In a single evening he had dropped fourteen thousand ducats, the price of a fortified town, to Cardinal Raffaello Riario. He was so unlucky that despite his revenues from Churchly offices and the pardon bank, increased by a recent concession for the legitimizing of bastards, he was always out of funds.

Naturally he was anxious to be the son-in-law of a man who was believed to be the richest citizen in Europe. The anxiety, however, was not betrayed. The Pope was a shrewd bargainer in his own simple way, and when at last in March, 1487, the marriage contract was drawn up, Lorenzo had promised to give with his daughter the usual splendid trousseau, four thousand ducats in cash, two of the old Pazzi residences, an estate at Spedaletto and title to the County of Anguillara. The total was so great that he had difficulty in raising it in time for the betrothal in May.

On his side he kept insisting that Innocent too should do something handsome for the young couple. He was proud of "the family connection concluded with me by His Holiness," but he wrote chidingly to the Pope that people would begin to talk if the Holy Father did not provide for his son "in such a manner that I may remain content and satisfied, as I shall when Sig. Francesco's affairs are in a state which conforms to the dignity of Your Holiness and the repose of my mind." Of course no one else should be despoiled for their sake, but:

"It seems to me unlike your goodness and kindness not to provide him with means to keep up his position without doing injury to others. I beg you in all humility to relieve yourself and me of this trouble, and to provide for him in such a way that I shall no longer need to approach you in this matter. By doing this you will perform a deed worthy of your clemency and goodness, not only a pious and reasonable act, but one that is necessary and most pleasing to me."

After the betrothal Maddalena remained at home, for she was a little young to be sent to her husband.

Innocent had not done his paternal duty in a financial way, but then he was always slow. No doubt he would be generous in the end.

Meanwhile Lorenzo was attaching himself to Naples by means of Piero, who at fifteen was betrothed to a distant cousin, Alfonsina Orsini, daughter of one of Ferrante's dearest friends and a favorite with the Roman members of the family. Lorenzo's opinion of his wife's kinsmen was low.

"The brains of these Orsini are of a strange and peculiar nature," he said after he had been married some years. "They are greedy and ambitious, and if not kept in order by necessity they are unstable."

Nevertheless they were a powerful clan, and Ferrante approved the match. Lorenzo was eager enough for it to cancel all the debts which the Neapolitan Orsini had contracted with his bank, and he was prepared to welcome a daughter-in-law who was, if Bernardo Rucellai could be trusted, by no means charming. Bernardo, as Ambassador to Naples, arranged the details of the marriage settlement. In order to catch a glimpse of Alfonsina before he made an offer he was obliged, much to his distaste, to consort with the very young bloods "so much that you would think I had gone back several years." At last he met a gawky child of fifteen—he was told she was only thirteen—whose throat was "somewhat thick at the back." This, however, proved to be only a temporary swelling, but Bernardo was not much impressed.

"Her arms, which are usually a guide to the legs, are good, and also her hands," he wrote dispassionately. "She seems to be straight, but about this and her height I will tell you another time. Her skin is good and she has a good natural color. Her eyes are light, she has a good nose and her mouth, though a little heavy, does not destroy her charm. But I may be mistaken, for I have only seen her once and then with respect."

Determined to be cautious in such a delicate undertaking as his nephew's marriage, he added:

"Anyhow I may be mistaken in some of the details I have given you, for you know how easy it is for a man to be deceived. A mother would rather show her daughter to ten men than to one woman."

The Medici were well enough satisfied with the description, but the negotiations were long and acrimonious. Lorenzo insisted that in exchange for cancelling the Orsini debts, Alfonsina should bring a large dowry. For months the plenipotentiaries wrangled and Piero waited.

Lorenzo turned his attention to finding husbands for his other daughters. He was also a little worried about Maddalena. Her real marriage was hurried on quicker than he liked. Clarice had gone to Rome to visit her family for the winter. Her favorite daughter went with her, and it was known that the girl would join her husband. None of the Medici children ever left home without a few parting words of advice from their father, who could on such occasions assume a pomposity with which Machiavelli could not quarrel.

"Remember," he told Maddalena, "the sacredness of the place where you are and what the Roman people expect of you. Consider that while it is shameful to neglect your duties, it is honorable to perform them well, and do not forget that your first duty is to please the Pope and to cherish your husband."

On a bleak November day the little girl went through the splendor of a Church wedding and almost at once learned that she had stepped from a carefree, comfortable home into a life filled with disillusionment. She had no friends in Rome save Matteo Franco, sent by Lorenzo to act as her chaplain, entertainer, instructor and man of business. The wit was very fond of his patron's daughter, but Franceschetto kept him so busy he had little time to amuse her. Most of her days were spent with Clarice, whose consumptive cough was bad that winter, making her a most querulous companion. By spring both women were eager to return to Florence. Maddalena was almost deprived of that pleasure, for Franceschetto liked to assert his conjugal authority and only yielded when Lorenzo asked as a special favor that the girl be permitted to accompany her mother.

Once at home they learned that all the family except the priestly Giovanni and little Giuliano had been taken to the matrimonial market. Despite gout so bad that he spent many anguished weeks at the baths, despite the press of foreign and domestic business, Lorenzo had put through the marriage settlements of his remaining three daughters, and the dowries were only two thousand ducats each, the usual portion of a Florentine maiden of good family. Furthermore all three girls would stay at home in Florence. Lucrezia, now eighteen, was destined to heal the last of the Pazzi conspiracy enmities. She was betrothed to Giacopo Salviati, cousin of the Archbishop. Luigia was to marry Giovanni de' Medici, her cousin. Contessina, although only eleven, was promised to Piero Ridolfi, whose family had adhered to the Medici without the faintest sign of disloyalty ever since old Cosimo's day.

While these settlements were being made, contracts signed, money passed and dates set, Piero was off to the south to bring home his bride. The Orsini had reluctantly consented to give twelve thousand ducats with Alfonsina. After nearly a year of bargaining the deal was finally closed by a brilliant ceremony in Ferrante's palace. The King, the Queen, all the nobles of the court attended in their best robes of state, but the bridegroom was not there. He was represented by proxy and saw his wife for the first time three months after the wedding. They met in Rome and returned together to Florence.

Celebrations designed to recall the splendor of Lorenzo's union to Clarice had been prepared but were never carried out. The bridal couple reached home only a few days after Luigia died, and the whole family was in mourning. Alfonsina entered a silent city and rode through it to Careggi without stopping. She did not see her famous father-in-law for some days. He had to see too many ambassadors, too many office seekers, too many merchants. When he could escape he did not go to Careggi. Not for a new daughter-in-law, certainly not for an Orsini, would he miss one of those protracted poetic sessions at Fiesole where the nights were cool and the soft breezes rustled the trees while the stars twinkled above the talk and from the walls of Florence the cries of the watchmen rose faintly to the group taking their wine on the hillside.

A son-in-law was different, and Lorenzo felt obliged to welcome Franceschetto Cibo and his dull companions from Rome in person. The Captain General of the Church was eager to sample the famous Medici hospitality, and he timed his arrival well. Even Lorenzo laid aside his mourning for San Giovanni's Day. There was more to it this year than the festival of Florence's patron saint. The betrothals in the Medici family were to be celebrated in the lapse from mourning. For days the studios had been working overtime to decorate the triumphal cars which Lorenzo had ordered for the pageant. Rare fireworks exploding above the floats gave the semblance of clouds, while from concealed traps painted demons popped out to be quelled by benignant angels in robes of silk and halos of gold.

The weavers, goldsmiths, carpenters and masons of Florence, connoisseurs in such displays, pro-

nounced the festival a great success. But Franceschetto Cibo was worried. He was lodged in the Via
Larga while his companions were accommodated in
other palaces. The Captain General was disappointed to return from dazzling spectacles outdoors
to very plain dinners. There were no wild parties,
no breathless gaming, no gay ladies in the Medici
Palace. Most of the guests were men and most of the
talk about books or some silly theatrical entertainment
for which, it appeared, his host had written the words.
The visitor was bored. Worse than that, he feared
the ridicule of his fellows to whom he had promised
a reception more magnificent than their dreams. At
last he became despondent enough to apologize for
bringing them to such simple homes. They were
amazed.

"If I were the Pope himself," one Roman cavalier
exclaimed, "I could not be more splendidly housed
or more highly honored."

Franceschetto was relieved, but he cherished some
resentment on his own account. He did not see why
he should have been allied to the only stingy man in
Florence. His feeling was so obvious that his host
felt explanations were due.

"Your friends," he said, "are strangers here, but
you are my son, and we would not treat you otherwise than as one of the family."

Outside the home Lorenzo was spending money
with a freedom which concealed the fact that in the
confusion following the death of Louis of France,

the Medici Bank at Lyons was unable to pay deposits, and Lorenzo was obliged to compound with his creditors. Such trifles should not be allowed to mar the enjoyment of the carnival. He borrowed some more money from his cousins and went on with the rehearsals of the play he had written for the family. There was a part for each one. It was the last time all the children would be together under his roof. Maddalena would soon be returning to Rome, the other girls to their husbands, Giovanni to complete his education at Pisa. They were making the most of it, and they were all young enough to enjoy playacting. They were exceedingly merry as they prepared their parts, all but Franceschetto. The title of the piece was "San Giovanni and San Paolo," the theme the apostasy of Julian. As given before a select audience of friends and relatives, the show was an immense success. The critics said it was not only genuine poetry but that the triumph of pure religion was complete when Lorenzo in the title rôle brought the performance to a laudably pious end with the wail:

"Oh Christ, the Galilean, thou after all hast conquered."

The playwright did not remain long to enjoy the applause. He was no longer strong enough to bear such rich festivities as had honored Saint John this year. The excitement buoyed him until the floats had been dismantled, the costumes put away, the guests departed. Then he collapsed, an old man of nearly forty, crippled by gout, tortured by indigestion, barely able to hobble from one room to another, but still doing as much work as was needed to keep the peace. Anne, the Regent of France, was trying to draw him into her struggle to prevent the Pope from crowning Maximilian of Austria. No one but himself could be trusted to compose the kind of despatches that would keep him neutral without losing French good will. He had written some of them between the acts of "San Giovanni and San Paolo." He wrote the rest at Filetta, a lonely little resort in the hills to which his physicians had ordered him so that he would find repose which he did not want.

He left Clarice sick, but not noticeably more so than she had been for months. Her consumption had pursued its normal course. Sometimes she was quite animated. Suddenly, a few days after Lorenzo departed, she took to her bed and a few hours later, with only Maddalena near her, she was dead.

"I had told you that Madonna Clarice was ill," the Ferrarese Ambassador wrote to his master. "She died three days ago, but I did not send the news at once as it did not seem of much importance. Now that I am despatching the courier with letters from Naples, I inform your Excellency."

At Filetta the news was received with composure. Lorenzo did not return for the funeral. He would have been too late, for Clarice was buried, simply and with very few mourners, in San Lorenzo the same day she died. More elaborate ceremonies, at

FIORENZA

The Florence of the Renaissance.   An Engraving
of 1490

which the foreign Ambassadors figured more prom-
inently than citizens of Florence, were held a few
days later, but the bereaved husband was still in
Filetta writing correct expressions of a sorrow which
he considered became him.

"Being thus deprived of her sweet accustomed
company," the Pope was informed by the man who
did not see his wife if he could help it for months on
end, "has grieved me so much that I can find no
remedy. However, I do not cease to pray God to
give me peace, and I have a firm hope in His divine
goodness and that He will make an end of my great
pain and will not thrust upon me more such trials
as I have suffered for some time past. And I most
humbly beg Your Holiness from the depths of my
heart to deign to pray for me, for I know how anxious
you are to help me. I commend myself to you and to
your Holy Feet."

Repose and the Filetta waters had wrought no
improvement in his own health. With a train of
secretaries to attend to the business which he insisted
on transacting, he wandered from Filetta to Poggio
to Spedaletto, where couriers on horseback brought
him the healing waters of Morba. None of them
availed, and at last he returned to Florence where,
if he must suffer, he could at least do it in congenial
company. He could also try the skill of a new physician, Petrus Bonus Avogarius, who was sure he
could cure gout by an infallible system of his own
invention.

[*289*]

Lorenzo submitted to the course of treatment hopefully. There was a soothing ointment for his inflamed joints and a most vile medicine, whose ingredients were not disclosed, to be taken at sunrise once a month. It meant getting up early, but anything for health. At the beginning of spring he was to take a violent purge, and always he was to wear on the third finger of the left hand a sapphire set in gold so that the gem would touch the skin.

"This is a certain preservative against both gout and rheumatism," the learned physician explained. "I have tried it myself and found that its properties are divine and miraculous."

Still the gouty inflammations persisted. Petrus could not understand it, but before Lorenzo returned to the ministrations of more conservative practitioners and their time-honored specific of pearls ground up in wine, Avogarius begged for one more chance. He would procure for his patient a bit of celandine, "a red stone that grows in the stomach of the swallow." If Lorenzo would wear this sewn in his shirt just under the left breast, recovery was certain.

In Florence Lorenzo had no time to coddle his illness. There were too many things to do. Ferrante and the Pope were quarrelling again, just because the King had broken his word and murdered a few of the barons who had encouraged Innocent to assert his claim to Naples. Lorenzo wrote many soothing letters urging everyone to be calm. To His

Holiness he felt called upon to point out that Franceschetto was still waiting for the estates which a
Pope's son ought to possess. Innocent was too timid
and his son too lethargic to attempt anything really
big in the way of nepotism. But the son had told
Lorenzo the only way to deal with his father.

"Like the ox, he needs the goad," said Cibo.

So Lorenzo prodded, very respectfully. He reminded His Holiness that even Popes do not live
forever but he hoped the delay in providing for the
young couple was due to carelessness.

"My daughter has to be stinted," he complained
to his Ambassador, "and I am in despair about the
little care that is taken of these matters there."

But his goading did no good, and he turned to
the task of conciliating Venice, for his envoy there
had informed him:

"The Venetians detest your name more than
Satan detests the cross."

They did not like to see anyone so powerful that
if he should take it into his head he might stir up all
Italy against them. Lorenzo had to convince them
that such a thing would never occur to him. In
addition to this diplomatic chore he was saying a
few prayers of thanks for the sudden death of
Girolamo Riario and composing a very nasty quarrel
between the Manfredi and the Bentivogli.

Ever since his father's death, Girolamo had been
living unobtrusively at Forli. He indulged his talents
for intrigue and cruelty at the expense of his subjects,

no wider field offering. He mulcted and humiliated them so severely that at last they rebelled, but it was not easy to get at him, for he never moved abroad without a guard of well paid, well treated mercenaries. Finally the leaders of the revolt hid themselves in his bedroom and stabbed him as he came in from supper. His stripped, mutilated corpse was thrown from the window as a signal to the citizenry to rise and assert their independence. The Count's wife, Caterina, and their three children were captured by the ringleaders, but the fortress on the hill above Forli was loyal to the Riario and the garrison was strong. Caterina offered to persuade them to surrender, leaving her children with the people as evidence of her good faith. Once inside the fortress she thumbed her nose at the rabble, telling them graphically just what her brother in Milan would do to them. The rebels replied by erecting a gallows on the hillside. They threatened to hang her children there in her sight one after another unless she surrendered.

"Hang them," retorted Caterina. "I can get more."

The children were spared to rule Forli under the protection of Duke Ludovico, but Lorenzo gave thanks to God that one more of Giuliano's murderers had been fittingly punished.

The affair of the Manfredi and Bentivogli was less pleasing. It was just another of those little disputes that were always being brought to Lorenzo for his decision. This one was his fault to begin with, for out of sheer love of meddling he had arranged a marriage between Galeotto Manfredi, Prince of Faenza, and Francesca Bentivoglio, daughter of a Bolognese condottiere often used by Florence. The husband was a huge, good natured, credulous soul with a taste for astrology and women. His wife, a shrewish dame with a poisonously witty tongue, resented both his hobbies. She upbraided him violently and constantly until he, slow of speech and unable to think of adequate repartee, beat her and locked her up.

Her father rode gallantly to the rescue. He kidnapped his daughter, escaped back to his own country and prepared for war. That brought the Manfredi domestic relations into the class of politics that concerned Lorenzo. He offered his mediation and persuaded Francesca to return to her husband. Galeotto promised to restrain his temper if she would hold her tongue. But he did not reform his other habits. He still consulted the stars to the accompaniment of mysterious incantations. He still carried on amorous intrigues with the ladies of the court. One night, returning late, he was informed that his wife was ill and wished to see him. As he approached her bed, four men sprang from under it and rushed him. Galeotto was a strong man, and though wounded had nearly gained the door when Francesca, attired only in her shift, jumped out of bed, seized a sword and ran him through from behind.

The murdered prince had been popular. His subjects were determined to punish his assassins. Bentivoglio was equally determined to protect his daughter. Again war threatened; again Lorenzo forced a compromise. Francesca was to go into a convent and meditate on the sin of jealousy. Her father was to go home and stop annoying Faenza. He did, but he did not stop annoying the arbitrator. Before long Lorenzo, wearied of Bentivoglio's importunities, was asking the Pope to release Francesca from her vows; her father had found her another husband.

Truly, Lorenzo murmured, the way of the statesman is hard. But the blessings of peace must be preserved.

XXIII

Once again Lorenzo was corresponding actively with the Pope, but this time Naples and Franceschetto's financial affairs were subordinated to the advancement of "our Messer Giovanni." He had been paving the way with hints for years, but now he was openly bidding for a Cardinalate. The ambition he had once entertained so hopefully for his brother should be realized in his son. Giovanni was only thirteen, but time was pressing. Innocent was subject to fainting spells; another Pope might not be so favorably inclined to the Medici.

Influence was brought to bear in many quarters. Franceschetto pleaded for his brother-in-law. Cardinal Sforza, Ludovico's brother, was enlisted. For a consideration Cardinal Borgia was willing to urge the appointment and no churchman had more success. Lorenzo was eager to use this man, although he was suspicious of the Spaniard. Rodrigo's ability to ingratiate himself with anyone made him formidable. He was so greedy he might become dangerous. Despite waves of anti-Spanish feeling which had swept through Rome at intervals since his uncle's death, he had remained high in the favor of every Pope. He had an uncanny sense for anticipating the direction in which conclaves would swing, and the successful candidate was always under obligations to him for leading the shift. He was popular with the mob for his good nature and with the worldlings for his lavish, riotous parties, to which husbands were never invited.

Presenting to the world this front of careless good fellowship, Rodrigo was unostentatiously amassing great wealth. He was supposed to spend most of his gains on his children, but a few knew that he was hoarding immense treasure. Lorenzo as a banker was one of the few, and he wondered about it. The energy, the ambition, the ruthlessness of Pope Alex-ander VI had not yet been displayed by Cardinal Borgia, but Lorenzo seems to have sensed them. Giovanni thought of his father's warnings a few years later when Rodrigo used his savings to buy the tiara.

"We are in the jaws of the wolf," the boy whis-pered to a kinsman. "He will gulp us down if we do not make good our escape."

Meanwhile His Eminence could be useful. He was most obliging in the matter of the Cardinalate, and the process of goading Innocent went on apace.

In Florence Lorenzo was taking on a few new hobbies to beguile his old age. With only the peace of Italy, the affairs of his banks and farms, the manipulations of the Monte, the Platonic Academy, poetry and painting to interest him, he found some spare time at his disposal. His grandchildren claimed a little of it. He had to write many letters and select suitable presents when Maddalena bore her uninterested husband a daughter. Lorenzo was pleased that they named the child Lucrezia out of regard for his mother, but his real delight was saved for the birth in September of Piero's son. Here was an heir to all his greatness. The proud grandfather, looking at the unimpressive morsel of humanity, was sure that this little Lorenzo would outdo him magnificently. With the ruler of Florence for a father and a Pope— why not?—for an uncle, there could be no limits to his possibilities. Yet all the gods had reserved for this child was a miserable, futile ascendancy during which he was really ruled by his mother and his uncle, and such flickers of fame as he derived from being the grandfather of the family's most prominent woman, Catherine de' Medici, Queen of France.

Lorenzo's other idle moments were divided between Filippo Strozzi and the encouragement of sculpture in a serious way, for he suddenly realized that this one of the arts was lagging behind in the development of Florentine culture.

The cautious Filippo had been bitten by the bug of ambition. He wanted to build the finest palace in Florence, but he was afraid. Every time he walked beyond the Arno he could see the huge ruinous emptiness that was to be the Pitti Palace. Old Luca had been ambitious too, and see what had happened to him. Of course Strozzi was no politician, but Lorenzo might not understand if his desires were too openly expressed.

"He feared," wrote the ambitious one's son, "that the man who was at the head of the government might take it into his head that the reputation of another would put his own in the shade, and Filippo was in great dread of exciting envy."

After all, he had spent many years in exile, and he had grown timid. He did not want to be driven back to Naples just for the gratification of his ambition. So he dissembled beautifully. He mentioned to everyone he met, and his voice was mournful, that his family had grown so large he would have to build a new house. Fortunately, and here he seemed to cheer up a trifle, he had a plot of ground near the Mercato Vecchio across the street from the Tornabuoni Palace. Cherishing the dream of a building that would put all other private houses to shame, Filippo said aloud that of course his place would be nothing like so grand as his neighbor's.

"Just a home for my family," he explained, and went on to moan grievously about the expense.

He was, he lied, a poor man. It was a great blow to him to have to build at all. But his face brightened as he suggested that perhaps he might have shops on the ground floor. That would help. Benedetto da Majano, as architects will, proposed more elaborate designs, far less imposing than what Filippo had in mind, but he feigned a great reluctance to give up the idea of shops. By this time Lorenzo heard of it, and he fell hard into the trap which Strozzi had so neatly laid for him.

"He who then governed the destinies of the city," wrote the builder's son, "began to meddle in the matter and asked to see the plans."

This was nothing unusual—he meddled in everything—and just what Filippo wanted. For once Lorenzo got started, he developed an enthusiasm equal to and much more loudly expressed than Filippo's own. He egged the cautious one on with great gusto. He suggested and advised. He insisted that here was a great opportunity to adorn the City of Flowers worthily, to surpass all other buildings in beauty and set a new style. Filippo pleaded poverty. Lorenzo ignored him. Filippo objected that grandeur like this ill became a simple citizen. Lorenzo brushed the argument aside.

So at last it worked out as Filippo had always meant that it should. He allowed himself to be persuaded. He even made a few suggestions himself. At last one August morning as the sun rose—the horoscope casters had selected that hour as propitious—the cornerstone of the Strozzi Palace was laid with much formality. Lorenzo strolled by much later in the day to felicitate Filippo, and each of them looked upon the palace as his own work as they watched it rise in an unparalleled beauty of stonework to fulfill the old merchant's dream, a dream he did not live to see completed.

While Lorenzo stood with the other idlers watching the workmen, a handsome lad of fourteen was exclaiming with incoherent cries of pleasure over

the beauties of the Medici art collections to which
he had just been introduced. Young Michelangelo
Buonarroti was entering on the only truly happy
period of a long, glorious career. He had been given
the privilege of working in these lovely gardens,
where men he had learned to revere spent their days
walking, sketching or talking with enthusiasm about
art. The boy's fingers itched for a chisel. Michelangelo had looked forward to the changes in his life
with more than the normal joy of youth in new
surroundings. Home had been for him a rather unpleasant place. His father, Ludovico, was a ruined
gentleman, and that was his sole occupation. It
provided only a precarious livelihood for his family.
He cared nothing at all for the beauties of line and
form of which his son dreamed passionately.

At thirteen Michelangelo was very glad to escape
from the wretched paternal abode to become one
of the great Ghirlandaio's apprentices. He had expected the whole world to unfold for him at once,
and indeed in the immense *bottega* where the popular
master lived and worked things were a little better.
But the boy was disconcertingly swift to learn. He
distanced his companions easily and, although the
most kindly of boys outside the studio, he could
never cure himself of saying unpleasant truths, made
more unpleasant by the sting of sarcasm, about the
work of others. Even after Piero Torrigiano used a
fist as repartee and broke Michelangelo's nose, the
habit persisted.

Within a year he was chafing under the slow progress permitted him as an apprentice. Naturally he was speechless with joy when Ghirlandaio told him he might finish his term under the eye of the Magnificent Lorenzo. A new school was being formed in the gardens of San Marco where old Bertoldo, with his interminable stories of the great Donatello, under whom he had studied, had been assigned the task of raising the standard of Florentine sculpture. Michelangelo and Francesco Granacci, also one of Ghirlandaio's apprentices, were his youngest pupils. It was as near Heaven as the ardent young sculptor could imagine. The only real work he had was blocking out some marble for the Library of San Lorenzo which his new master was building back of the parish church. All the rest of his time was his own to dream, to study, to chisel. He looked with adoration upon his patron, and before long his patron was looking with interest upon him.

The boy was so absorbed in copying in marble a faun's head, a grinning bit of antique sculpture that had long fascinated him, that he did not hear Lorenzo approaching up the garden path. For some time the great man, unobserved, watched in silence.

"You ought to know that the old never have all their teeth," he said at last, and passed on leaving the boy shivering with joyous excitement. The patron had noticed him!

A few days later Lorenzo strolled that way again and was pleased. The faun was grinning toothlessly now. Michelangelo had an instinctive suppleness in dealing with the mighty which was lacking in the older da Vinci. Lorenzo nodded his head approvingly as he looked, but he was still sparing with words.

"Go and tell your father that I wish to speak to him," was all he said.

The elder Buonarroti wasted no time in hurrying to the Medici Palace. He was a little disappointed that Lorenzo wanted to talk only about the boy's future, not about the father's unrecognized abilities. Ludovico had never been able to distinguish between a stone-cutter and a sculptor; it ill became a gentleman's son to be either, he believed. But he knew a gentleman's duty to the powerful, so he told Lorenzo:

"In faith, not Michelangelo alone but all of us with our lives and all our abilities are at the pleasure of Your Magnificence."

Lorenzo did not think much of the abilities of the rest of the family, but he took the hint. He asked Ludovico whether he would not like to serve the State and if so in what capacity. Buonarroti missed an excellent opportunity. He did not know how high a value Lorenzo set upon art, and he had little faith in his son's talents. He asked modestly for a place in the customs house, a position involving as little work as he was accustomed to, but paying only the miserable pittance of about eight scudi a month. Lorenzo was surprised, and a little contemptuous, at such moderation.

"You will always be poor," he said, but Buonarroti got the job he asked.

For the son more generous provision was made.
He was given a room in the Medici Palace, told to
draw on his patron for his clothes and allowed five
ducats a month for pocket money. He moved in at
once, receiving from his father this bit of advice
which Ludovico considered suitable for a gentleman's son starting out in the world:

"Above all things take care of your head and keep
it moderately warm, and see that you never wash.
Have yourself rubbed down, but do not wash."

Michelangelo moved into a household rendered
exceptionally good natured by success. Innocent had
at last felt the goad. Giovanni was to be a Cardinal,
but on certain conditions. The new Prince of the
Church was to be reserved *in petto* for at least three
years. Until then no one was to know that His
Holiness had given the Red Hat to a child not yet
fourteen, for Innocent had promised the conclave
that elected him to create no Cardinals under thirty.
It was a hard blow, for it meant there could be no
celebration. Lorenzo had planned something quite
out of the ordinary. The Pope also insisted that
Giovanni was to pursue his studies diligently. Perhaps if he were a good boy he would not have to
wait the full three years to be proclaimed.

On this understanding the deal was closed, and
Lorenzo felt once more the glow of triumphant
achievement, a feeling which had eluded him for

years and which he would never feel again. He had placed his family in such security, he thought, that they could not fail to go on to splendors greater than anything he had known. He was in an extremely pious frame of mind, for he had been thinking much of spiritual affairs in the course of the negotiations for the Cardinalate. As usual his emotions found expression in poetry, and in a burst of tuneful gratitude to God for the favors he had showered upon the family Lorenzo wrote in paraphrase of the Hebrew singer:

> *Let all of good this bosom fires*
> *To Him, sole good, give praises due.*
> *Let all the truth Himself inspires*
> *Unite to sing Him only true.*
> *To Him my every thought ascend,*
> *To Him my hopes, my wishes bend.*
> *From earth's wide bounds let louder hymns arise,*
> *And His own word convey the pious sacrifice.*

The poet's piety was genuine, despite his detailed knowledge of how the Church operated in its spiritual functions. Intelligent men made a very real distinction between their religion and the Church. As a sensible, reflective human being, Lorenzo regarded his relations with God as quite personal. For the Church, recognized as the traditional medium of communication with Heaven, he had affection without respect. With the direct clear-sighted simplicity which men were beginning to apply to such problems, he expected the Lord to understand that he was dealing with life as he found it, not as he would like it to be. To him no material good in life was any the less tasty for having been acquired by doubtful means. He did not see why the same rule should not apply to spiritual goods. So, on both counts, he rejoiced in Giovanni's Cardinalate.

Within a few weeks news of the boy's elevation leaked out. Innocent was furious; Lorenzo quite well pleased that the world should know to what heights he had been able to raise his son. Nevertheless, there was a momentary coolness in his relations with the Holy See for Innocent accused the Florentines of boasting while Lorenzo insisted the leak could only have been in Rome, and Giovanni went unostentatiously to Pisa to carry out the Pope's exhortations that he study hard and fit himself for his exalted station. No lad of fourteen could have taken the dignity more seriously. Giovanni was naturally studious and he knew his father was keeping a close watch on him.

Pisa had changed greatly from the dull, deserted little town in which Lorenzo had planted a university seventeen years before. It had grown; life had returned; it was possible to be quite gay. Many students took advantage of the opportunity. During Giovanni's attendance there he saw plenty of riotous living, for to Pisa came the young Cesare Borgia, bringing with him a reputation for brilliant scholarship at Perugia. Later came Alessandro Farnese, with no reputation for scholarship as yet. Both young men maintained elaborate establishments at the expense of Cardinal Borgia, for Cesare was his favorite son and Alessandro was the brother of Giulia la Bella, Rodrigo's then mistress. Both were accustomed to the dissipations which were rather more open in Rome than in Florence. They were handsome, engaging young devils and quickly took the lead in all the pleasures of university life.

Giovanni, plump, plain and temperamentally grave, was not much in their society. All three were destined for the Church, but the Medici, though the youngest, was already a Cardinal; the others were not even protonotaries, although Lorenzo, returning Borgia's favors in the matter of his son's elevation, wrote letters of recommendation for young Farnese's advancement saying:

"I wish you to know that this gentleman, besides coming of such a noble family has many distinguished qualities, among them unusual learning and excellent morals, being at once very accomplished and a model of virtuous conduct. I recommend him to you as if he were my own son."

This was not quite Alessandro's reputation at Pisa, and Lorenzo's own son saw little of him, keeping to his books and his lectures, distinguishing himself in learned debates on legal and theological subjects while Borgia and the future Pope Paul III drank and hunted and organized parties for the ladies.

Giovanni was so obviously being a good boy that his father thought he had earned public recognition of his rank. Innocent's fainting spells were more frequent and alarming. Once he had been sunk so long in a stupor that it was rumored he was dead. If he should die with Giovanni still *in petto* the whole long intrigue would be to do all over again. Lorenzo became importunate, but Innocent, grown more slippery and dilatory with increasing age, could hardly ever be prevailed upon to make decisions. He still had scruples about admitting such a child to the Sacred College, although Lorenzo pretended to believe that the mere appointment had conferred upon the boy some divine grace which made him worthy of his honor.

"Messer Giovanni," he wrote to his Roman Ambassador the day after he heard of the nomination, "has grown and changed since yesterday. I pray that this dignity may be prosperous and happy for him, that he may prove a column of strength to the tottering Church."

XXIV

Over his wine in the Medici Palace, Pico was getting eloquent. He had been travelling again, this time without exciting any scandal, and at Reggio he had heard a Voice. It had stirred him wonderfully, for with all his inquiring nature, he was susceptible to emotional appeals. Furthermore, the impression of mystic power which the Voice had left had not faded, and Pico could talk of nothing else. Never, he declared with emphasis, was there such a preacher as Fra Girolamo Savonarola.

Most of the other men at the dinner table had ceased to listen to him, but sitting near the patron Michelangelo saw that Lorenzo was interested. He heard Lorenzo asking questions about the object of Pico's admiration, and the conversation returned to that subject. A few of the guests remembered the man, a Dominican friar from Ferrara, who had preached with but little success in Florence six or seven years ago. Perhaps Lorenzo recalled his Lenten sermon in San Lorenzo about that time? No, if he had heard it, the patron had not been impressed.

But Pico's enthusiasm was contagious. Florence must have the best of everything if Lorenzo was to justify his existence to himself. He could get anything he wanted from any monastic order, and he asked for Fra Girolamo. There was only a little delay, and on the first of August, 1490, at San Marco His Magnificence heard for the first time the Voice which was to call down ruin on everything he loved. He listened critically to the harsh, vibrant tones, observed without emotion the fierce gestures, analyzed disapprovingly the fanatic doctrine of imminent, terrible punishment which was to descend upon the city of wickedness. Lorenzo did not share Pico's admiration for this type of oratory. He thought Fra Mariano, the Augustinian, a far better preacher, Fra Mariano spoke like a man of the world as well as a priest, ardently at times and stirringly, but with a polish, a delicate wit, a restrained force much more effective, coldly philosophical hearers maintained, than the wild fury of the reformer.

However, Lorenzo had not yet brought the general taste for oratory to such a discriminating level. It became not only popular but fashionable to attend the sermons in which Savonarola so confidently predicted woe and doom for a godless generation lost in the impious pursuit of pleasure. But while they listened, no one except a few impressionable mystics like Pico allowed themselves to be diverted from the chase.

In his youth Fra Girolamo had been horrified by the lavish lasciviousness of the Este court. He left home to enter the monastery, certain that God would smite the blasphemers who surrounded the Duke in his big red castle. Florence, he thought, was even worse than Ferrara. The whole city lived only for the pleasures of the flesh, and to Savonarola all such pleasures were equally damned. All art unless devoted to religion, all song except sacred music, all laughter, all conviviality, all adornment of the person were denounced with a fervor surpassing anything his audiences had ever witnessed. Besides, this strange man spoke in terms of Holy Writ instead of deriving his learned discourses from the Greek and Roman philosophers. He was a decided novelty. He sent shivers of delicious fear rippling down almost every spine in Florence, and the excitement was increased by Fra Mariano, who took it upon himself to deny the foreigner's theory that God was angry.

Lorenzo took no part and but little interest in the theological dispute. He had built for the Augustinian a magnificent new convent close to the San Gallo gate, had favored him above all Florentine preachers. But the Medici were also the patrons of San Marco, and their donations largely supported the Dominican establishment.

Lorenzo was inclined to dismiss the whole controversy as the vaporings of an ignorant or hypocritical mind. It was impossible that he should consider seriously Savonarola's denunciations and warnings. He had made Florence what it was, and he was proud of his work. He had only scorn for those who refused to pay homage to beauty. He believed that the amusements of the people, their pageants, their gambling, their merry evenings in the taverns were quite harmless. Certainly they were better than the gloomy meditations which seemed to be Fra Girolamo's only substitute.

The warnings of the Dominican preacher made far less difference in his life than a new treatment he was trying for the gout. Dr. Pier Leoni had written out these instructions for the avoidance of those ever increasing maladies which tormented Lorenzo's days:

"Beware of cold and damp feet, of moonlight and of the air at sunset, and do not eat pears or swallow grape pips."

While Fra Girolamo declaimed against the frivolities of the world, Lorenzo continued to enjoy as many of them as he could. As for the prosperity which Savonarola denounced, the peace of which he predicted the speedy end, the ruler of Florence wrote proudly:

"I have contributed to the welfare of my country, the prosperity of which may now rival that of any other state, however flourishing."

It was also a source of much self congratulation to him that in spite of the temptations which great accumulations of wealth offered, crime was almost abolished. In a day when no man travelled without armed escorts, when Rome was represented as a den of thieves and cutthroats, a traveller wrote with amazement of Florence:

"We have here no robberies, no nocturnal commotions, no assassinations. By night or by day every person may transact his concerns in perfect safety. Spies and informers are here unknown. The accusation of one is not suffered to affect the safety of the many, for it is a maxim with Lorenzo, 'It is better to confide in all than in a few.'"

Of course the millennium was not yet. The fierce watch dogs were still trained to bite; the bars on the merchant's windows were thick; the dagger was still universally worn, and there were enough brawls going that young Piero de' Medici, untamed by family cares, "found himself present at the death of a man or two," Guicciardini remembered.

Not since before the Pazzi conspiracy had Lorenzo been so free to devote himself to his favorite amusements. Indeed, he was even indulging in dreams of complete retirement from active participation in affairs. His youthful craving for power, which even in youth he had deplored, had at last been surfeited. One evening after a particularly satisfying meeting of the Fiesole colony he amazed Poliziano by declaring quite calmly and without the petulance with which he sometimes commented on a statesman's troubles, that he intended to resign all his authority, retreat to one of his country places "far from the tumult of the city" and devote himself to study with his learned friends. Poliziano cried out that the State could never do without him, the natural thought of all his friends, for they had never known a Florence in which the Medici were not all-powerful.

"I shall provide a substitute in the person of your pupil," Lorenzo answered with a smile, "and entrust the burden to his shoulders."

Poliziano was doubtful. It was his habit on all occasions to exaggerate Piero's ability and intelligence, but in his heart he knew that the young man, reckless, addicted to sports and fighting, was not fit to rule Florence. He was a bright lad, but far from the precocious youngster his father had been. Besides, there was the Orsini heritage of pride and greed. Piero liked to push himself forward at all times, and one day would push into trouble. And always his tactlessness was encouraged by that hard, grasping little person, Alfonsina. On this night Lorenzo argued that his son was quite competent, but he ended with a sigh, for he knew Piero's limitations. His own desire for a rest, however, persisted, and as usual he put it into writing, expressing what he conceived to be the convictions of all sensible men.

"What can be more desirable to a well regulated mind than the enjoyment of leisure with dignity?" he asked. "This is what all good men wish to obtain, but which great men alone accomplish. Having now obtained the object of my cares, I trust I may be allowed to enjoy the sweets of leisure, to share the reputation of my fellow citizens and to exult in the glory of my native place."

As an ideal it was admirable; as a practical programme it proved to be impossible. Lorenzo consoled himself by having a new organ installed in his

house, making five in all, and by sketching a plan
for the façade of the Cathedral. He spent many
hours with his music, trifling at the four little organs
or attempting ambitious sounds on the big one with
the carved wooden case. His plan for the façade was
carefully filed away to be forgotten, Lorenzo himself
urging the builders to be in no hurry to select any
design.

He even found time as spring wore on to interest
himself in the sayings and doings of Savonarola.
After his first few outbursts the preacher had devoted
himself to the instruction of novices and the writing
of some philosophical treatises remarkable for their
cruel theological mysticism. But soon he returned to
the pulpit. The crowd of his admirers was too great
for his own church and he had to preach his Lenten
sermon in Santa Maria del Fiore. Stimulated by
success, he grew increasingly violent in his denunciations. His warnings of the horrors to which the people
were exposing themselves by their sins became ever
more picturesque. His predictions of divine vengeance were soon alarmingly specific.

They became so specific that at last Lorenzo
thought it time to interfere. Savonarola had singled
him out as the epitome of all that ailed Florence, and
at first Lorenzo had tolerantly remarked that so long
as the good monk was improving the conduct of
the people, he could forgive any libels against himself. But when the preacher extended his remarks to
attack the principles which Lorenzo had been trying

to teach the mob for years, the ruler decided upon action. He sent a delegation of five, headed by Bernardo Rucellai, to advise Savonarola to moderate his language. Fra Girolamo turned upon them in his best pulpit manner. They would be far better employed, he told them bitterly, if they were advising Lorenzo to repent of his sins. The delegation reminded him there was a law making attacks upon Lorenzo equivalent to attacks upon the State. They had been authorized to give some gentle hints about the possibility of exile, but they only aroused the monk's prophetic spirit.

"Lorenzo is a Florentine citizen and I am a stranger," he exclaimed in an exalted tone, turning his face towards Heaven, "but he will go and I shall remain."

Once started he was not easy to stop, and Lorenzo's emissaries were treated to one of Fra Girolamo's most effective sermons, that in which he predicted wholesale death and destruction, the passing of powerful Popes and kings, the ravages of war, the sacking of cities, all the barbarities of a retribution which he believed to be the aim of an all-merciful, all-loving God. The five returned to their leader with word that the Dominican was incorrigible. Some of them suggested punitive measures, but Lorenzo refused to be alarmed. He put aside with gestures of distaste all proposals for teaching the preacher his place. He did not even object—and his least word would have put an end to all Savonarola's prospects for advancement—when his enemy was elected Prior of San Marco. The convent had been a particular object of Medici generosity for nearly a century. The head of the family was regarded as the patron of the Dominican Order in Florence, and three generations had been accustomed to receive a formal visit of respect from every new prior. Such a tradition could find little favor with Savonarola. He scornfully rejected the idea of showing any marks of courtesy to the man he believed to be Satan's most valued instrument in the corruption of the people.

"I hold my election from God alone," he cried with a pride which he believed to be sinful. "To him alone I owe obedience."

Lorenzo's views on the responsibility for Savonarola's election and the monk's debt of gratitude were rather different.

"A stranger has come into my house and does not deign to visit me," he commented.

Still he made no move against the Prior. His gifts to the monastery continued as before, although Savonarola was careful to pass his gold pieces on to other charities. There was nothing mercenary in the preacher's fanaticism; he was quite sincere in all his delusions, and perhaps no part of his creed was so far from that of his brethren as his principle that silver and copper were good enough for the support of true Christianity.

Lorenzo, regarding San Marco as "my house," saw no reason for discontinuing his walks in the gardens. Resolutely on days when his gout permitted him to walk he paced the shaded paths, but he never met the Prior face to face. Fra Girolamo always shut himself up in his cell whenever his patron was on the grounds.

XXV

The incorruptible Prior was not often forced out of his garden, for only a few more days of walking were left to Lorenzo. Frequently he complained that his feet were in such pain that he could not write.

"Feet and tongue are indeed far apart, yet they interfere with each other," he explained, resuming a correspondence interrupted by gout.

In the summer and fall of 1491 he had to be carried by litter to the baths. He returned, little benefited, and in January, a few days after his forty-third birthday his whole body was tortured by pains which no amount of pearls crushed in wine could alleviate. The man who all his life had been accustomed to think of a score of things at once lost the power of thought altogether. He could only feel. He could see no one. Ambassadors waited in vain for his pleasure and wrote home that nothing could be done until His Magnificence was well. At last he reappeared, his face lined and old and contorted by suffering, to be carried to the Palazzo Publico. Once more the affairs of Italy were taken into his stiff, swollen fingers.

But not for long. A few days in the drafty, damp rooms of the Palazzo, shivering with cold and pain inside his violet cloak, sent him back to his bed in greater agony than ever. The gossipy Ferrarese envoy reported that the entire city suffered in sympathy. From Naples Ferrante, knowing that only Lorenzo's influence kept the Pope from drifting into war, expressed the greatest alarm.

"Exhort His Magnificence," the King instructed his Ambassador, "to arm himself with patience and thus overcome the evil."

Of more comfort to the sufferer than anything the Neapolitan could say was the arrival of the day when Giovanni was at last to be given the right to wear the red hat. On the eighth of March Lorenzo's friends trooped into his bedroom with congratulations. He replied with something of his old gayety and actually smiled. Giovanni had come down from Pisa, but although his formal entrance into the Sacred College took place no further away than the Abbey of Fiesole, Lorenzo was too weak to attend. He could only listen, his pain almost forgotten in a glow of paternal pride and satisfied ambition, while they told him how well everything had gone. He beamed upon them as they described Giovanni's grave, dignified bearing, the solemnity of the mass, the blessing of the Cardinal's robes, the kneeling youth's acceptance of the insignia of office. He exclaimed approvingly as they repeated Matteo Bosso's final words:

"May it be for the good of God's church, of our country and of your House! This day, Giovanni Medici, the three years' delay appointed by the bull and this brief for your dignity as Cardinal is expired. Whosoever will read, let him read; all is fulfilled."

Holiday had been proclaimed in Florence, and as Giovanni rode down into the city through a drizzle of rain, an immense crowd at the San Gallo gate broke into delighted shouts, pushing forward through the escort to beseech the blessing of His Eminence. Scattering benedictions in all directions, the boy rode at the head of a constantly growing procession to pray at the Cathedral and then on to assure the Signoria, met in special session to receive him at the Palazzo Publico, that he was still theirs to command.

Only after his public duties had been thus performed did he turn back to the Via Larga for a word with his father, but he had time for no more than the word and a hasty embrace before he had to dash out again into the celebrating city. It was a fête worthy of the dying master, for Lorenzo had put all his remaining energies into directing the carnival. For three days he lay quietly in his bed listening to the revelry, proud of the never flagging commotion. Shouting, singing, laughing processions, bright with all the silks of the Por' Santa Maria, swept through the Via Larga day and night, bellowing Lorenzo's own songs as they marched up to drink his wine. Feasting and pageants followed each other in rapid succession. Every street was lined with banners and paved with flowers. From every window streamers fluttered down towards the heads of the paraders. At night the sick man's room was illuminated by the

Giovanni Greets His Father After Receiving
"the Greatest Dignity We Have Ever Enjoyed"

fireworks which flared in mad profusion until dawn. Around huge bonfires in every square the people danced and shouted to the carnival music. No one slept, no one worked, everyone was merry. It was all so splendid that when the bills had been paid from the public treasury, the Monte Commune five per cent. bonds dropped from 27 to 11½.

The three days culminated in a great banquet at the Medici Palace with Piero and Giovanni maintaining the honors of the house magnificently as they had been taught to do. Towards the end servants carried Lorenzo into the hall so that he might see for himself that the feast was worthy of the occasion. Even his exacting taste was satisfied, and he returned to his room to compose his thoughts for transmission to paper.

It was the last work of his pen, a letter to Giovanni who was off to Rome tomorrow to show himself at the Vatican. Never had Lorenzo so completely, and so unconsciously, revealed himself. In his carefully selected phrases appear the solicitude of a father, the pride of a banker whose son has been raised to princely dignity, the tact of a diplomat, the modesty of a showman who knows just how far ostentation is valuable, the piety of a professing Catholic, the good taste of a connoisseur and the facile eloquence of the poet.

He thought it proper to begin by acknowledging the family's debt of gratitude to divine Providence "for having conferred upon us in your person the greatest dignity we have ever enjoyed." The only way that debt could be repaid was "by a pious, chaste and exemplary life."

"Endeavor to alleviate the burden of your early dignity by the regularity of your life and by your perseverance in those studies which are suitable to your profession," he urged. "It gave me great satisfaction to learn that in the course of the last year you had frequently, of your own accord, gone to communion and confession; nor do I conceive that there is any better way of obtaining the favor of Heaven."

The writer realized that there was something a little ponderous in these words of advice, and he offered as a sort of apology the explanation:

"As you are now to reside at Rome, that sink of all iniquity, the difficulty of conducting yourself by these admonitions will be increased."

Then came a few fatherly warnings against evil companions "as there is at present less virtue among your brethren of the College." He hoped, however, that Giovanni might by careful search discover a few worthy comrades there, but he named no likely names.

"Listen to others rather than speak yourself," he admonished, and added that while he was to preserve the interests of the Church above all, he was never to forget "to favor your family and your native place."

With even more fervor he appealed for modesty and good taste, saying:

"A handsome house and a well ordered family will be preferable to a great retinue and a splendid residence. Silk and jewels are not suitable for persons in your ſtation. Your taſte will be better shown in the acquisition of a few elegant remains of antiquity, or in the collecting of handsome books, and by your attendants being learned and well bred rather than numerous."

Lorenzo was not above giving some advice which he had always scorned himself.

"There is one rule," he said, "which I would recommend to your attention above all others: Rise early in the morning. This will not only contribute to your health but will enable you to arrange and expedite the business of the day."

The moſt practical advice was reserved for the end. In his closing sentences the ſtatesman and diplomat disclosed the secret of a Churchman's success in the severely worldly atmosphere of Rome.

"With respect to your speaking at the consiſtory," the letter concluded, "it will be moſt becoming for you at present to refer the matters in debate to the judgment of His Holiness, alleging as a reason your own youth and inexperience. You will probably be desired to intercede for the favors of the Pope on particular occasions. Be cautious, however, that you trouble him not too often, for his temper leads him to be moſt liberal to those who weary him leaſt with their solicitations. This you muſt observe leſt you should give him some offence, remembering also at times to converse with him on more agreeable topics and if you should be obliged to request some kindness from him let it be done with that modesty and humility which are so pleasing to his disposition. Farewell."

When he wrote that last word he knew it was a real and lasting farewell. But one last service he could perform for the new Cardinal. That was to send with him as advisers Filippo Valori and Pietro Delfino, who as General of the Order of Camaldulensians knew his way about Rome as well as any man could.

"I entrust my son to you," he told Filippo. "As for me, you will see me no more."

A few days later, as Florence recovered slowly from the grand spree, Lorenzo endured the agony of the journey to Careggi in order once more to be in sight of his beloved gardens, fresh with the beauty of spring. Men and women drew aside silently and respectfully as his litter, the curtains closely drawn, was carried carefully through the narrow streets and out over the rough road to the villa.

Pier Leoni went with him, but the doctor was in despair. All his charms were worthless. None of his medicines seemed to be of the slightest use. And on the fifth of April lightning struck the cupola of the Cathedral, several marble blocks falling through the roof in the direction of Careggi. It was a sinister sign. His patient, however, was quite resigned. He had suffered enough, and he had the consolation of

knowing that he had accomplished almost everything he had set out to do. His children were in a
position to carry on still further. In rare moments of
relief from pain, he had visions of the glories to which
Florence and the Church would be carried by Piero
and Giovanni. He was spared any foretaste of the
future, the future that held for Piero two years of
arrogant rule, an ignominious surrender to men
whom his father had always referred to as "ultra-
montanes and barbarians," nine years of debauchery
and futile plottings in exile, all to end with an early
death in the floods of the Garigliano.

Giovanni, it was true, was to attain to those
heights which Lorenzo had seen for him in the distance, was to wear the tiara as Leo X and was to
confer upon Henry VIII of England the title of
"Defender of the Faith." The young Cardinal's
struggle upwards from the moment when he fled
from a hostile Florence in the disguise of a Franciscan
monk until he mounted the throne of Saint Peter
would have gratified his father. So would the encouragement of that brilliant band of scholars, artists
and musicians who made the Vatican their home and
conferred upon the pontificate of Leo the adjective
"glorious." But the sagacious Lorenzo would have
been ashamed of the shameless rapacity of the Pope's
relatives, disgusted by the split in the Church which
followed the excommunication of Martin Luther
and shocked that the temporal power of the Holy
See was exerted over Florence only to pave the way

for Pier Francesco's descendants to assume almost royal dignities.

Even less admirable to him would have been the vulgar squabbles over money with which his daughters enlivened Rome. He would have no cause for pride in the reign of the legitimized Giulio, who as Clement VII was to make the name of Medici hateful and involve himself in the queer domestic tangles of Henry of England. Only of the quiet life and obscure death of Giuliano would he have approved, for Giuliano was happy. Nor would he have considered it sufficient compensation for the shattering of his dreams that less than a century after his death the last of his descendants to bear his name would confer a not altogether desirable fame upon it as Queen of France.

No premonitions of all this troubled Lorenzo as he prepared to die. He only knew that there was one more chance to give good advice, and he called his eldest son to him.

"The citizens will doubtless recognize you, my Piero, as my successor, nor do I doubt that you will obtain the same authority as I myself have exercised," he said. "But since the collective state is a body with many heads, remember always to follow the course which appears to be the most honorable and study rather the good of all than individual and particular interests."

The traditional last words of a dying Medici thus uttered, he could at last and with a clear conscience throw off for the few hours that remained to him all thought of politics, of the balance of power, of the future of Italy. He had only one more duty, to make his peace with God, and as his confessor was announced, he struggled to rise, crying:

"It shall never be said that my Lord who created and saved me shall come to me in my room. Raise me quickly, that I may go to meet Him."

Supported on either side, he tottered into the next apartment and fell on his knees before the Host. They carried him back to bed and there he quietly confessed, prayed and partook reverently of the body and blood of Christ. His mind was at rest, and all through the night he discoursed cheerfully with Poliziano just as if they were sitting again on the terrace at Fiesole with the talk flowing even more freely than the wine. The doctors, hopeless but professionally unable to permit their patient to die peacefully, fussed about with draughts and potions. The famous Lazarus of Pavia had arrived to reinforce Pier Leoni, but when Lorenzo asked what medicine he was preparing the physician had to admit that it was only another paste of precious stones. But, he added optimistically, they were more valuable than any hitherto pulverized.

"Do you hear that, Agnolo?" Lorenzo asked brightly, for it pleased him to have such splendid medicines, even though he knew they were useless.

The poet burst into tears and rushed from the room. When he returned Pico was with him, for

Lorenzo had expressed a desire to listen to the young philosopher's conversation once more. For hours the three talked of books.

"I wish," Lorenzo murmured wistfully to Pico, "that death had spared me until your library had been complete."

It was his only regret, and he had just finished expressing it when another visitor came to Careggi. Savonarola, who would never consent to meet the ruler of Florence in health, considered it his duty to intrude upon the dying man, preaching repentance if he were really dying or reform if it seemed he would live. But Lorenzo's dark, wasted face and calm courtesy softened even Fra Girolamo's fierce fanaticism. Quite mildly, for him, he explained his mission. He actually refrained from arguing when Lorenzo replied that he had been guided throughout life by religion. The Prior of San Marco was turning to go when Lorenzo called him back.

"Oh, Father, before going give me your benediction," he asked.

Savonarola paused, then suddenly sank on his knees at the bedside. There, while a tearful circle of friends and servants drew closer around the pair, the apostle of gay autocracy and the prophet of gloomy democracy prayed fervently together. They ended and, bestowing his blessing, Fra Girolamo went off to his sermon.

For it was a Sunday, the eighth of April, and while Lorenzo lay dying, Florence watched the portents of his doom. At San Marco Savonarola delivered his usual sulphurous predictions. At Santa Maria Novella a woman sprang up screaming that a monstrous bull with blazing horns and fiery breath was charging down upon the city. Marsilio Ficino swore that while meditating on his grief he had seen ghosts of unearthly size wrestling in his garden. In the Piazza della Signoria the tame, over-fed lions suddenly, unprecedently sprang, roaring, upon each other in unaccountable frenzies of rage.

While these strange events were taking place, Lorenzo was growing weaker. He swallowed patiently what the physicians put between his lips, but he begged that no one trouble himself further. Finally as darkness fell he asked that someone read aloud from the Gospels the story of the Passion of Christ. As long as he could speak he repeated the sacred words, but in the midst of it his voice failed although his lips still moved. The reader faltered and stopped, and an attendant slipped a silver crucifix into the dying man's hand. He had just strength enough to grasp it.

Outside the villa, the watchers on the terrace saw a meteor streak overhead, hang motionless for a moment and, as Lorenzo with his last gesture lifted the crucifix to his lips, plunge downwards across the heavens into the darkness.

Three hours later the body of the Magnificent Lorenzo was carried through the night to San Marco. The next day with a simplicity which he had requested he was placed beside his brother in the sacristy of San Lorenzo. The whole city was silent in his honor and couriers galloped day and night over the peninsula with the news. Everywhere they were heard with dismay, and Ferrante exclaimed:

"His life has been long enough for his own death-less fame, but too short for Italy."

His mourning fellow citizens felt that the life must be its own memorial, for none of them could suggest a tribute worthy of his greatness. The Sig-noria, indeed, summing up his accomplishments in an official proclamation, declared:

"It had seemed good to the Senate and people of Florence to establish a public testimonial of gratitude to the memory of such a man in order that virtue may not be unhonored among Florentines."

There was much debate over the nature of this testimonial, and at last it was framed in a way that his friends knew would most have pleased him.

"The memory of Lorenzo," the Signoria an-nounced, "needs no outward adornments as it has struck deep root and blooms fresher every day. There-fore it has been determined to transfer to Piero, the heir of his father's dignity and successor to his fame, the public honors due to his ancestors."

So for many years there was not even an inscrip-tion on the plain marble slab under which the brothers Medici lay. At last one work of art, deemed worthy of the great patron of all arts, was found and above the grave was placed Michelangelo's figure of the Madonna, bowed lovingly towards the two young men whose bones were crumbling beneath her feet.

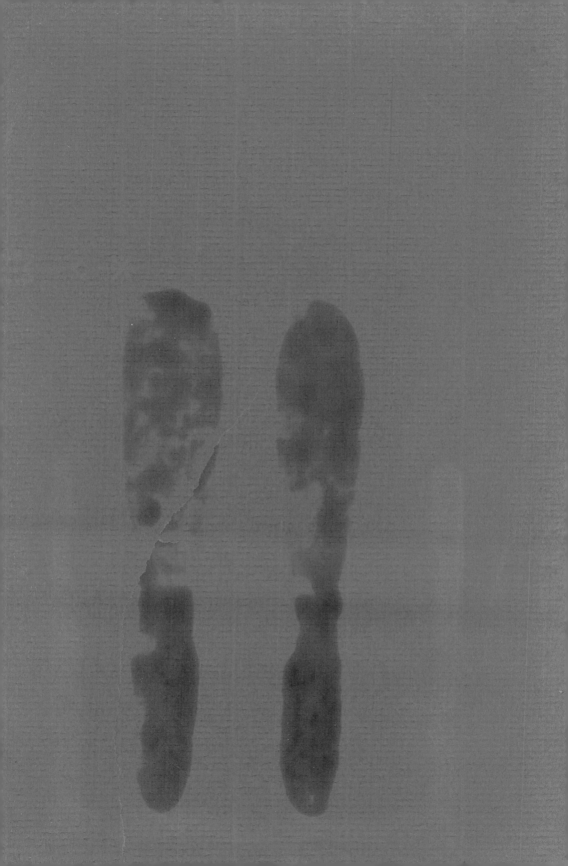

DATE DUE	
NOV 28 2018	

GAYLORD   PRINTED IN U.S.A.